winter chill
November to March

beetroot
broccoli (Calabrese;
  purple sprouting)
Brussels sprouts
cabbage (January king;
  red; Savoy; tundra)
carrots
cauliflower
celeriac
Jerusalem artichoke
leeks
onions
parsnips
potatoes (Cosmos; King
  Edward; Orla; triplo)
spring greens
squashes (butternut; crown
  prince; kabocha; spaghetti)
swede
watercress
winter leaves

hungry gap
March to April

dandelion leaves
cabbage
carrots
kale
onions
potatoes
  (Lady Christl; valor)
spring onions
watercress
wild garlic
winter leaves

autumn
and
winter
veg

RIVERFORD ORGANIC FARMERS

guy watson

with kirsty hale, anna colquhoun, rob andrew, francesca melman and other riverford cooks

To the customers whose trust allows us
to farm and do things the right way

16

32

46

64

82

100

112

124

142

156

168

182

196

216

234

248

256

272

282

286

contents

introduction 9
the Riverford Cooks 12
store cupboard essentials and kitchen kit 14

beetroot 16

Brussels sprouts 32

cabbage 46

carrots 64

cauliflower and romanesco 82

celeriac 100

Jerusalem artichokes 112

kale 124

leeks 142

onions and shallots 156

parsnips 168

potatoes 182

pumpkin and squash 196

purple sprouting broccoli 216

radicchio (and other bitter leaves) 234

salsify 248

spinach and chard 256

swede 272

garlic 282 / fresh herbs 286
useful basics (including stock, soups, risottos and dressings) 290

index 298 / acknowledgements 303

You will find the veg below in our
Spring and Summer Veg book:

artichokes and cardoons
asparagus
aubergines, peppers
 and courgettes
broad beans and green beans
cucumbers
fennel
kohlrabi and summer turnips
new potatoes
spring greens
sweetcorn
tomatoes and tomatillos

introduction

the book

I want this book to bridge the gap between aspiration and reality; to make a cabbage or cauliflower exciting and to prevent radicchio or romanesco or from being intimidating. My dream is that a veg box will seem like an allotment without the work, and that this book will help make veg the stars of your eating. Most of the recipes are quick and simple, with lots of possible variations, suitable for those weekday nights when you're tired but want to get something on the table that's good, seasonal, in budget and uses what you have in the house. Our cooks have not been able to resist a few more challenging ones, which I hope will appeal to the more seasoned and less time-pressed cooks among you. Our intention is above all to make veg box cooking easy and pleasurable. I hope that, in a year's time, your copy of this book will be grubby, dog-eared and stained beyond recognition.

farm and kitchen

My four siblings and I grew up watching and helping my father farm and my mother cook and garden. Growing, preparing and sharing food was the arranging force of our lives. My mother was a fantastic cook who drew her inspiration from the ingredients in the hedgerows or produced in her garden or on our Devon farm. She was deeply unfashionable: in the 1950s and 60s, as the nation emerged from the tedium of post-war food rationing to embrace the exotic (which came in tins, cans, jars and bottles), her cooking celebrated seasonality, provenance and tradition. We wanted Hellmann's but she made mayonnaise from her own eggs, baked infuriating bread that crumbled under often-rancid home-made butter, and made her own bacon and preserves. On top of raising five children and countless calves and chickens, this was a feat that would have been feted by today's foodies, though I suspect she would not have appreciated their attention.

My father wasn't from farming stock. He was restlessly experimental and, like many pioneers, frequently incompetent. The parish and his neighbours didn't expect him and his new-fangled ideas to last, but he demonstrated dogged determination and proved them wrong. The farm was run from the kitchen table, giving us all a keen appreciation of the tribulations of business. We learned as much from his failures as from his triumphs, and watched as he lost faith in the post-war rush to intensive farming and sought a better way. Above all we absorbed his optimistic belief that anything was possible given enough determination.

Six decades after he came to Riverford, after a little experimentation in the outside world, all five of his offspring are back on the farm: Ben, who runs the farm shop and a very creative production kitchen, two dairy farmers (Oliver and Louise), my sister Rachel (who had the idea for this book series) and me, still as obsessed with growing and selling vegetables after 30 years.

veg boxes

I started growing vegetables in 1986 with an ancient borrowed tractor, a wheelbarrow and a field next to our farmhouse. After 30 years of trial and error, Riverford now packs and delivers veg boxes across the country. It's been a rollercoaster ride of insane gambles and hard work, but it feels like a blink since I was picking ingredients from the garden with my mother, washing the mud from them at the sink and waiting hungrily for her to transform them into a feast-like supper for the family and farm staff. Essentially nothing has changed; the veg box scheme is all about sharing veg at its freshest and seasonal best, with the minimum of fuss, packaging and marketing.

a long winter

Autumn and early winter see an abundance of veg, with the last of the salads and peppers overlapping with the first parsnips, kale and Brussels sprouts. As temperatures drop and days draw in, the variety reduces and the less hardy romanesco, chard and radicchio drop out of the box availability list. Things start to get more repetitive as the shortest day approaches, but we find most customers are still enjoying the hearty winter veg through to the first sunny days in February and March when most kale and cabbages start to run to seed. In South Devon, we are blessed (and sometimes cursed) by our mild, damp winters, which allow us to cut cauliflower, purple sprouting broccoli and spring greens right through the winter.

Planning the contents of your box can start 18 months before it arrives on your doorstep. Every potato, parsnip, squash and radicchio, every head of kale and beetroot has a box and week allotted to it before the seed is sown (even if these well-laid plans rarely run to schedule). Our aim is to push you as far towards seasonal eating as we dare without losing you. I reckon a truly committed and experienced seasonal cook could eat 90 per cent UK-grown vegetables without hardship, but 20 years of checking out friends' and customers' fridges in February has taught me that even the most die-hard proponents of seasonal eating will rarely manage to go all the way. By March, as we slip into the 'hungry gap' and wait for the new season's plantings to mature, we make pragmatic compromises and import from our own farm in France and direct from growers we know and trust further south, mainly in Spain, to maintain variety. Counter-intuitively, our sums with Exeter University suggest that it can be 10 times less damaging to the environment to import a Spanish pepper than to buy one from heated glass in the UK. But we never airfreight and always enjoy the UK season to the full.

Riverford Cooks

Notwithstanding all the cooking on TV, and in the glossies and recipe books, cooking can

be hard if you didn't grow up around it – and many people didn't. Back in the 1990s, when I delivered the first boxes to friends and family, it quickly became obvious that some customers needed a helping hand. With my mother's aid I created sporadic recipe newsletters, photocopied at the last minute. Just as my repertoire was getting exhausted, we opened the Field Kitchen, our farm restaurant, and I was able to call on a real chef for help.

Riverford Cooks is a determined, if absurdly utopian, plan to address the reality gap between celebrity chefs proclaiming their enthusiasm for seasonal veg in the media and people really learning how to enjoy practical,

affordable cookery at home. It's a loose affiliation of professionals and proficient amateurs who share our style of cooking and enthusiasm for seasonal veg; they run events and give informal classes to our customers. The major contributions to this book have come from Anna Colquhoun, a founder Riverford Cook; Kirsty Hale, who creates the recipes that come with our veg and recipe boxes; Rob Andrew, ex-head chef at the Field Kitchen; and Francesca Melman, another long-standing Riverford Cook. Thanks to them all, and a good few others besides who have contributed and tested the recipes.

Guy Watson

the Riverford Cooks

The eclectic mix of cooks and chefs who work with Riverford have one thing in common: an enthusiasm for cooking with fresh seasonal produce and making vegetables the star of the plate. Riverford's founder **Guy Watson** is an enthusiastic amateur cook who has honed his skills over 30 years cooking veg for breakfast, lunch and dinner. He is supported by the chefs in our farm restaurant (the Field Kitchen) and a community of professionals inspired by the quality of the farm's produce and style of cooking who devise the recipes that appear in the veg boxes and work up and down the country at Riverford events. Below is an introduction to a few of those who have contributed to this book. Thank you to all the others who have contributed ideas and recipes over the years. Please keep them coming.

Kirsty Hale is something of a recipe-writing legend at Riverford. Resolutely dubbing herself a cook rather than a chef, Kirsty has been devising the weekly and seasonal collections of recipes that give inspiration to our veg box customers for many years, as well as running cooking events, food demonstrations and conjuring up menu ideas for Riverford's new recipe boxes. Kirsty is a champion of simply cooked, seasonal food that never compromises on flavour, with a bias towards vegetarian cooking (although she's not one!).

Anna Colquhoun, aka The Culinary Anthropologist, is a cooking teacher, food consultant and writer with a fascination for the anthropology of food. Something of a food nerd, Anna has travelled far and wide to research her subject, having first trained as a chef in San Francisco and at Alice Waters' legendary restaurant, Chez Panisse, in Berkeley, California. She continues anthropological studies and research at SOAS (the School of Oriental and African Studies in London). Anna is author of *Eat Slow Britain*; consultant on BBC Radio 4's *The Kitchen Cabinet* and is Riverford's preserving guru. She offers cooking classes in London, including popular bread-making and preserving workshops. Her supper club, the Secret Kitchen, is a convivial dinner at which people share a surprise seasonal menu. Anna is also renovating a stone farmhouse in Croatia where she will host culinary holidays. www.culinaryanthropologist.org

Rob Andrew is becoming a Riverford fixture. He joined us to head up the enormously popular Travelling Field Kitchen (housed in a yurt), and then took over as head chef at the stationary version on the farm in Devon – the pioneering Riverford Field Kitchen. Rob's grounded but creative culinary background suits our philosophy of good food and good farming. His experiences include working in a seafood restaurant in Melbourne, living off-grid on an organic smallholding in Tasmania and working as part of the vibrant restaurant scene in Brighton.

Francesca Melman has spent more than 15 years working as a chef in some of London's top restaurants, including The River Café and Alistair Little, as well as doing stages at Chez Panisse and Rick Stein's Seafood Restaurant. She now works as a food photographer and recipe writer at www.francescamelman. com but is still very active as a Riverford Cook. Francesca's blog is at: www.checkyskitchen. blogspot.co.uk

Guy **Watson**

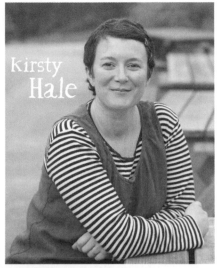
Kirsty **Hale**

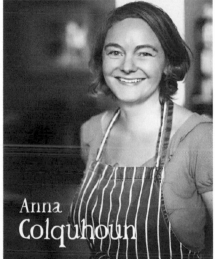
Anna **Colquhoun**

Rob **Andrew**

Francesca **Melman**

store cupboard essentials and kitchen kit

Essential to any cook is a well stocked store cupboard. The list below will help transform your veg box and will put you well on the way to making the most of the recipes in this book.

grains, seeds and pulses

* dried pasta and noodles

* rice (long grain, basmati and Arborio)

* couscous and/or bulghur wheat

* lentils (Puy and a red or yellow split lentil)

* flour (plain and self-raising; gluten-free absorbs more liquid so recipes may need a splash more if you use this)

* quinoa

tins and jars

* tinned chickpeas, white beans (cannellini, haricot or butter) and red kidney beans

* tinned tomatoes (we generally find chopped the most useful)

* tomato purée/concentrate

* mustard (English/Dijon and/ or wholegrain)

* olives (in brine or oil)

* capers (in brine or salted)

* anchovies (in oil or salted)

* tinned coconut milk

bottles

* oils (extra virgin olive oil for salads or drizzling; light olive oil for roasting or frying; sunflower/rapeseed for deep-frying)

* vinegars (red wine, white wine and balsamic)

* soy sauce (use tamari for gluten-free)

* Worcestershire sauce (Biona do make an organic vegetarian version)

flavourings

* ground spices (use as fresh as possible for the best flavour; grind whole spices in a pestle and mortar or spice/coffee grinder; a ✿ indicates where we think whole are best): caraway seeds✿, cardamom pods✿, coriander seeds✿, chilli flakes, cinnamon (whole sticks and ground), cumin seeds✿, medium curry powder, fennel seeds✿, mustard seeds✿, nutmeg✿, paprika (unsmoked and smoked sweet), saffron threads

* dried herbs (bay leaves, mint, thyme oregano or marjoram)

* fine and coarse or flaky sea salt

* peppercorns

* sugar (caster, soft light brown and dark muscovado)

* honey

* Good vegetable bouillon (for a quick stock)

fridge

* Parmesan (or vegetarian alternative and/or other hard cheeses)
* feta, halloumi and a soft sheep's or goat's cheese
* lemons and limes

frozen

* stock (chicken, beef and/or vegetable; stock cubes will do but fresh/frozen stock is usually better)
* pastry (puff and shortcrust)

kitchen kit

You can tackle most vegetables with a sharp knife and a sturdy chopping board. Below are a few other recommended items for your vegetable tool box.

* good vegetable scrubber
* big, heavy, sharp cook's knife for chunky veg like squash
* small serrated knife for tomatoes
* swivel peeler (for potatoes)
* box grater (for cheese and veg)
* very fine, sharp grater or Microplane (for Parmesan, horseradish, ginger, citrus zest and nutmeg)
* stick blender (for blitzing soups)
* kitchen paper (for draining vegetables and fried food)
* salad spinner (to get salad leaves dry without mess)

* pestle and mortar (for grinding spices and smashing garlic)
* potato ricer or masher
* cast-iron griddle pan (for griddling; especially useful if you do not have a good oven grill)
* mandolin (for thinly slicing veg; very useful for gratins amongst other things)
* spider or wire skimmer/strainer (handy for fishing out batches of greens when blanching, or when deep-frying)

beetroot

october to april

Riverford has converted many a veg phobe, but judging by customer comments, no veg has converted as many as the humble and much-maligned beetroot. Its current renaissance is well deserved as its deep earthy sweetness is full of culinary potential; whether as young, tender, thin-skinned new season beets in June in a salad or thumping barn-stored roots whizzed into a winter borscht. The root is vitamin- and mineral-rich and the tops even more so – if they're fresh they're as good as their close relative, chard, and can be used in much the same way but need a bit more cooking.

Equally important for us at Riverford, beetroot is easy to grow in our climate, having few pests and diseases, and stores extremely well; the first crops are ready in June with successive sowing keeping us going until October when we lift and barn-store the remaining crop for use through to April.

Beetroot can come as the traditional deep purple; yellow; striped Chioggia (pretty but not such good flavour) or even white. They can look wonderful as a mixture on the plate, but with my slightly grumpy aversion to all forms of veg faddery and over-tasteful cooking aesthetics we tend to stick mainly to the purple ones.

Guy

storage

When your beets arrive, separate the leaves or they'll draw up water, softening the roots. Unless they're really manky, remove the stalks and leaves, wash them well in cold water, spin or shake dry and store in the fridge in a plastic box or bag lined with kitchen paper. When they're small and young, they're delicious raw in salads; if slightly older, sweat them gently in butter with a little garlic, as you would spinach. For the best shelf life, leave the roots muddy and store in a paper bag in the fridge or somewhere cool and dark – they'll keep for several weeks.

prep

Clean your beetroot with a scrubbing brush and water. Don't top and tail them with a knife since they'll bleed from cuts, losing flavour and colour. If using raw in salads, peel with a veg peeler at this stage. Otherwise, the skin is easier to remove after the beet has been cooked: simply rub it or slip it off like a jacket.

Depending on age and soil bacteria, beetroot vary in flavour and texture, from sweet and dense to quite bitter and a little soft. Small and sweet, they're excellent raw and in salads; bigger and older ones need more help from sugar, vinegar and spices.

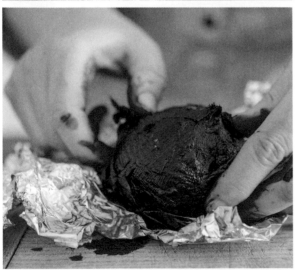

TIP

A pair of plastic or rubber gloves will save your hands from being dyed purple when preparing beetroot.

eating beetroot raw

Raw beetroot excels in salads. Peel and grate, or cut into matchsticks or small cubes with a sharp knife.

IDEAS FOR RAW BEETROOT

* Finely slice, dice or grate and mix with cottage or feta cheese, seeds or nuts, horseradish and dill. Dress with a simple vinaigrette (see page 296) or with cider vinegar and rapeseed oil.

* Combine with other vegetables for a gorgeous purple slaw. It pairs particularly well with the sweetness of carrots and apples, but cabbage, parsnip, swede and celeriac are also good partners. To dress, mix lemon juice and chopped herbs into yoghurt, to taste, or try toasted seed and tahini dressing (see page 53).

* Add finely grated raw beetroot to a basic risotto recipe, just after you've toasted the rice (see recipe on page 294).

---

cooking

Roasting beetroot – on its own or with a medley of other root veg – is easy, adaptable and plays well to beetroot's character. Boiling works very well too. Cooking time varies hugely, depending on size, season and age, but is often much longer than you might expect because of the density of the flesh. Cooked beetroot is good in salads (see overleaf). If you have lots in your kitchen, it's economical to roast or boil your beets en masse while they're fresh. They'll then last very well in the fridge for a few days.

salt-baking beets

Baking beetroot in a salty dough crust gives them a gentle hint of seasoning and is a novel way to present them. Serve as part of a roast dinner; they would go particularly well with beef or venison. To bake 6 medium-sized beetroot, mix 500g coarse sea salt and 500g plain flour in a large bowl. Add cold water gradually (around 10 tablespoons in total) until the mixture forms a sticky, stiff dough. Cover and chill for 30 minutes. Heat your oven to 220°C/Gas 7. Roll out the dough to about 1cm thick. Cut into 6 pieces and fold each around a washed beetroot (skin on), pressing together to seal any folds and cracks. Arrange in a baking dish and bake for 1 hour. To serve, crack open their crust and slip them out (but don't try eating the crust).

beetroot

roast

Scrub the beetroot clean, lay in a single layer in a roasting tin, drizzle with oil, season with salt and pour in about 1cm of water. If you like, add flavourings, such as a cinnamon stick, strips of orange zest, some thyme sprigs. Cover tightly with foil – the tighter the better as this will speed up the cooking. Alternatively, wrap beetroots individually in foil. Roast at 190–200°C/Gas 5–6 until tender. This will take anything from 45 minutes to 2 hours, depending on your beetroot. They are done when they feel slightly soft when squeezed and are easily pierced with a knife. Rub off the skins with your hands while they're still warm.

boil

Scrub the beetroot clean. Boil in plenty of water until tender. Again, this will take anything from 45 minutes to 2 hours depending on your beetroot. Make sure they are always covered with water. Test and peel as above.

IDEAS FOR BOILED/ROASTED BEETS

* Combine with cooked potato and blitz to make a stunning purple mash.

* Make a simple dip: blitz 800g chopped beets with 1 teaspoon of cumin, the juice of ½ a lemon, 2 tablespoons of yoghurt and a little salt and pepper. Transfer to a bowl and stir in more yoghurt, lemon juice, cumin and seasoning to your own taste and desired consistency. Serve with toasted warm pitta or crudités.

* Grate finely and mix with yoghurt, lemon juice, cumin, cayenne and chopped mint for a refreshing salad to go with a mezze selection.

* Grate and stuff into a pitta with some grated carrot, Greek yoghurt and a little harissa or ground cumin for a quick lunch. Add tinned chickpeas to bulk it out.

* Go Scandinavian: dice with pickled herring, onion, potato and apple and dress with a mustardy vinaigrette (see page 296).

* Dress warm wedges of beetroot with a dash of red wine vinegar, salt and pepper, mix with watercress and serve with sour cream.

ROASTED BEETROOT SALADS

Roasted beetroot add a dash of colour and sweetness to hearty salads. Cut them into wedges and dress while still warm for best absorption. For the maximum flavour, dress with the vinegar first, allow the beetroot to soak it up, then add the oil. Here are some ideas to try:

* One part red wine vinegar to three parts olive oil, with orange juice and zest, ground cumin, a touch of ground cinnamon and cayenne to taste. Serve with dollops of yoghurt and torn mint leaves. Season to taste.

* Balsamic vinegar and walnut oil (about one part to three) and a little crushed garlic. Gently mix with crumbled blue cheese, toasted walnuts and parsley or lovage. Season to taste.

* One part red wine vinegar to three parts olive oil, orange juice and a little cayenne gently mixed with orange segments, watercress and toasted hazelnuts and served with goat's cheese. Season to taste.

works well with...

* cheese – cottage cheese, blue cheese, goat's cheese and feta
* dairy – soured cream, yoghurt and crème fraîche
* cumin
* herbs – dill, parsley, mint and lovage
* horseradish
* nuts – hazelnuts and walnuts
* oily fish – cured salmon, smoked mackerel and pickled herring
* orange
* seeds – pumpkin, sunflower and sesame, including tahini
* vinegar

roasted beetroot, carrot, lentil and cumin seed salad

easy

vegan

Cooked lentils are useful for throwing together a quick salad. This one would also work with other root veg, such as parsnips or celeriac (see pages 171 and 103 for how to roast).

SERVES 2

2 medium beetroot (about
    300–350g), scrubbed well
3 medium carrots (about
    300–350g), peeled and cut
    into quarters lengthways
5–6 tbsp olive oil
1 tsp cumin seeds
100g Puy lentils (or other
    small green lentils)
2 tbsp freshly squeezed
    lemon juice, or to taste
bag of salad leaves, e.g.
    rocket or watercress
salt and black pepper

Heat the oven to 190°C/Gas 5.

Wrap the beetroot in foil and roast it in the hot oven (see page 20) – this may take an hour or more, depending on their size. When you can easily insert and remove a knife, they are cooked.

About half an hour before the beetroot are cooked, toss the carrots in a roasting tin with 1 tablespoon of the oil, the cumin seeds and some salt and pepper. Add to the oven and roast for 20–25 minutes, until beginning to caramelise.

Meanwhile, put the lentils into a pan of cold water and bring to the boil. Simmer for about 20 minutes, until tender. Drain and dress with 1 tablespoon of the olive oil and a little salt while still warm.

Mix the lemon juice and 3–4 tablespoons of olive oil with a little salt to make a simple dressing. Taste and adjust the balance of lemon to oil if necessary.

Allow the beets to cool so you can handle them, then slip off the skins. Cut into bite-sized chunks and toss with some of the dressing. Dress the salad leaves, scatter over the lentils and top with the carrots and beetroot.

VARIATION
For a heartier dish, double the quantity of lentils, omit the leaves and finish with a scattering of crumbled feta and chopped parsley.

beetroot salad with cottage cheese and horseradish

quick & easy

vegetarian

SERVES 4 AS A SIDE

50g dried cherries (optional)
4 medium beetroot
    (400–500g), peeled and
    cut into matchsticks
½ tsp salt
1½ tbsp red wine vinegar,
    or to taste
200g cottage cheese
1 tsp horseradish, freshly
    grated or from a jar
about 8 fresh mint leaves
salt and black pepper

This punchy salad works well as a quick dish at any time of year and in autumn and winter makes a good match for heavy meat stews. It's an excellent way to use beetroot without having to boil or roast it for an hour first. The recipe comes from Danish food writer Mia Kristensen, who, with Anna, runs popular Nordic cooking classes in London. She is known for her home cook's approach to the 'New Nordic' food movement, which uses northern European ingredients in place of Mediterranean staples such as olive oil, lemons and chillies.

Soak the dried cherries, if using, in warm water until they have plumped up, about 15 minutes, then drain and roughly chop.

Toss the beetroot and cherries with the salt and vinegar. Mix the cottage cheese with the horseradish and a little salt and pepper. Taste and add more horseradish if it needs more punch.

Stack the mint leaves in a pile, roll up like a cigar and then cut crossways into thin ribbons.

Check the beetroot for acidity and seasoning, then garnish with spoonfuls of cottage cheese and the mint.

borscht-style stew with soured cream

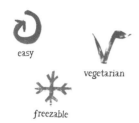

easy

vegetarian

freezable

Variations of borscht are found all over Eastern Europe and down through Turkey to Israel and Syria. It's most commonly a beetroot and potato soup, with cabbage or other greens, made with a meat stock. Some are served hot, some cold. This vegetarian version uses similar flavours. It's good with rye bread or on rice or quinoa to mop up any sauce.

SERVES 2

1 tbsp sunflower or
    light olive oil
1 onion, finely diced
2 medium potatoes (250g),
    peeled and cut into
    2cm dice
2 medium beetroot (350g),
    peeled and cut into
    2cm dice
1 garlic clove, finely
    chopped or crushed
1 tsp dried dill
½ tsp caraway seeds (lightly
    crush in a pestle and
    mortar if you have one)
½ tsp dried thyme
½ x 400g can of chopped
    tomatoes
250ml vegetable stock
salt and black pepper
soured cream, to serve

Heat the oil in a good-sized, heavy-based saucepan with a lid and fry the onion on a low heat, stirring now and then, for 10 minutes, until softened. If it starts to catch, add a splash of water and turn the heat down.

Add the potatoes, beetroot and garlic and cook on a very slightly higher heat for 3 minutes, stirring constantly. Add the dill, caraway and thyme. Stir, then add the chopped tomatoes and stock. Season with salt and pepper.

Bring the veg up to a low boil, cover and simmer for 20–25 minutes or so – the potatoes should be nice and soft and the beetroot tender but with more bite than the potato. Stir now and then and keep an eye on the liquid; add a splash of water, particularly towards the end of cooking if it looks like it's drying out too much.

Check the seasoning, then serve with a dollop of soured cream.

VARIATIONS
* Add a handful of boiled, refreshed and chopped spinach, chard or kale leaves for added greens.
* Add some cooked, tinned beans to make it a one-pot dish.
* If you can find fresh dill, add a small handful of roughly chopped leaves at the end of cooking instead of the dried dill.
* Add more stock and blitz into a smooth soup.

beetroot, potato and horseradish röstis

quick & easy

vegan

A sure-fire hit for breakfast, brunch or lunch. You can cook the beetroot first, but using it raw lends the röstis a nice bit of bite. If you have any leftover cooked beetroot or potato these would work fine too, or swap the beetroot for parsnip, celeriac or squash.

SERVES 4

2 large potatoes
1 large beetroot, peeled
1 small red onion
5cm piece of horseradish, peeled or 1 tsp grated horseradish from a jar
1 large garlic clove
small bunch of dill, roughly chopped
small bunch of tarragon, roughly chopped
small bunch of parsley, roughly chopped
1 tbsp plain flour (or rice flour to make it gluten-free)
sunflower oil, for frying
salt and black pepper

Put the potatoes in a pan of cold salted water and slowly bring to the boil, then reduce the heat and simmer for 5 minutes. Turn off the heat and leave the potatoes in the hot water for 15 minutes so that they are half cooked. Drain and peel.

Coarsely grate the potatoes, beetroot and onion into a large bowl. Finely grate the horseradish into the same bowl.

Bash the garlic into a fine paste using a pestle and mortar, or crush in a garlic crusher, then add it to the bowl with the herbs. Season with salt and pepper, sprinkle over the flour and mix well.

Heat the oven to 190°C/Gas 5. Shape the veg mix into four burger-sized patties. They should hold together well, but add a bit more flour if not.

Heat a good slug of oil in a non-stick frying pan and fry the röstis until golden brown on each side (don't be tempted to flip them more than once or move them much). Transfer to a baking tray and finish cooking in the oven for 15 minutes, until crisp and cooked through.

SERVING IDEAS
* Serve as a great substitute for your average side of potatoes; try them with a slice of roast beef or venison and some wilted kale.
* Top with smoked salmon, a dollop of crème fraîche and a handful of chopped green herbs.
* Use the same mix to make mini patties and serve as fancy hash browns with a full English breakfast.
* Crumble blue cheese on top, with a sparing drizzle of runny honey and a small pile of peppery watercress leaves.
* Top with wilted spinach or chard and a poached egg.

spiced pickled beetroot

vegan

This is like a more flavoursome, much-improved version of those jars of pickled beetroot you can buy. Full of mulling spices, the beetroot can be tossed into salads or served as a dish on its own. It's not a true pickle, so won't last indefinitely, but will keep well in the fridge for a week or so, submerged in its vinegary liquid.

SERVES 4

3 medium beetroot,
    scrubbed well
100ml red wine vinegar
75g light muscovado sugar
1 star anise
2.5cm piece of
    cinnamon stick
6 cloves
4 allspice berries
juice of 1 orange
1 bay leaf
8 peppercorns

Put the beetroot in a snug-fitting pan. Add all the other ingredients and top up with water until the beetroot are just covered. Bring to the boil and simmer for an hour or so until the beetroot is tender to the tip of a knife.

Remove the beetroot from the pan, strain the liquid to remove the spices (discard them), then return the liquid to the pan. Bring the liquid to the boil over a high heat and leave it to bubble and reduce until sweet and syrupy.

Peel the beetroot when they are cool enough to handle, then slice thinly. Pour over the sweet spiced liquid and allow to cool completely before serving or refrigerating for later.

roast beetroot and potatoes with red onions, balsamic vinegar and rosemary

easy

vegetarian

This simple recipe works best with smaller beetroot as they don't need to be peeled, just scrubbed really well. It requires your attention for 10 minutes on the stovetop but can then just be stuck in the oven.

SERVES 4-6 AS A SIDE

1kg waxy potatoes (see page 184 for varieties), scrubbed well
500g small beetroot, scrubbed well
4 red onions, peeled
150g butter
6 garlic cloves, peeled
300ml balsamic vinegar
leaves from 6 fresh rosemary sprigs, very finely chopped
salt and black pepper

Heat the oven to 200°C/Gas 6.

Cut the potatoes into medium-sized wedges and the beetroot into halves or quarters, depending on size. Cut the onions in half and then into wedges (don't cut off the base as this is what holds each wedge together).

Heat a large roasting tin on the stovetop, add the butter and let it bubble. Add the potatoes, beetroot, onions and garlic. Cook for at least 5–10 minutes so that the vegetables soak up the butter and start to colour a bit.

Add the balsamic vinegar and rosemary, season well with salt and pepper and gently stir the vegetables around so they soak up the vinegar.

Place the tin in the oven and roast for 45 minutes, until the beetroot are cooked and the potatoes are dark and sticky. Adjust the seasoning if needed.

VARIATIONS
* Swap red onions for brown onions or try using whole or halved shallots.
* Try fresh thyme instead of rosemary.
* Swap potatoes for carrots or other roots.

beetroot and pink peppercorn gratin

a bit fancy

vegetarian

Comforting and colourful, this hearty gratin gets its mild warmth and fruity, spiced edge from the pink peppercorns. A food processor or mandolin will make quick work of the prep, otherwise settle down with a very sharp knife.

SERVES 6 AS A SIDE

2 large garlic cloves, peeled
400ml double cream
800g beetroot, peeled and
    cut into 2mm slices
175g sourdough bread, sliced
    (best if slightly stale)
20g cold butter, diced
1 tsp sunflower, rapeseed or
    olive oil
1 tbsp pink peppercorns,
    finely ground
1 tbsp red wine vinegar
salt and black pepper

Heat the oven to 180°C/Gas 4.

Lightly crush the garlic cloves with the flat of a knife and put them into a small pan with the cream. Slowly bring to a simmer and cook for 10 minutes.

Strain the cream through a sieve, pressing the garlic with the back of a spoon to extract its flavour. Season generously with salt and mix well.

Pack the beetroot flat into a roasting dish and pour over the cream. Cover tightly with foil and bake for about 1 hour, until the beetroot is just tender.

Meanwhile, pulse the bread in a food processor or blender until reduced to coarse crumbs. Add the butter and oil and pulse again until the butter is evenly distributed.

Remove the foil from the roasting dish, then stir in the ground peppercorns and red wine vinegar. Taste and adjust the seasoning if necessary. Cover with the breadcrumbs and return to the oven for 25 minutes or so, until golden brown on top.

VARIATIONS
* Instead of the peppercorns and vinegar, add a little freshly grated horseradish or a spoonful from a jar.
* Stir in some fresh or dried herbs, such as thyme, sage or finely chopped rosemary.
* Replace half the beetroot with potato or another root veg.

Brussels sprouts

november to january

Sprouts are the most bitter of the edible brassicas (cabbage, cauliflower, swede and broccoli), but bitter can be good provided it is not combined with the abuse of overcooking. It is the harnessing of this bitterness that gets sprouts singing through a dish. Contrast it with the sweetness of chestnuts; pair it with the acidity of balsamic vinegar, the richness of honey and the toasty crunch of pine nuts; or balance it with cream and bacon in an oozy gratin.

Sprout tops can be picked and treated as a mini, open-hearted cabbage. This encourages the plant to put its energy into filling the sprouts higher on the plant, rather than into growing new sprouts. But the tops do tend to be a bit tough and bitter, and often host a colony of sheltering aphids, so we seldom send them out in our veg boxes unless other greens are in very short supply.

We pick the first varieties in August and the season runs through to March at a stretch, but we have found that sprouts are usually at their best from November to January and we concentrate our harvest then. Growing a cosmetically perfect organic sprout is nigh on impossible – the dense canopy of leaves above the stalk traps a layer of humidity, providing the perfect breeding ground for slugs, aphids and fungal diseases. Even after being picked through by hand, our sprouts are never perfect, but the slower growth does make them taste better! Don't be put off by a few tatty outer leaves: it's pretty hard to avoid these without a barrage of fungicides and pesticides; peel them off and you'll find that the sprout within is usually just fine.

Guy

eating Brussels sprouts raw

This quick option has converted some staunch sprout haters, but should only be tried with very fresh veg. Slice the sprouts as finely as you can: this is easiest if you cut them in half first so that you have a flat surface for them to sit on. Toss with one of the following dressings and season to taste:

* German style: one part cider vinegar to two parts rapeseed oil, a good dollop of soured cream, a little wholegrain mustard, finely sliced apple and toasted hazelnuts.

* Vietnamese style: Sriracha or other chilli sauce, lime juice, rice wine vinegar, fish sauce, sunflower oil, sugar, crushed garlic, finely sliced shallots, toasted peanuts and coriander leaves.

* Japanese style: soy sauce and toasted sesame seeds.

storage

Sprouts on the stalk will keep somewhere cool for a couple of weeks. Off the stalk, they are still good for a week or so.

cooking

Whether boiling, frying or roasting, the main hazard with Brussels sprouts is overcooking them – they'll become a soggy, sulphurous mush. Avoid this pitfall and you have a winter veg that is versatile, delectable and filled with folic acid.

boil/steam

Prepare your sprouts as described above and drop into lightly salted boiling water – leave the lid off to preserve their colour. They're done when just tender to the tip of a sharp knife, usually less than 5 minutes. You could

prep

Remove any ragged or tough outer leaves. Trim the base if it is long or discoloured. Unless your sprouts are huge, there's no need to score a cross in them to speed up cooking – it may make them a little mushy. Rinse in cold water and don't be tempted to save the trimmings for stock unless you want a kitchen smelling of school canteen cabbage.

also steam them, which takes a couple of minutes more. Either way, they're nicest when the core retains some texture – less than crunchy, but not soggy. For the simplest dish, drain and toss with butter, salt and pepper. If you want to reheat and serve them later, refresh them immediately in a bowl of cold water to halt cooking and preserve their bright green.

fry

Slice your sprouts into fine rounds or half moons. Heat oil or butter in a wide pan, add the sprouts, season and fry over a moderate heat, stirring frequently, until wilted – about 5 minutes. Adding some acid really lifts their flavour, so include a dash of lemon juice or vinegar a minute or so before they come out of the pan. Eat as they are, or jazz them up by:

* Frying some bacon lardons until just starting to colour then adding the sliced sprouts. If there is enough bacon fat in the pan you may not need extra oil or butter. This is good topped off with toasted flaked almonds or for a sumptuous pasta sauce, wait until the sprouts have cooked then stir through a spoonful of cream, letting it bubble up and reduce for a couple of minutes.

* Stir-frying the sprouts quickly over a high heat with a pinch or two of chilli flakes, some slivers of garlic, fresh ginger and a splash of soy sauce.

* Stir dried cranberries, chopped pecans and parsley through fried sprouts for a festive side.

IDEAS FOR BOILED OR STEAMED SPROUTS

* Toss or top with flavoured breadcrumbs: fry finely chopped streaky bacon until browned, add finely chopped mushrooms and fry for another couple of minutes, then add breadcrumbs and fry until crispy. For a festive vegetarian version, use chopped pre-cooked chestnuts instead of the bacon and mushrooms.

* Gently melt some butter in a pan and let it brown, swirl in lemon juice or white wine vinegar and pour this over warm, cooked sprouts. Garnish generously with chopped herbs such as parsley, chives and tarragon.

* Fry some lardons until the fat runs, add cooked sprouts and toss everything together to reheat the sprouts.

* Dress boiled, halved or quartered sprouts in vinaigrette while they're still warm, then serve at room temperature. This is good with a really mustardy dressing that includes a generous spoonful of Dijon (see vinaigrette recipe on page 296). You could also blend in some roasted garlic (see page 284).

roast

Roasting sprouts intensifies and caramelises their flavour and averts any risk of sogginess. It's a good option if the oven is on anyway for something else. Toss whole sprouts with just enough oil to coat, season with salt, spread evenly over a baking tray or roasting tin and roast in a hot oven (190°C/Gas 5) for about 20–30 minutes, until the sprouts are tender to a knife tip and lightly browned. Mix a dash of lemon juice or vinegar (balsamic or sherry is particularly good) through the roast sprouts before serving. They are also beautiful mixed with slow-cooked onions and the saltiness of bacon, pancetta or goat's cheese.

work well with...

* acid – vinegar and lemon juice
* anchovies
* dairy – butter, cream, strong hard cheeses, and blue cheese
* herbs – parsley, chives and tarragon
* garlic
* nuts – hazelnuts, chestnuts and almonds
* mustard
* onion (especially roasted)
* pork – bacon, sausage meat and chorizo
* spices – black pepper, caraway, chilli, nutmeg and mustard seeds

Brussels sprouts with cream, lemon and parsley

quick & easy

vegetarian

With sprouts dressed in a luscious, creamy sauce and finished with lemon, which cuts through the richness, this is an indulgent side dish, or it can be made into the main event by following one of the variations. Taste as you go when adding the lemon zest – a little goes a long way.

SERVES 4

300ml double cream
1 bay leaf
10 peppercorns
2 garlic cloves, peeled
    and smashed with the
    back of a knife
500g Brussels sprouts,
    trimmed and halved
zest and juice of ½ lemon
pinch of nutmeg
salt and black pepper
handful of flat-leaf parsley,
    roughly chopped,
    to garnish

Put the cream in a high-sided pan with the bay leaf, peppercorns and garlic. Bring slowly to the boil, then lower the heat and simmer until reduced by half, stirring frequently so it doesn't catch. Meanwhile, steam or boil the sprouts for 3–4 minutes, until just tender.

Strain the cream into a clean pan and place over a low heat. Add the sprouts and about half the lemon zest and leave until warmed through. Finish with nutmeg, salt, pepper and lemon juice to taste, adding the remaining lemon zest if you like. Serve garnished with the chopped parsley.

VARIATIONS

* The creaminess of this dish makes it a great pasta sauce – it's particularly good if you add some fried smoked bacon lardons.
* Reduce the quantity of cream a little and pour the mixture into a gratin dish. Stir in some blanched, squeezed spinach and/or a bit of grated cheese (a good melting one such as Gruyère or Parmesan). Top with ordinary or chestnut breadcrumbs (see page 35) and bake at 190°C/Gas 5 for 10 minutes, until nicely browned.

roasted Brussels sprouts with sage and chestnut butter

quick & easy

vegetarian

You will make more butter than you need for this recipe, but it's not worth making any less. It will keep in the fridge for a week or so, or can be frozen and sliced as you need it.

SERVES 4 AS A SIDE

500g Brussels sprouts,
    trimmed and cut in half
oil for roasting, e.g. sunflower
    or light olive
125g salted butter,
    at room temperature
100g cooked and peeled
    chestnuts (or use pre-
    cooked), finely chopped
8 sage leaves, finely chopped
salt and black pepper

Heat the oven to 190°C/Gas 5.

Put the sprouts in a baking dish and toss in just enough oil to coat. Season with salt and pepper and roast for 20–30 minutes, until just tender but still with some bite. Toss once during cooking.

Meanwhile, put the butter in a large bowl and beat with a wooden spoon until very soft. Stir in the chestnuts and sage. Lay a piece of cling film on your work surface. Spoon the butter in a line down the middle. Fold the cling film over and twist both ends to form a taut sausage. Chill until needed.

When the sprouts are roasted, toss with about six thin slices of the chestnut butter. Check the seasoning before serving.

VARIATIONS
* Add a few unpeeled garlic cloves to the sprouts before roasting.
* Toss the sprouts with other cooked greens or stir them through a risotto (see page 294 for a simple risotto recipe).

Brussels sprout salad with balsamic and Parmesan

quick & easy

vegetarian (if you use a
vegetarian alternative
to Parmesan)

SERVES 2

200g Brussels sprouts,
   outer leaves removed
2 tbsp good, aged
   balsamic vinegar
2–3 tbsp extra virgin olive oil
50g Parmesan, shaved (try
   using a vegetable peeler)
salt

This variation on a classic Italian recipe from the Emilia-Romagna region in northern Italy, home to both Parmesan cheese and balsamic vinegar, comes from Riverford Cook Francesca. It is one of those deceptively easy dishes that delivers more than the sum of its parts. As with most simple recipes, use the best ingredients you can. It's important to choose an aged balsamic as it is just used as a dressing - it should be syrupy. It may be expensive but a little goes a long way. Parmesan isn't vegetarian but you can substitute another salty hard cheese if you like.

Shred the Brussels sprouts – a food processor with a fine slicer attachment is good for this, or a very sharp knife.

Mix the vinegar and oil to make a dressing and season to taste with salt. Adjust the balance of oil to vinegar as required; how much oil you will need depends on the quality and age of your balsamic vinegar. Pour over the shredded Brussels sprouts and toss. Crumble the Parmesan shavings over the top.

VARIATION
Serve with slices of Parma ham (also from Emilia-Romagna).

sausage, sprout and potato hash with poached eggs

quick & easy

SERVES 2

2 large all-rounder potatoes
    (unpeeled), cut into
    2cm chunks
2 tbsp sunflower oil
1 large red onion, sliced
2 celery sticks, finely diced
4 good-quality pork sausages
    (or 8 chipolatas), each cut
    into 6 or 8 chunks
100–200g Brussels sprouts,
    raw or cooked
leaves of 1 thyme sprig
1 garlic clove, chopped
2 eggs
2 tsp wholegrain mustard
salt and black pepper

A quick brunch, lunch or dinner, this is a good way to use up leftover cooked sprouts and gives a wonderful range of texture and flavour from hardly any ingredients. If poaching eggs fills you with dread, fry them instead but leave the yolks runny. Most potatoes will do here, but the ideal is an all-rounder, such as Marfona, Orla or Triplo, that holds its shape a bit when cooked.

Put the potatoes into a pan of cold, salted water and bring just to the boil. Remove from the heat and leave submerged for 20 minutes.

Heat the oil in a wide frying pan over a medium heat and fry the onion and celery for 5 minutes, until they start to soften. Drain the potato and add to the pan. Turn up the heat and fry for a further 5 minutes, stirring frequently.

Add the sausages and cook for a further 10–15 minutes, until they begin to brown. Don't worry if they break up.

If your sprouts are raw, remove the outer leaves and steam or boil them for 3–4 minutes, then quarter them. Add the cooked sprouts to the frying pan along with the thyme leaves and garlic and cook for a further 5 minutes, until everything is heated through. Meanwhile, poach your eggs (see page 223).

Add the mustard to the hash, check the seasoning, then divide it among two bowls and top each with a poached egg.

VARIATIONS
* Use bacon, chorizo or chunks of leftover roast pork in place of the sausages.
* Replace the sausages with large, sliced portobello mushrooms for a vegetarian alternative.
* Substitute Brussels sprouts for cabbage or kale.

Brussels sprout and pancetta pasta with sage and roast garlic cream

easy

SERVES 4

1 whole garlic bulb
200ml double cream
1 tbsp olive or sunflower oil
250g pancetta or streaky
   bacon, diced
1 onion, very finely sliced
6–8 sage leaves,
   finely shredded
small glass of white
   wine (optional)
400g dried spelt or
   other pasta
500g Brussels sprouts, outer
   leaves removed, halved or
   quartered, depending on
   size (keep a little of the
   core intact so the pieces
   hold together)
4 tbsp Parmesan,
   finely grated
salt and black pepper

Roasting garlic gives it a sweet, caramelised flavour that suits this dish, but it does take a little time, so you might as well roast several heads and save some for other dishes (see page 284 for suggestions). If you're short of time, just add a couple of crushed or finely chopped garlic cloves towards the end of the onion cooking time. We've gone for a spelt pasta because we like its nutty flavour alongside the sweet garlic sauce, but any pasta will do.

First, roast your garlic. Heat the oven to 180°C/Gas 4 and follow the method on page 284. Once cooked, leave to cool slightly, then separate the cloves and squeeze the skin to release the flesh. Save half for another day and mix the remainder with the cream.

Heat a tablespoon of oil in a frying pan, add the pancetta and fry, stirring now and then, to brown it. Remove to a plate with a slotted spoon. Add a splash more oil if the pan seems dry, lower the heat, add the onion and fry very gently for 10 minutes until softened. Stir now and then to stop it catching. Add the pancetta and sage to the onion. Turn up the heat and stir for 2 minutes.

If using the wine, add it now and let it reduce for a couple of minutes, then add the garlic cream and let it bubble away for a couple more minutes.

Meanwhile, put two pans of salted water on to boil. While the onion and pancetta are cooking, add the pasta to one pan of boiling water and cook according to the packet instructions. Drain, reserving a little of the pasta cooking water. Meanwhile, blanch the Brussels sprouts in the other pan for 3–4 minutes, depending on size. Drain.

Stir half the Parmesan into the sauce, then toss in the cooked pasta and sprouts, adding a little reserved pasta water to thin the sauce if needed. Season with salt and pepper to taste then serve sprinkled with the rest of the cheese.

Indian spiced pan-fried Brussels sprouts

quick & easy

vegan

All brassicas work well with Indian spices, especially mustard seeds and chilli. This makes a good side dish for an Indian meal along with some boiled basmati rice. Or try stuffing it into a pitta bread with a dollop of yoghurt for a quick lunch.

SERVES 4 AS SIDE

2 tbsp sunflower or
  coconut oil
½ tsp brown mustard seeds
1 large or 2 small garlic
  clove(s), chopped
1 or 2 green bird's eye chillies,
  slit with a sharp knife
2 or 3 curry leaves (optional)
500g Brussels sprouts, outer
  leaves removed and halved
¼ tsp ground turmeric
¼ tsp garam masala
¼ tsp salt, or to taste
2 tsp fresh lemon juice
handful of fresh coriander,
  chopped

Heat the oil in a pan, but don't let it smoke. Reduce to a medium heat and add the mustard seeds, garlic, chillies and curry leaves (if using); there should be a sizzle and a crackle – watch out for splattering hot oil.

Add the sprouts and stir to coat with the spiced oil, then sprinkle over the turmeric, garam masala and salt. Add a tablespoon of water, turn the heat down, cover and let the sprouts cook in steam for 5 minutes, or longer if you prefer them very soft.

Pour over the lemon juice and chopped coriander. Serve warm and watch out for the whole chillies!

cabbage

october to march

In season for 52 weeks of the year, cabbage is a kitchen faithful with magnificent culinary potential. Ranging from the slow-growing hardy Savoy to the sweet and delicate hispi, it lends itself to quick cooking, slow braising and being eaten raw in thinly sliced slaws.

Strangely, as a nation we spend more money on peppers than we do on all cabbages and kale combined – this despite the fact that the former is in season here for only six weeks, is many times the price and is far less versatile and nutritious. A good part of the Isle of Thanet in Kent, once a major region for cabbages, has been glassed over to create Planet Thanet, where vast quantities of gas are burnt to coax peppers from a plant that never touches the soil. Such is the loss of connection with our own food culture and agriculture that many feel intimidated by a hearty Savoy in their kitchen. So, yes, we are on a bit of a mission to change that, to re-embrace our horticultural heritage, to rehabilitate the humble cabbage and to banish the memory of that sulphurous stench of abused white cabbage to distant memory.

Cabbages are members of the brassica family and ancestors of cauliflowers and Brussels sprouts. The original kale-like sea cabbage from which today's cultivars are descended is still found growing among the pebbles on our beaches, between the high-tide mark and the cliffs. The cabbages we grow vary in their winter hardiness. Apart from in April and May, when we find ourselves arguing with the pigeons over the last of the greens, you should receive a steady flow but lots of variety year-round.

Guy

cabbage

identifying

Many recipes that call for cabbage could use any variety, or be made with spring greens or kale. However, some cabbages are suited to particular dishes.

① SPRING GREENS (February to April) are a group of varieties grown at high density to produce loose heads that are harvested when still immature. They are at their best from February to April, a time when other greens are in short supply. Organic crops are particularly good – grown more slowly, they are smaller and more flavourful than the non-organic versions which receive regular boosts of nitrogen fertilizer throughout the winter to keep them going.

② TUNDRA (February to March) is a cross between a white cabbage and a Savoy. This is the most reliable green cabbage for late winter and often the only option in February and March when Savoy and January King have finished. They are less flavoursome than some other varieties, so we try to go easy with them in the veg boxes.

③ HISPI (May to November) is a pointed cabbage with a delicate, sweet flavour. It is good steamed, stir-fried or simply cooked in butter. We sometimes harvest immature hispi as 'summer greens', before the heart forms – they are meltingly tender and delicious.

④ RED CABBAGE (July to December but can be barn-stored through to May) is particularly good braised for a long time until soft and caramelised. Sliced very thinly, they enliven green salads and slaws.

⑤ SAVOY (October to February) is the slowest growing cabbage, with deep-green, crinkly, loosely furled leaves. It can be in season from July but is at its best in colder weather. Savoy has a robust texture and flavour and is good for slow-cooked soup and stews, stuffing and roasting in wedges. It is often interchangeable with cavolo nero (black kale).

⑥ CELTIC/GREEN (July to December) is the generic name for a host of high-yielding solid green cabbages with dense, cannonball heads. They are easy to grow, and they dress up well with strong flavours such as chilli, ginger and garlic.

⑦ JANUARY KING (October to February) is a purple-green, sweet-tasting, tender and hardy cabbage. They are great in the kitchen but hard to manage in the field; from the same sowing date they can mature any time between October and February, making it very hard to plan box contents. Like hispi, January King is good steamed, stir-fried or simply cooked in butter.

⑧ WHITE (July to January and can be barn-stored until May) has good texture for coleslaw or when quick-cooked with butter and caraway seeds.

storage

Generally the harder the cabbage the better it will keep. Red and white cabbage can be kept in the fridge for a week or more, though this probably doesn't do much for their nutritional value. Hispi should be used within a week, and spring greens last only three or four days.

prep

Slice the cabbage into wedges or gently separate the leaves, depending on your recipe. If you have chunky central ribs, cut them out and discard or add, sliced, to the pan before the more delicate leaves.

The easiest way to rinse is after cutting up: place your prepared cabbage into a big bowl or sinkful of cold water, swish around a couple of times, then let it rest for a few minutes so any dirt sinks to the bottom. Lift out the cabbage and drain.

eating cabbage raw

Good cabbage (generally hispi, red, white or the heart of a pointed cabbage) is the foundation of coleslaw. Slice as thinly as you can, then try:

* adding something from the allium family for punchiness – onion, shallot, spring onion or chives.

* dosing with plenty of acidity in the form of vinegar or citrus.

* sweetening with a little sugar, honey or maple syrup.

* keeping it simple with a plain vinaigrette (see page 296).

* going Middle Eastern with a tahini dressing (see Toasted Seed and Tahini Slaw, overleaf).

* going Vietnamese by combining with daikon (or turnip or kohlrabi) and a fiery dressing made with Sriracha chilli sauce and crushed garlic (see Vietnamese-style Carrot and Cabbage Slaw, page 80).

* mixing with plenty of lime juice and zest, green chilli and fresh coriander and serving with spicy pulled pork in a soft bun.

* using up the other winter veg in your box by grating them in too: beetroot, swede, parsnip, turnip, carrots and celeriac.

cooking

Cabbage is more versatile than you might think. Shredded and used in stir-fries, curries, soups and stews, it adds a healthy bulk of greens, or try raw shredded cabbage in salads. Simply steamed or braised and buttered, it's a good foil for meat dishes. Make it the star of the show in a gratin, or use larger cooked leaves as wrappers for rice, grains and other vegetables or mince.

fry

The simplest method of cooking cabbage is to shred it finely then stir over a medium heat for about 10 minutes with a good dose of oil or butter.

braise

Nothing beats soft, sticky braised red cabbage as a pairing for game in winter. It does take time though – see page 63 for full instructions. Savoy cabbage is also good braised and in soups and stews.

boil or steam

Delicate hispi and January King are best steamed for 3–5 minutes and served with a little butter, salt and pepper. For sturdier Savoy, boil for 4–5 minutes in plenty of salted water, keeping the lid off to help maintain the colour.

works well with...

* alliums – onions, shallots, garlic, spring onions and chives
* anchovies
* beef
* apple
* lamb
* mustard
* pork – bacon, sausage meat and chorizo
* smoked fish
* soy sauce
* spices – caraway, chilli, coriander seed, ginger, juniper, mustard seed, nutmeg and pepper

toasted seed and tahini slaw

quick & easy

vegetarian

Mixed toasted seeds add extra crunch, flavour and nutrients to coleslaw. You needn't stick to cabbage and carrots - try grating any other root veg you have in your box. This one's good served with chicken wings and potato wedges.

SERVES 4-6 AS A SIDE

4 tbsp mixed seeds
   (e.g. sunflower, sesame,
   pumpkin, linseed)
4 tbsp plain yoghurt
1 garlic clove, crushed
   or grated
1 tbsp light tahini
   (sesame) paste
juice of 1 lemon
½ Savoy cabbage, core
   and tough ribs removed,
   leaves very finely shredded
2 carrots, peeled and
   coarsely grated
1 small or ½ larger
   onion (red or white),
   very finely sliced
salt and black pepper

Toast the mixed seeds in a dry frying pan for 1–2 minutes over a medium heat, until fragrant.

Mix the yoghurt, garlic, tahini and lemon juice in a large bowl.

Add the cabbage, carrot, onion and toasted seeds, season with salt and pepper and toss gently to combine.

VARIATION
This also works well with shredded red cabbage.

winter rainbow coleslaw

quick & easy

vegetarian

SERVES 4 AS A SIDE

¼ red cabbage

¼ white cabbage or
   green cabbage

500g mixed root veg
   (e.g. swede, turnip,
   parsnip, celeriac, carrot,
   beetroot), peeled

1 small red onion or
   2 sizeable shallots

For the dressing

3 tbsp olive oil

2 tbsp mustard, smooth
   or wholegrain

3 tbsp cider vinegar
   or freshly squeezed
   lemon juice

3 tbsp yoghurt

¼ tsp chilli flakes, or to taste

1 tsp sugar or honey, or
   to taste (optional)

large handful of fresh herbs
   (parsley, lovage, dill,
   chervil or chives), chopped

salt and black pepper

This zingy salad, which brings welcome freshness and crunch to a winter table, comes from Riverford Cook Anna Colquhoun. It is a great way of using vegetable odds and ends and with its rainbow colour it is particularly spectacular served in a bowl lined with the purply green outer leaves of a January King cabbage. Let it sit for an hour before serving so that the dressing has time to penetrate and soften the vegetables. It keeps well in the fridge for a couple of days.

Cut each cabbage quarter in half lengthways into two wedges. Discard the cores and then finely slice each wedge crossways. Cut the root vegetables into very thin matchsticks or coarsely grate – this is quickest with a mandolin or food processor. Slice the onion or shallots thinly.

Mix all the dressing ingredients together then toss with the vegetables, giving them a good massage with your hands. Adjust the dressing to taste, then leave to sit for at least an hour before serving to absorb the flavours.

Savoy, brown butter and red onions

quick & easy

vegetarian

A good accompaniment for white fish, veal, pork or chicken, especially if served with chopped capers and a squeeze of lemon juice. Any leftover brown butter goes well with cooked carrots or stirred through mash.

SERVES 4 AS A SIDE

2 tbsp sunflower or
   light olive oil
2 red onions (3 if they're
   small), finely sliced
1 small Savoy cabbage,
   quartered, cored and
   shredded (make sure you
   remove any tough ribs
   in the outer leaves)
125g butter
1–2 tsp balsamic vinegar
salt and black pepper

Heat the oil in a large saucepan or frying pan. Add the onions and cook over a low heat for about 20 minutes, until soft and very slightly coloured.

Steam the Savoy cabbage (see page 51) or add directly to the pan of onions and fry until tender.

Make the brown butter: melt the butter in a small pan over a medium heat – a silver-coloured rather than a non-stick one will enable you to see it change colour more easily. Swirl the pan to keep an even heat. As the butter begins to foam, it will change colour from golden to a nutty brown. When it gets to this stage, remove the pan from the heat immediately so it doesn't burn and add a very small dash of balsamic vinegar. Carefully spoon or pour the brown butter from the saucepan, leaving behind the milk solids at the bottom. Add the brown butter and cabbage to the onions, toss, season and serve.

VARIATIONS
* Toast caraway seeds in a dry frying pan for a couple of minutes and add them with the butter at the end.
* Add chopped capers and a squeeze of lemon juice.

keralan cabbage thoran

quick & easy

vegan

This is a dry cabbage stir-fry that is delicious eaten with just a poppadum or two. Cabbage pairs brilliantly with chilli, mustard seeds and ginger and this dish is one of many regional Indian variations on the theme. Don't worry if you don't have the curry leaves or coconut – the recipe will work well without them.

SERVES 2

3 tbsp coconut oil or
   vegetable oil
2 tsp black mustard seeds
10 fresh curry leaves, roughly
   chopped (optional)
1 tsp cumin seeds
2 dried red chillies, each
   broken into several pieces
30g (or 4cm piece) fresh
   ginger, peeled and very
   finely grated
2 fresh green bird's-eye
   chillies, sliced into very
   thin rounds, with seeds
½ tsp ground turmeric
good pinch of salt
½ tsp coarsely ground
   black pepper
250g hispi or pointed spring
   cabbage (or spring greens),
   shredded into 5mm pieces
2 carrots, peeled and cut
   into fine matchsticks
   or coarsely grated
100g fresh grated coconut,
   or 2 tbsp desiccated
   coconut (optional)
handful of fresh coriander
   leaves, finely chopped
juice of ½ lemon (optional)

Heat the oil in a heavy-based saucepan or wok over a medium heat, and, when hot, add the mustard seeds followed by the curry leaves (if using), cumin seeds and dried chillies. Stir for about 30 seconds, then add the ginger, fresh chilli, turmeric, salt and pepper and fry for another 30 seconds. Watch out – the mustard seeds will pop and spit.

Stir in the cabbage and carrots and cook, covered, over a medium heat for 5–7 minutes, until the vegetables are tender, adding a splash of water if they start to stick to the pan. Scatter over the coconut, if using, and coriander and sprinkle with the lemon juice (if using) then serve.

VARIATION
You don't have to stick to cabbage – this will make a light, healthy dinner with any of your veg box greens – spinach, chard, kale or even shredded Brussels sprouts.

spicy greens with mung beans

quick & easy

vegetarian

This is an easy, one-pot dish that will warm you up on a winter's night. The recipe comes from Riverford Cook Anna Colquhoun, who is a big fan of dals. If you don't have all the spices on the list, use what you do have, perhaps adding in one or two more Indian spices of your choice.

**SERVES 2 AS A MAIN
OR 4 AS A SIDE**

200ml hulled and split mung
   beans (moong dal)
1 medium green cabbage
a good slug of sunflower oil
1 onion, sliced
3 garlic cloves, sliced
2.5cm piece fresh ginger,
   peeled and finely chopped
2 dried red chillies, left whole
½ tsp black mustard seeds
½ tsp nigella (black onion)
   seeds
½ tsp fenugreek
½ tsp turmeric
juice of ½ lemon
a generous knob of butter
   or ghee
salt and black pepper
naan bread or chapatis,
   to serve (optional)

Rinse the mung beans in a couple of changes of water then place in a pan, cover with water and leave to soak for an hour or so.

Quarter the cabbage then finely slice crossways. Put in a big bowl of water, swish around to wash and leave to soak.

Heat the oil in a wide pan over a medium–high heat. Add the onion, garlic, ginger, chillies and mustard seeds and cook for 4–5 minutes, stirring frequently, until the onions start to soften and caramelise at the edges. The mustard seeds should start to pop. Add the remaining spices and cook for a further 2 minutes until everything is fragrant and golden.

Lift the cabbage out of the water and add directly to the pan. Stir to coat with the spicy oil and season with salt and pepper.

Drain and add the mung beans. Stir and add enough water to cover. Bring to a boil, cover with a lid, reduce the heat to low and simmer until everything is tender but not disintegrating – about 30 minutes. Keep an eye on the pot and add more water if it seems too dry, or cock the lid a little if it seems too wet. You're aiming for a thick dal-like consistency. Taste and add more salt and pepper if needed. Finish by stirring in the lemon juice and a generous knob of butter or ghee. If a main course, serve with naan or chapatis.

VARIATIONS
* You needn't stick to green cabbage – this also works well with shredded spring greens.
* Swap the mung beans for yellow split peas or red lentils. The split peas will also need soaking, but red lentils only require a quick rinse.

smashed potatoes, cabbage, crème fraîche and chives

quick & easy

vegetarian

A versatile and indulgent dish of potatoes and greens, which you could serve with sausages, chops or steak, or just some grilled or pan-fried Portobello mushrooms for a quick mid-week dinner.

SERVES 4-6 AS A SIDE

1kg potatoes, peeled
  and chopped
50g butter
1 tbsp sunflower or light
  olive oil
1 medium leek, shredded
1 green cabbage, such as
  Savoy or January King,
  tough core and ribs
  removed, finely shredded
125ml crème fraîche
2 tsp Dijon mustard
a small bunch of chives,
  finely chopped
salt and black pepper

Put the potatoes in a pan of cold, salted water. Bring up to the boil and cook until tender, about 8–12 minutes, depending on size. Once cooked, drain, leave in the colander for a couple of minutes to let the excess heat evaporate, then tip them back in the pan. Mash them coarsely, leaving them a little chunky.

While the potatoes are cooking, melt the butter with the oil in a large frying pan. Add the leek and cook on a low heat for about 8 minutes, stirring now and then, until softened. If it looks like it's catching at any point, add a splash of water and turn the heat a little lower.

Add the cabbage and keep cooking for 3 minutes or so, stirring now and then, to wilt the leaves.

Add the mashed potato to the leek and cabbage. Mix the crème fraîche with the mustard, then stir into the veg along with the chives, salt and pepper to taste. If you like a creamier taste, add more crème fraîche.

turkey meatball broth with greens

easy

SERVES 2

50g bread, blitzed
    into crumbs
1 tbsp milk
250g minced turkey
1 large egg yolk
4 large sage leaves,
    finely chopped
leaves from a small bunch
    of parsley, finely chopped
sunflower or light olive oil,
    for frying
1 large or 2 small onions,
    finely diced
1 large carrot, peeled and
    finely diced
1 celery stick, finely diced
300g shredded green
    cabbage (e.g. Savoy
    or January King)
1 litre chicken stock
salt and black pepper
25g Parmesan, finely grated

Easy to scale up to serve more, these meatballs could be made with chicken or pork mince, but turkey is a good lean meat and is often available from Riverford over the winter months. Its leanness makes it prone to drying out, so adding milk-soaked breadcrumbs keeps the meatballs moist, as does poaching them in the stock. The onion, carrot and celery add an extra flavour, but a good stock is really essential here – we of course recommend the chicken stock we sell, if you don't make your own.

In a large bowl, stir the breadcrumbs into the milk. Add the turkey, egg yolk, sage and parsley. Season with salt and pepper and use your hands to mix and squidge it together well.

Roll into walnut-sized balls. Heat a thin layer of oil in a large, deep frying pan and fry the meatballs to lightly brown them all over (cook in batches if they don't all fit). Transfer to a plate.

Add the onion, carrot and celery to the same pan and cook for 15–20 minutes on a low heat, until tender but not coloured, stirring now and then. If the veg looks like catching at any point, add a splash of water.

Add the meatballs, cabbage and stock. Simmer for 5–6 minutes, until the meatballs are cooked through (cut one open if you're not sure) and the cabbage wilted. Check the seasoning and serve sprinkled with the Parmesan.

VARIATIONS
* This works equally well with shredded kale or even Brussels sprouts.
* Try minced chicken or pork.

braised red cabbage

long, slow cook

vegetarian (if using
butter and veg stock)

freezable

A classic recipe for red cabbage braised with apples, this makes a wonderful accompaniment to game and roast meat. It's worth making a big potful as it reheats very well; try the leftovers in a baked potato with a dollop of crème fraîche and some horseradish.

SERVES 4-6

a good knob of lard, duck
   or goose fat, beef dripping
   or butter
1 large onion, finely chopped
1 red cabbage, quartered,
   cored and shredded
2 tbsp dark brown sugar
3 tbsp cider vinegar
250ml chicken or
   vegetable stock
1 tbsp flour
4 tbsp crème fraîche
1 tsp English mustard
   powder
2 apples (Bramley, if you
   can get them), grated
salt and black pepper

Heat the oven to 150°C/Gas 2.

Heat the fat in a heavy casserole, then gently sweat the onion for 10 minutes, until softened.

Add the red cabbage, sugar, vinegar and stock, season with salt and pepper, cover with the lid and cook in the oven for 1½ hours.

Mix the flour with the crème fraîche and mustard powder in a large bowl to a smooth paste.

Remove the casserole from the oven and stir in the apple and crème fraîche mixture. Cook on the hob for 10 minutes over a low heat, stirring regularly, to heat the crème fraîche.

Check the seasoning. The fresh acidity of the grated apple should come through.

october to january
carrots

Carrots are more highly bred than our royal family. Through 500 years of intensive selection, the Dutch have selected out all the freaks so that what we have left are fast-growing, uniform, bland-tasting roots with 'robust handling characteristics', meaning that you can drop them out of an aeroplane without them breaking – crucial for mechanical harvesting, grading, washing and packing. I once visited a carrot variety trial and throughout the day I never saw anyone taste a carrot or even mention flavour. As a nation we've been trained to expect blandly uniform carrots – at best a bit watery, at worst rather bitter – and to pay very little for them; the Nairobi variety accounts for over half the market even though it comes near the bottom in every taste trial. Many of the most flavourful varieties we used to plant at Riverford are no longer available. (If you are a gardener try Autumn King; they grow huge, are brittle and tend to crack but taste great.)

There ends the rant. We try hard to do better and customers often cite the flavour of our carrots as a reason to recommend us. It's hard to prove, but I attribute this to growing them on loamy soils without irrigation to push them on (as happens on the sands and peats where most carrots are grown). The best carrots tend to be those grown in a dry year when the sunshine and slow growth can lead to incredibly intense flavour. The lack of moisture in the soil may mean they occasionally arrive a little floppy but don't reject these – they are often the sweetest.

Lifting from the February sowings starts in late June; we normally put these in the boxes as bunches. The main crop is sown in May and harvested any time from October to April. We find they taste better if lifted in October and barn-stored in bins rather than leaving them in the field.

Guy

carrots

storage

Washing can damage carrots' protective skin, so they're best stored muddy – they'll keep well in a paper bag in a cool place for several weeks. Once washed, they're likely to deteriorate faster and are best stored in the fridge and eaten within a week. Don't worry too much about a little softening – it's often a sign that they've been grown slowly and without irrigation. Slightly floppy carrots can be fantastically sweet.

If your carrots arrive with their tops on (likely in the summer), twist them off to avoid water being sucked from the roots. Keep the tops fresh in a glass of water, like cut flowers, and use sparingly in salads, as a garnish, or whizzed into pesto along with a leafy herb such as parsley or basil.

prep

Clean carrots with a scrubbing brush in cool water. If they're really caked in mud, soak them for a few minutes before washing.

TO PEEL OR NOT TO PEEL?

As the winter progresses, the skins can become discoloured and bitter tasting and are better discarded, but the autumn crop scrubs up well and the skin adds lots of flavour and nutrients. If in doubt, a quick scrape with a knife is a good compromise that doesn't waste too much carrot.

eating carrots raw

Really fresh young carrots are often best appreciated raw. Scrub them clean or peel if you prefer (a swivel peeler will make the lightest work), then grate, cut into matchsticks ('julienne'), or shave off strips with a peeler or mandolin.

* Make a Moroccan salad with grated carrot, 1 part lemon juice to two of olive oil , pumpkin seeds, sultanas, toasted cumin seeds and a little sugar.

* Try a sweet-and-sour Vietnamese-style dressing made from the juice of 1 lime, 1 1/2 teaspoons fish sauce and chilli, crushed garlic, sugar and fresh coriander to taste.

* Pair raw carrots in a salad with other raw veg: grated beetroot, shredded cabbage, grated kohlrabi, turnip or even swede.

* For a healthy snack or lunchbox, grate a carrot and mix with a handful each of cooked quinoa, whole unsalted almonds and mixed seeds. Add a little freshly grated ginger, a splash of soy or balsamic vinegar and a drizzle of oil.

* Raw carrots are also ideal for juicing – apple and ginger are classic partners.

cooking

The best way to accentuate carrots' natural
sweetness is to keep them away from water.
Try roasting or braising, or add them to
a stir-fry to preserve their fresh crunch.

soffrito

The Italian 'soffritto' (or the French
'mirepoix') is the term for the holy trinity
of classic Mediterranean cooking – carrots,
onions and celery – that makes an excellent
base for soups, stews, braises, pot-roasts and
stocks. It's a good idea always to leave one
carrot in the bag for such dishes – you never
know when you might need it.

For soffritto, cut carrots into regular dice
so that they cook evenly. Fry gently along
with diced onions and celery in oil or butter.
Usually recipes call for them to be completely
soft and sweet but not browned. This takes
longer than you might think – 10–20 minutes
on a low heat.

For chicken or vegetable stock, carrots,
onion and celery can be added raw in
chunkier pieces since they will simmer for
a long time. As the base of a pot roast or
oven-braised hunk of meat (e.g. shoulder
of lamb or pork), the trio can be included
raw, although frying them until lightly
caramelised adds extra depth of flavour.

roast

If the carrots are small, leave them whole or
cut them in half lengthways; if they're bigger,
cut them into quarters lengthways, or 'roll-
cut' them (see box on page 69). Toss the
pieces with olive oil and salt, spread over

a roasting tin and roast at 200°C/Gas 6 for about 30 minutes, until cooked through and lightly caramelised.

Roast carrots can be pepped up with flavourings: add spices such as fennel seeds, cinnamon, cumin; robust fresh herbs like thyme and rosemary with the oil; or a little sugar or honey towards the end of cooking for extra sweetness (see 'work well with' overleaf for more ideas).

braise

Braised carrots are best sliced regularly so that the pieces cook evenly. Simmer them slowly with butter, herbs, salt, a good pinch of sugar and just enough water to cover. As the carrots reach tenderness, let the water evaporate so they're glazed in the buttery residue (see Carrots Braised with Cider and Thyme on page 71). For a fresh finish, stir through chopped parsley. Or a favourite Riverford Field Kitchen variation is to melt 50g butter and a spoonful of honey in a heavy-based pan, add 1kg carrots cut into 2cm chunks, and 50ml water. Cook over a high heat for a couple of minutes until the mixture is simmering, then turn the heat right down, cover the pan with a tight-fitting lid and simmer for 15–20 minutes or until tender. Stir frequently so the carrots don't catch on the bottom. You can also add a tablespoon of balsamic vinegar to cut through the sweetness – pour it over the carrots when they are nearly done, then increase the heat and cook for another couple of minutes.

ROLL-CUT YOUR CARROTS

Roll-cutting gives even-sized pieces the length of the carrot and exposes more surface to the heat. Start at the tapered end, make a diagonal cut, roll the carrot away from you a quarter turn, cut again, keeping the knife at the same diagonal. Continue rolling and cutting to the end. This technique is good for roasting or braising carrots as it gives nice caramelised edges; it can be applied to other cylindrical vegetables such as courgettes and parsnips.

boil

To boil carrots for a salad (such as the Moroccan salad on page 74), leave them whole and they'll retain more of their flavour – you can cut them up afterwards. Medium-sized whole carrots take 15–20 minutes to cook, in salted boiling water; test by inserting a sharp knife into the thickest part of a carrot – it should meet no resistance.

A FEW LEFTOVER CARROTS?

* Grate lone carrots into a salad or sandwich for a bit of texture, or into dishes such as Bolognese sauce for complexity of flavour.

* If you have a sweet tooth, turn those last few carrots into a carrot cake or muffins.

* Leftover roasted carrots lend a lovely sweetness to salads, lentils, dal, hummus and risottos; if you've got a larger quantity, whizz them into soup (see page 292).

* Carrot trimmings are good for stock (see page 290), so don't automatically throw them away.

steam

Steaming carrots is the healthy option and very quick and easy. Cut into slices or batons – they'll take 10–15 minutes to steam, depending on how al dente you like them. Serve immediately, drizzled with a little olive oil and seasoned, or plunge them into a bowl of iced water to keep the colour vibrant.

work well with...

* acid – vinegars and lemon juice
* citrus – lemon, orange
* herbs – bay, chervil, coriander, dill, mint, parsley, rosemary and thyme
* honey and sugar
* nuts – almonds, hazelnuts and pistachios
* raisins, currants and sultanas
* sesame, including tahini
* spices – black onion seeds, cardamom, cinnamon, coriander seeds, cumin and fennel seeds
* ginger, paprika, star anise

carrots braised with cider and thyme

quick & easy

vegetarian

SERVES 4

2 tbsp sunflower oil
600g carrots, peeled and
    cut on the diagonal into
    2cm chunks
350ml cider (or half wine
    and half vegetable stock)
30g butter
leaves from 4 large
    thyme sprigs
salt and black pepper

The trick with braising carrots is to use just enough liquid to cook them through, but not so much that they're swimming in it. By the time the carrots have cooked the liquid should have evaporated, leaving the carrots glistening in a buttery glaze. We use a great cider called Ashridge, made just up the hill from the farm in Devon. If you don't have any cider, you could replace it with a mixture of wine and vegetable stock.

Heat the oil in a large, heavy-based saucepan with a tight-fitting lid until just smoking. Tip in the carrots, being very careful not to splash yourself – they'll spit and hiss violently. Add a good pinch of salt and stir well for a couple of minutes.

Add the cider and butter – it will bubble and foam a bit. Keep on a high heat until the cider reduces to a syrupy glaze.

Stir the carrots well before covering with the lid and turning the heat down to medium. Cook the carrots for about 15 minutes, checking them every 5 minutes to make sure that they aren't sticking, until nearly tender. Add a dash of water if they are drying out. Add the thyme leaves and cook for another 5 minutes without the lid to evaporate any excess liquid and give the carrots a little colour. Check the seasoning and serve.

VARIATIONS
* Replace the cider with chicken stock.
* This method also works well with butter in place of the oil, and some bay: place the carrots in the pan with the butter, a teaspoon of sugar and a good pinch of salt, crumbling in a couple of bay leaves (fresh if possible). Just cover with water and simmer until tender, letting the water evaporate slowly. Top up if they dry out, then, when they're nearly done, let all the water boil away and you'll be left with a nice buttery glaze. Add a dash of white vermouth or white wine with the water if you like.

carrot and coriander soup

easy

vegan

freezable

**SERVES 4 AS A MAIN
OR 6 AS A STARTER**

2 tbsp vegetable oil
2 onions, chopped
1kg carrots, peeled
   and chopped
1 potato, peeled
   and chopped
large bunch of fresh
   coriander (leaves and
   stems), roughly chopped
salt and black pepper

This 1980s pairing seemed very cutting edge back then, but it has stood the test of time. Carrot and coriander are a good match and the soup has become a classic.

Heat the oil in a large pan then add the onion and carrots and sweat them gently over a low heat for 20–30 minutes, being careful that they don't catch. They should be no more than lightly browned. This is the most important stage as it is when the vegetables release most of their flavour.

Add the potato, season with salt and pepper and cook for another 3 minutes, stirring frequently. Cover the ingredients with water and simmer until the potato is fully cooked, about 15–20 minutes.

Finally, add the chopped coriander and whizz with a hand blender until the soup is really smooth.

GARNISH IDEAS
* a dollop of crème fraîche or cream
* toasted almonds
* toasted and lightly crushed cumin seeds
* a couple of drops of orange flower water
* walnut, hazelnut or sesame oil
* 1 heaped teaspoon of ground mixed Moroccan spices,
such as caraway and cumin with a little hot chilli
* chopped parsley or chervil

Moroccan carrot salad with cumin and orange

quick & easy

vegan

SERVES 4 (AS ONE OF A
SELECTION OF SALADS)

600g carrots (about 6
    medium-sized), peeled
3 tbsp olive oil
3 tbsp lemon juice
zest of ½ large orange
1 tsp cumin, freshly toasted
    and ground if possible
½ tsp paprika
¼ tsp icing sugar
⅛–¼ tsp crushed garlic
leaves from a small bunch
    of parsley, finely chopped
salt and black pepper

'Kemia' – various salads, often made with cooked vegetables – are served at the start of a Moroccan meal to stimulate the appetite. They are nearly always beautifully presented and subtly flavoured with herbs, spices and citrus. Riverford Cook Anna Colquhoun learned this recipe while travelling for culinary research in Morocco. It is easy to make and lasts well in the fridge for a couple of days. Don't be tempted to leave out the icing sugar – it enhances the natural sweetness of the carrots and pairs well with the spices.

Boil the carrots whole in salted water for 15–20 minutes, until just tender. Meanwhile whisk all the other ingredients except the parsley together in a bowl.

While warm, cut the carrots into chunks (or roll-cut them, see page 69) and mix them with the dressing. Check the seasoning and add more salt and pepper as desired, and perhaps some more olive oil or lemon juice.

Let the salad sit for an hour so the flavours blend, or chill and bring back to room temperature before eating. Stir in the parsley just before serving.

bulghur wheat salad with carrot, date and pomegranate

easy

vegan

SERVES 4

150g bulghur wheat

1 litre hot vegetable stock, or hot water from the kettle

4 good-sized carrots, peeled and grated (or finely shredded on a mandolin)

1 small red onion, very finely diced

handful of toasted, chopped nuts (e.g. almonds, hazelnuts or pistachios, or a mixture)

handful of pitted and chopped dates

2 good handfuls of finely chopped parsley leaves

juice of 1 lemon, or more to taste

4–6 tbsp good olive oil

seeds from 1 pomegranate (optional)

salt and black pepper

To remove pomegranate seeds (if you are using them), cut the fruit in half crossways, turn each half upside down and lightly bash with a rolling pin over a bowl. The white membrane is bitter, so pick out any pieces that fall in. Bulghur grains are pre-cooked and cracked so can be quickly prepared by soaking in hot liquid. For salads, medium or fine grain usually work best.

Put the bulghur in a heatproof bowl and pour over the hot stock or water. Leave to soak for 45 minutes for medium bulghur or 10 for fine. (Our experience is that longer soaking makes bulghur easier to digest but you can get away with soaking medium bulghur for 25 minutes.)

Drain the soaked bulghur in a sieve, pressing it down with a wooden spoon to remove any excess liquid.

Transfer to a bowl and add the carrots, onion, nuts, dates, parsley, lemon juice, olive oil and half the pomegranate seeds, if using. Season with salt and pepper. Gently toss, adding more lemon juice, olive oil and seasoning to taste. Serve sprinkled with the remainder of the pomegranate seeds, if using.

VARIATION

Replace the bulghur with rice or quinoa, cooking the grains according to the packet instructions and missing out the soaking.

roast carrots with honey and fennel

quick & easy

vegetarian

This is a simple side dish that works particularly well with roast pork – both honey and fennel are great partners for the pig. If you are a fennel fan, rub crushed fennel seeds into the scored pork skin (with the salt) to make fantastic, aniseed crackling.

SERVES 4 AS A SIDE

1kg carrots, peeled
2–3 tbsp olive or rapeseed oil
1½ tsp fennel seeds
4 tbsp honey
a good pinch of salt

Heat the oven to 200°C/Gas 6.

Cut the carrots into long wedges or roll-cut them into angular pieces (see page 69). If they are small and slender, leave them whole or cut them in half lengthways. Toss with the oil, fennel seeds, honey and salt.

Spread the carrots in a single layer over a roasting pan lined with baking paper. Roast for around 30 minutes until cooked through and caramelising in places – check after 20 minutes and turn over to ensure even roasting. Serve hot or warm.

VARIATIONS
* Add a few sprigs of thyme to the roasting tray.
* Swap carrots for beetroot or celeriac – or use a combination of root veg.
* Instead of fennel seeds, try cumin seeds or lightly bashed coriander seeds.

carrots in a bag

quick & easy

vegetarian

We originally used this method in the Field Kitchen for new potatoes in the summer, then found that it works brilliantly for carrots and Jerusalem artichokes too. It's a nifty technique that seals in the flavour and lets the veg cook in its own moisture. You'll need baking parchment and a stapler.

SERVES 4

2 rosemary sprigs
2 garlic cloves, unpeeled
2 bay leaves
knob of butter
8 good-sized carrots, peeled and chopped on the diagonal into 1cm chunks
2 tbsp olive oil
salt and black pepper

Heat the oven to 180°C/Gas 4.

To make the bag, spread out a rectangle of baking parchment, approximately 60 x 30cm, with the longer side towards you. Fold it in half from left to right. Double-fold the top and bottom ends and staple the folds closed with two staples.

Using a pestle and mortar, bash the rosemary, bay leaf and garlic roughly (you can also do this using the back of a knife on a chopping board). Put the mixture into the bag with the butter.

Put the carrots in a bowl, season well with salt and pepper and drizzle over enough of the olive oil so that the seasoning sticks to them. Tip into the bag.

Double-fold the open edge of the bag and staple in both corners and in the middle. Lay in a roasting tin and bake for about 25 minutes; the bag should puff up. Turn out into a bowl or open at the table like a big bag of crisps. Watch out for the staples!

VARIATIONS
* Replace the rosemary with thyme sprigs.
* Stir in a few 5mm discs of chopped leek.
* Add a few strips of orange or lemon zest.
* Add some spices (see the 'work well with' list on page 70) and brown butter (see page 55).
* Try adding a scant drop of rosewater or orange flower water, especially if you're using cumin or coriander.

Vietnamese-style carrot and cabbage slaw

quick & easy

SERVES 4 AS A SIDE

For the dressing

2 garlic cloves, chopped

1 shallot, chopped (or a quarter
　of a red onion
　if you have no shallots)

1 tsp sugar

¼ tsp salt

4 tbsp rice wine vinegar

3 tbsp fish sauce

2 tbsp lime juice

1 tbsp Sriracha chilli
　sauce, or to taste
　(or omit altogether)

3 tbsp vegetable oil

For the slaw

3 medium carrots, peeled
　and cut into fine matchsticks,
　or coarsely grated

¼–½ green or white cabbage,
　depending on its size
　(the firmer and crunchier
　the better), cored and
　finely shredded

4 shallots, finely sliced

2 red chillies, halved, seeded
　and finely sliced

large handful of coriander
　leaves, or Thai basil leaves

large handful of roasted
　unsalted peanuts, coarsely
　chopped or pounded in
　a mortar

This salad packs a punch. Sriracha is an Asian hot sauce that's typically made from chilli peppers, distilled vinegar, garlic, sugar and salt. It is increasingly available in supermarkets and Asian food shops in the UK but replace with a hot chilli sauce if you can't find it, or reduce or omit entirely if you're not keen on the heat. Riverford Cook Anna Colquhoun developed this recipe while living in San Francisco, inspired by the city's many talented Vietnamese chefs. You need to taste the dressing as you go, adjusting the sugar, salt and lime juice to taste.

First make the dressing: use a pestle and mortar to grind the garlic, shallot, sugar and salt until you have a paste. Alternatively, blitz them in a spice grinder, or bash them in a sturdy bowl with the end of a rolling pin.

Transfer to a large bowl and whisk in the vinegar, fish sauce, lime juice, Sriracha and oil. Taste and add more sugar, salt or lime juice as you like.

Toss all the prepared vegetables together with the dressing. If possible, leave to sit for an hour or even overnight – this salad improves with time. Give another good mix and serve garnished with the coriander leaves and peanuts.

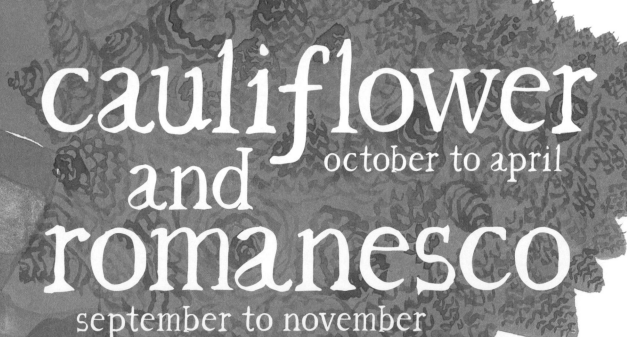

cauliflower
october to april

and
romanesco

september to november

After years in the culinary doldrums, condemned by sulphurous memories of school dinners, cauliflower is back; and quite rightly so. Treated kindly, this sturdy brassica is fit for a feast and is much prized in Italy, Asia and Africa – in fact most places apart from where it grows best: in the UK.

Cauliflowers love our damp, mild maritime climate, particularly in the mild West, and it is consequently pretty cheap for most of the year. It's possible to harvest cauliflower 11 months out of 12 in frost-free coastal areas. Riverford is not quite on the coast of Devon but some of our co-op growers are. Although easiest to grow in the late summer and autumn, this is when we have an abundance of other veg; our boxes need them most in the winter and early spring so this is when we concentrate our cropping plans.

Romanesco cauliflower (also called romanesco broccoli) has beautiful, fractal-patterned green curds. You might think it is a fancy modern invention – the latest supermarket gimmick – but actually it's an old Italian variety. It's at its best from September through to November and can be treated pretty much like white-curded cauliflower, though it is slightly more crunchy and nuttier in flavour.

Guy

cauliflower and romanesco

storage

Greengrocers often peel cauliflower and romanesco leaves back to display the head, but this means the curds brown and dry more quickly so it's best to keep the leaves on. Store your cauliflower and romanesco in the fridge until cooking. Don't wait too long: they're at their very best eaten within a couple of days, although they'll be fine for up to a week.

prep

Approach cauliflower and romanesco in the same way. Strip off the outer leaves until you are left with the curd on the stalk. Crop the stalk as near to the base of the gathered florets as you can. The stalk can be used in

most dishes – cut into slices or batons and cook with the rest of the florets. Cut the whole curd lengthways into halves or quarters – this will allow you to clip out even-sized florets. If the leaves are fresh cook them too – the outer ones may need to be discarded but those near the core are sweet.

eating cauliflower raw

Raw cauliflower and romanesco have a delicate, radish-like heat and a satisfying crunch. There are three preparation techniques: breaking each down into bite-sized florets; slicing large florets into very fine shards using a sharp knife or mandolin; or pulsing the curds in a processor until you have what resembles couscous. This last option makes a trendy alternative to pasta, rice or couscous, especially good for low-carb diets – but raw cauli is delicious in its own right as a salad. Try it:

* Finely sliced with lemon juice and olive oil (one part to three parts), parsley, Parmesan shavings and toasted hazelnuts.

* Finely sliced or broken into very small florets with white wine vinegar, olive oil (one part to three parts), capers, Dijon mustard, diced red onion and parsley or chives.

* Finely sliced or broken into very small florets with cider vinegar, rapeseed oil (one part to three parts), toasted walnuts, crumbled blue cheese and cress.

* Blitzed to 'couscous' (see overleaf) and mixed with lemon juice, chopped tomatoes, mint and lots of parsley – like a tabbouleh.

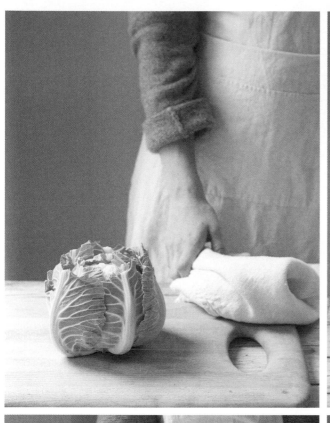

cauliflower and romanesco

CAULIFLOWER COUSCOUS

For a couscous or rice alternative, pulse cauliflower florets in a food processor until it resembles couscous (don't over-process it or you will end up with a paste). If you don't have a processor, grate it instead for a chunkier finish. You can leave it raw or roast it lightly by thinly spreading it out on a baking tray(s) and placing in a hot oven for 10–12 minutes, until lightly toasted. You can add other flavours as it toasts – ginger, garlic or chilli are good, as are Indian spices like cumin, coriander or garam masala. This goes well with curries (see pages 179 and 210), but avoid lots of liquid as this will result in soggy cauliflower.

cooking

However you cook your cauliflower, just don't overcook it – it should have a nice bite. The following applies to both cauliflower and romanesco, but the latter takes fractionally less time to cook.

boil/steam

If you're boiling or steaming 5–6 minutes should suffice for average-sized florets, but start checking after 3 or 4, especially if the florets are small.

With such a stunning fractal pattern, a head of romanesco is impressive (and very quick and easy) to serve whole. Pare away the base and leaves and boil or steam the whole head for 10–12 minutes, until just tender. Refresh in cold water to keep its bright colour.

roast

Intensely flavourful, roast cauliflower or romanesco is a great alternative to roast spuds, and much faster. Break the head into medium-sized florets, add a generous slug of oil, salt and pepper and spread out in a roasting tin. Don't cram too much in or the cauliflower will steam instead of roast – use two tins if necessary. Roast for 10 minutes in an oven heated to 190°C/Gas 5, until just starting to brown at the edges.

You can also roast your cauli whole, which gives a caramelised top and a bit of a veg wow factor: cut off any leaves and trim it so it sits flat in a baking dish. Drizzle with olive oil and sprinkle with sea salt. Roast at 200°C/Gas 6 for 1 hour or until golden and tender. Serve with a roast, or as a main with tomato sauce.

purée

A classic way to prepare cauliflower that pairs well with meat or scallops, a purée makes an interesting change from mashed potatoes. It can also be thinned down with stock for a simple soup. Sweat a sliced onion in a little butter for 10 minutes, or until tender. Add cauliflower florets and just enough milk to cover, along with 2 bay leaves and peeled garlic cloves. Cook for 8–10 minutes, or until soft, then strain in a colander over a bowl to catch the milk. Discard the bay and garlic (leave in some or all of the onion if you want). Blitz, adding milk, until you have the consistency you want. Season well and serve.

cauliflower and romanesco

deep-fry

Deep-fried cauliflower is a Riverford Field Kitchen favourite. The florets hold their shape well and have lots of nooks and crannies to hold added flavours. Boiling or steaming them for a few minutes first means you can cook the florets fierce and fast for maximum crispiness, and the residual water also helps any flour or flavouring stick to them. In the absence of a fryer in your kitchen, follow these rules for mastering the art of deep-frying in a pan:

* Cut veg into bite-sized pieces so the outside isn't overdone before the inside is ready.

* Fry in your deepest, highest-sided pan – you need at least 10cm of space from the top of the oil to the top of the pan. Use only enough oil to cover the batch you are cooking.

* Use flavourless oil with a high smoking point. Vegetable and sunflower oils are ideal.

* Heat the oil, slowly, so you have control over the heat, to 180–190°C. Invest in a thermometer for checking this – they're pretty cheap. Never leave the pan unattended and keep a constant eye on the temperature.

* If the oil catches light (because it got too hot), cover the pan with a lid or fire blanket and turn off the heat. Don't move it or lift the lid until it has cooled, and never throw water over it.

* Fry in small batches – this stops the oil temperature dropping and keeps the cooking fast and the veg crisp.

* Use a slotted spoon to lower food into the oil and remove it once cooked. Drain on kitchen paper to soak up the excess oil.

* If the oil isn't murky or heavily flavoured, once it has cooled, strain it through a sieve and store for next time. When it's been used two or three times, discard by pouring it back into its plastic bottle using a funnel. Don't pour it down the sink or you'll clog the pipes. If possible, take to a recycling centre; if not, seal the bottle and add to your household rubbish.

work well with...

* butter
* capers
* cheese
* chillies
* citrus
* mustard
* nuts, especially hazelnuts and pine nuts
* olives
* spices, especially cumin, coriander and turmeric
* vinegar

deep-fried Szechuan cauliflower

quick & easy

vegan

SERVES 4 AS A SIDE

15g Szechuan peppercorns
2 heaped tbsp plain flour
1 cauliflower, broken into
    bite-sized florets
vegetable or sunflower oil,
    for deep-frying
flaked sea salt
½ lemon, or 1 lime, to serve

Fast, easy and delicious, this is best appreciated immediately –
while it's almost too hot to eat.

Lightly toast the peppercorns in a dry pan until they start to
smell fragrant – a couple of minutes. Roughly crush them in
a pestle and mortar, or bash them in a tea towel with a rolling
pin, but avoid reducing them to a powder.

Mix the flour and peppercorns with a few good pinches of
sea salt in a large plastic bag.

Steam or boil the cauliflower florets for around 4 minutes,
until just cooked and retaining plenty of bite. Drain, but don't
let them dry too much as residual water helps the flour stick.

Add the cauliflower to the plastic bag, seal tightly and shake
vigorously.

Dust off any excess flour and deep-fry in small batches until
golden brown (see opposite for deep-frying instructions).
Serve with a squeeze of lemon or lime juice.

VARIATIONS
* This can be done with almost any veg that deep-fries in a few
minutes: try chunks of roasted squash, steamed batons of parsnip
or celeriac or florets of purple sprouting broccoli.
* All sorts of dry spices can be added in place of the peppercorns:
try garam masala for a curry twist or a few teaspoons of sweet or
smoked paprika for a quick tapas plate.
* Use gram flour (chickpea flour) instead of plain for a deeper,
mealier flavour; this will also make it gluten-free.

roasted cauliflower with butter, lemon and cumin

quick & easy

vegetarian

The cumin gives this dish an Indian feel but the spicing is so subtle that it works in the most traditional of meals. The flavour combination suits roasted parsnips too.

SERVES 4 AS A SIDE

1 cauliflower, split into florets
zest and juice of 1 lemon,
    plus the juice of another
80g butter, diced
2 rounded tsp cumin seeds,
    toasted and ground (or
    2 tsp ready-ground cumin)
handful of flat-leaf parsley
    leaves, roughly chopped
salt and black pepper

Heat the oven to 190°C/Gas 5.

Season the cauliflower with salt and pepper and spread it out in a roasting tin. Roast in the oven for 12–15 minutes until lightly golden. Cover with foil if it's browning too much. Finish with a squeeze of lemon juice.

Stir in the butter, cumin and lemon zest and roast for a further 3–5 minutes, until tender but so it still has bite. Remove the tin from the oven and stir in the parsley, then add the remaining lemon juice a little at a time to taste.

VARIATIONS
* For extra spiciness add 1 teaspoon of ground coriander and nigella (black onion) seeds with the cumin.
* Replace the cumin with dried or fresh thyme leaves.
* Swap the cumin for chopped garlic and chilli flakes (or chopped fresh chilli) and the parsley for fresh coriander leaves.

---

cauliflower 'Polonaise'

quick & easy

vegetarian

Polonaise ('in the Polish style') refers to the tasty topping of grated boiled eggs, parsley and fried breadcrumbs. You can serve other cooked vegetables in the same way – try broccoli, leeks and, in spring, asparagus. It transforms a humble boiled vegetable into a flavoursome, texture-rich and satisfying meal.

*SERVES 4 AS
A LIGHT MAIN*

1 large cauliflower or
   romanesco, broken
   into bite-sized florets
60g butter

For the topping
2 hard-boiled eggs
leaves from a small bunch
   of parsley, finely chopped
1 tbsp capers, rinsed
   and chopped
30g stale or dried
   breadcrumbs
120g butter

Steam or boil the cauliflower (see page 86), making sure that it retains some bite.

Heat the butter in a frying pan over a medium heat and fry the florets until golden, about 2–3 minutes. Arrange in a warm serving dish.

For the topping, grate the eggs and mix them with the chopped parsley. Scatter the mix over the cauliflower with the capers.

Fry the breadcrumbs in the butter over a medium heat until golden brown and pour over the top.

Taffy cauliflower cheese

quick & easy

freezable

Soothing and reassuringly simple to make, plain cauliflower cheese is comfort food at its best, but there are also lots of possibilities for jazzing it up. The leeks here can be replaced by practically any greens you have in your veg box – see below for other variations.

SERVES 2 AS A MAIN OR 4 AS A SIDE

1 large cauliflower, cut into large florets
6 rashers of streaky bacon, diced
2 leeks, trimmed and cut into 1cm slices

For the cheese sauce
40g butter
40g plain flour
500–550ml whole milk
100g mature Cheddar, grated, plus extra for sprinkling on top
70g Parmesan, grated (or replace with more Cheddar, if you prefer)
pinch of grated nutmeg
1 tsp English mustard
salt and black pepper

Heat the oven to 200°C/Gas 6.

Boil or steam the cauliflower for about 4 minutes, leaving it with a good bite (see page 86).

Fry the bacon in its own fat until just turning crispy. Blanch the leeks in boiling salted water for 4–5 minutes, until just tender.

Make the sauce by melting the butter in a pan over a low heat. Add the flour and whisk for a couple of minutes. Gradually add the milk, stirring constantly with a whisk until you have a thick sauce. Let it bubble gently for a few minutes while still stirring. Stir in the grated cheeses, nutmeg and mustard and season to taste.

Combine the leeks, cauliflower and bacon in an ovenproof dish and pour over the cheese sauce. Sprinkle with the extra grated Cheddar and bake in the oven for around 15 minutes, or until golden on top.

- -

VARIATIONS
* Use blanched, squeezed and chopped spinach or kale in place of leeks.
* Fry a handful of stale or dried breadcrumbs in butter and scatter on top for a crispy finish.
* Replace the Parmesan with crumbled blue cheese.
* Substitute half the cauliflower for broccoli.
* Roast the cauliflower first instead of steaming or boiling (see page 86).

- -

cauliflower, butter beans and kale

quick & easy

vegan

A robust winter salad, this is best served warm or at room temperature so that the flavours from the dressing have a chance to infuse. For a heartier meal, eat with slices of cold roast beef or topped with a sizzling pork chop.

SERVES 2

200g cooked butter beans
   (use a tin, or see page 297
   for how to cook your own)
1 cauliflower, cut into
   small florets
100g kale leaves, blanched,
   squeezed and roughly
   chopped (see page 128)
1 tbsp capers, rinsed
   and drained
leaves from a small bunch
   of tarragon or flat-leaf
   parsley, roughly chopped
wholegrain mustard, to taste
vinaigrette (see page 296),
   to taste
salt and black pepper

If you are cooking the beans yourself, add a good pinch of salt when they have become tender and let them sit in their cooking water for 30 minutes off the heat. If using tinned, heat them gently but thoroughly in their liquid and a dash of water.

Lightly steam or boil the cauliflower (see page 86).

Drain the beans and put them into a bowl with the cauliflower, kale, capers, herbs, a generous blob of mustard and a good drizzle of vinaigrette and toss to combine. Taste and adjust seasoning if needed.

VARIATION
This is a great way to use up leftover or tinned pulses; lentils and flageolet and haricot beans will all work well – or for a more varied texture try a combination of all three.

aloo gobi

quick & easy

vegetarian

Aloo gobi – 'potato cauliflower' in Hindi or **Urdu** – should not be confined to the takeaway. It's easy to make it yourself and a good, inexpensive, vegan dinner. You need to use waxy or all-rounder potatoes (see page 184) so that they hold their shape.

SERVES 2

2 tbsp vegetable oil

1 onion, thinly sliced

2 garlic cloves, very finely chopped

4–5cm piece of fresh ginger, peeled and grated

1 tsp black mustard seeds

¼ tsp ground turmeric

½ tsp ground cumin

½ tsp ground coriander

1 small green chilli, deseeded if you prefer less heat, chopped

6–8 curry leaves

1 small or medium cauliflower, broken or cut into large bite-sized florets (keep any light-coloured inner green leaves)

1 tomato, diced

juice of ¼ lemon, plus a little extra to finish

400g waxy potatoes, peeled and cut into even chunks

handful of fresh coriander leaves, roughly chopped

sea salt

warm naan bread, to serve

mango chutney, to serve

Heat the oil in a large heavy-based pan. Add the onion and fry on a low heat for 10 minutes, stirring now and then to stop it catching. If it does start to catch, add a splash of water and turn the heat a little lower.

Add the garlic, ginger, mustards seeds, turmeric, cumin, coriander, chilli and curry leaves. Turn the heat up a little and fry, stirring, until you hear the mustard seeds pop.

Add the cauliflower florets and leaves, the tomato and lemon juice and a splash of water. Cover and cook on a very low heat, stirring now and then, for 10 minutes or until the cauliflower is tender. Add a splash more water if the veg starts to catch on the bottom of the pan.

Meanwhile, cook the potatoes in boiling water for 8–10 minutes, until just tender. Drain and set aside.

When the cauliflower is almost tender, add the potatoes and stir to warm them through. Remove the pan from the heat, stir in the fresh coriander, season with salt and add more lemon juice to taste. Serve with warm naan bread and mango chutney.

Sicilian romanesco

quick & easy

vegan

SERVES 2 AS A MAIN
OR 4 AS A SIDE

150–200g couscous,
   depending on appetite
1 romanesco or cauliflower,
   cut into even, bite-
   sized florets
a generous slug of good
   olive oil
25g currants
50g pine nuts
1 red chilli, deseeded
   and finely chopped
zest of 2 lemons
handful of fresh parsley
   leaves, finely chopped
sunflower or light olive oil,
   for frying
salt and black pepper

The combination of chilli, pine nuts, lemon and currants is often found in traditional Sicilian cuisine – the influence of trade across the Mediterranean from the East. It gives a lovely sweet-and-sour combination. You can use ordinary couscous but giant couscous, which can often be found in large supermarkets, is even better.

Heat the oven to 190°C/Gas 5.

If you're using normal couscous, spread it out in a roasting pan, just cover it with boiling water and a pinch of salt and leave it for 30 minutes, then fluff it up with a fork. If you're using giant couscous, follow the instructions on the packet.

Meanwhile, toss the florets with the oil, salt and pepper. Spread out evenly on a roasting tray and roast for 10–15 minutes until tender and just beginning to brown (see page 86). While the florets are roasting, soak the currants in boiling water for about 10 minutes to plump them up, then drain.

Toss the pine nuts into a small dry frying pan and heat them gently, stirring often, for a couple of minutes until they start to turn golden. Remove from the heat and tip into a small bowl to stop them cooking.

Put the couscous in a large mixing bowl and stir in the currants, pine nuts, chilli, lemon zest, parsley and enough oil to give it a good gloss. Season with salt and pepper to taste, then gently stir in the romanesco.

VARIATION
This makes a really good pasta dish with cooked penne or fusilli replacing the couscous.

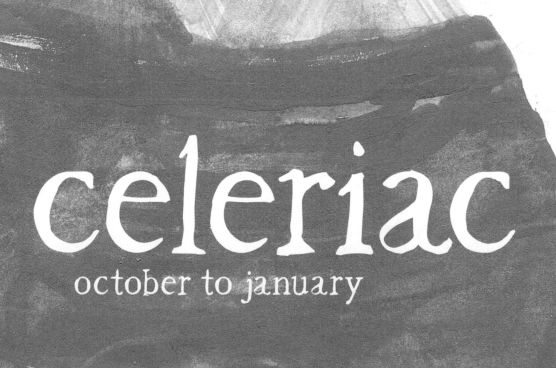

celeriac

october to january

With its craggy, irregular shape and deep folds and crevices, celeriac must be a contender for ugliest veg. In our weekly newsletter I once compared it to something between an elephant turd and Iain Duncan Smith's forehead on a bad day – a potential Ratner moment made worse by IDS resigning as party leader between my writing and the box delivery, thus him being instantly being forgiven everything, including his towering wrinkled forehead. A few Tory-voting box customers cancelled that week.

Appearance isn't everything and celeriac certainly has its share of inner beauty – under the skin lies a smoky, earthy flavour with some of the sweet freshness of its summer-loving cousin, fennel. This brings a host of culinary possibilities and a most welcome variation to the winter diet of a committed localvore. That strong and deep flavour is generated through slow and steady growth; seeded in February and planted in May, the roots do not reach a decent size until October and really need to be left in the ground into November. They can take a light frost but the prudent grower will have them harvested and in store well before Christmas; with care, good fortune and cold storage they keep well to April or May.

Guy

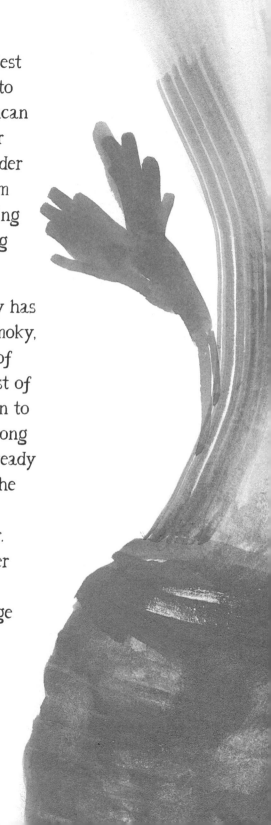

storage

A whole celeriac has a long shelf life and will sit in the bottom of your fridge for a month or more. It will be happiest loose or in a paper bag – never in plastic. Once cut, a celeriac chunk will be good for a week or so, but you may need to shave off the exposed surface if it has dried out.

prep

Knobbly and knotted, celeriac is a bit of a challenge to peel. Sometimes a veg peeler works fine, but if the skin is too tough and uneven, use a sharp knife to trim back the most awkward bits. Don't be shy: the washed trimmings are very good for the stockpot, as are the stalks and leaves (see page 290 for more on making stock).

Rinse the celeriac well after peeling, then, if you're not cooking straight away, drop chopped pieces into a bowl of cold water mixed with a dash of lemon juice or white wine vinegar, otherwise the exposed flesh will quickly discolour.

eating celeriac raw

Raw celeriac adds interest and flavour to vibrant winter salads and slaws without trucking in salad ingredients from sunnier climes. Grate it coarsely on a box grater or in a food processor, or cut into slices (a mandolin is good for this) and then into slender matchsticks. For a softer finish, blanch the matchsticks for a minute in boiling water.

cooking

Celeriac has remarkable versatility, both in texture and flavour. It can be made into velvety mash, a rich soup, tender gratins and pies, and in the Riverford Field Kitchen one of our favourite ways to bring out its mellow aniseed notes is simply by roasting it.

roast

Peel as described above and cut into evenly sized cubes or batons. Toss with olive oil and salt, then spread in a single layer over a roasting dish (use two if you don't have room – it needs a little space so that it roasts rather than steams). Roast at 190°C/Gas 5 for about 40 minutes, until tender and starting to caramelise round the edges.

To reduce the cooking time to 20 minutes, you could also blanch the celeriac for 5 minutes in boiling salted water beforehand.

fry

For crisp, golden cubes or chips, cut your celeriac up small and parboil it in salted water for 5–10 minutes, until just tender. Drain and let it steam dry for a few minutes. Heat a centimetre or so of oil then fry for 10–15 minutes, flipping gently with a spatula so that the pieces are browned on all sides.

celeriac

boil

Plain boiled celeriac with a bit of butter, salt and pepper is a tender treat in its own right. If you're roasting or frying celeriac in a hurry, boiling it for 5–10 minutes in salted water will also speed matters up.

* For mash: boil chunks of celeriac in salted water until completely tender, 15–20 minutes depending on their size. Drain and combine with an equal quantity of cooked floury potatoes and some butter, cream and mustard. For further variation, cube a couple of apples and add to the cooking celeriac; or boil your celeriac in milk with a few peeled garlic cloves then drain and blitz with a little of the cooking milk. Eat as a purée or mash with potatoes.

* For a luxurious, velvet-smooth soup: gently sweat a chopped onion in butter or oil until very tender, then add a peeled and roughly chopped medium celeriac. Stir in a bouquet garni (thyme, bay and parsley tied together) and enough stock just to cover. Peeled apple or potato and slices of leek are good additions here. Simmer until tender, remove the herbs, then blitz, seasoning well and adding a glug of double cream if you like. Garnish with walnut oil or chopped toasted hazelnuts.

'smash'

For a rustic-looking side with a nice bit of uneven texture (see left): heat a glug of olive oil in a pan over a high heat then add chunks of celeriac. It will hiss and spit – keep it moving so it doesn't catch or burn. After a few minutes, add 50ml of water, a knob of butter, a tablespoon of white wine vinegar or lemon juice and a good pinch of salt. Give it a final stir, cover with a lid and turn the heat to medium. Keep checking every 5 minutes, adding a dash more water if it looks like catching. Cook until the edges are soft but the middle retains its bite – about 20 minutes. Remove the lid for the last 5 minutes to evaporate off any excess liquid, then season to taste. Use the back of a wooden spoon to smash the celeriac – as much or little as you like. Good additions include:

* a couple of finely chopped garlic cloves added halfway through cooking.

* a slosh of white wine, red wine or Marsala part way through cooking, since celeriac is strong-flavoured enough to stand up to a bit of booze – as the liquid evaporates its taste will intensify.

IDEAS FOR ROASTED CELERIAC CHUNKS

Serve roasted cubes or batons simply, with a squeeze of lemon and some chopped dill or parsley. This goes well with white fish.

* Mix with robust cooked grains (such as spelt or pearl barley) or lentils. Add chopped apple, crumbled blue cheese, peppery leaves and a mustardy vinaigrette (see page 000) for a hearty, healthy salad.

* Fold into a risotto a few minutes before the rice is done, just to warm the celeriac through.

* Whizz up with some fried onions and stock to make a quick soup; or whizz into a purée with butter or cream and salt and pepper and serve alongside strong-tasting meats – beef, venison or game – or seared scallops and bacon.

* sprinkling over finely chopped rosemary and chilli, or thyme and sweet paprika, when the celeriac's nearly done and cooking for another few minutes with the lid off.

* an extra squeeze of lemon juice to brighten the taste at the end.

braise

For a popular (though long-cooking) Turkish technique, gently heat 4 tablespoons of olive oil, the juice of 1 lemon, 1 teaspoon of sugar and a pinch of salt in a medium pan. Add a diced medium celeriac (about 700g cut into 1–2cm dice) and just enough water to barely cover. Simmer, covered, on a low heat until tender – usually 45 minutes to 1 hour, depending on size. (The lemon and oil in the water means the celeriac takes longer to cook than just in water.) When the celeriac is nearly cooked, take the lid off and let the liquid evaporate so that you're left with a rich sweet–sour juice coating the veg. Serve at room temperature mixed with plenty of chopped dill. This is even more delectable eaten the next day.

works well with...

* apple and pear
* caraway
* cheese – blue cheese and Parmesan
* cream or crème fraîche
* fish – especially white fish such as bass or bream, mackerel and scallops
* herbs – chives, lovage, parsley, rosemary, sage and thyme
* horseradish – from a jar, or finely grated horseradish root
* lemon
* mustard
* nuts – especially hazelnuts and walnuts
* pork – roast pork, bacon, cold ham

celeriac, kale and mushroom pie

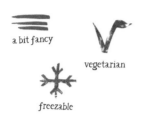

a bit fancy

vegetarian

freezable

This winter warmer gives the heartiest of meat stews a run for its money. Cooking the component parts may seem a bit fiddly but it ensures each ingredient retains its perfect flavour and texture. We've suggested some additions to the filling below but go easy with them - the veg is more than enough to carry the show.

SERVES 4

4 tbsp light olive or
   vegetable oil
1 large celeriac (about 1kg),
   peeled and cut into
   1cm chunks
1 tbsp white wine vinegar
60g butter
2 large red onions,
   roughly sliced
500g flat mushrooms,
   thickly sliced
1 glass of red wine
3 garlic cloves, finely
   chopped
150g cavolo nero (black kale),
   leaves stripped from their
   stalks and washed
100ml double cream
¼ whole nutmeg,
   finely grated
1 x 300g ready-rolled
   sheet all-butter puff
   or flaky pastry
beaten egg, for brushing
salt and black pepper

Turn the oven to 190°C/Gas 5. Heat 3 tablespoons of the oil in a pan, add the celeriac and follow the instructions for making 'smash' on page 104, adding the vinegar and half the butter during cooking.

Meanwhile, melt the remaining butter in a frying pan with the remaining tablespoon of oil and fry the onion on a medium heat until starting to soften, about 10 minutes.

Add the sliced mushrooms and cook until they start to release their moisture. Pour in the wine, add the chopped garlic and let the liquid bubble and reduce until you have a dark, sticky mess. Season with salt and pepper.

While the mushrooms cook, blanch the kale in salted water in two batches for 1½ minutes each. Remove with a slotted spoon and plunge straight into ice cold water to stop the cooking and fix the colour. When cool, squeeze out the water and roughly chop.

Combine all the component parts in a large bowl. Add the cream and nutmeg, mix gently and check the seasoning.

Pack the mixture snugly into a shallow pie dish. Cut out the pastry to the size of the rim of your dish and place it over the top of the filling, tucking it around the sides. Brush with the egg and slash a couple of holes in it for the steam to escape. Bake for 20–25 minutes, until the pastry is golden and the filling is bubbling around the edges.

VARIATIONS
* Make it festive by adding a handful of chopped pre-cooked chestnuts.
* Add diced and fried streaky bacon.

potato and celeriac gratin

quick & easy

vegetarian (if using a vegetarian
substitute for Parmesan)

freezable

**SERVES 4 AS A MAIN
OR 6 AS A SIDE**

butter, for greasing
200ml double cream
150ml milk
1 bay leaf
2 garlic cloves, crushed
600g potatoes
400g celeriac
100g Parmesan
    (or vegetarian
    equivalent), grated
salt and black pepper

If the rain is lashing the windows, a voluptuous, comforting root gratin should be on your menu. This does well either as a side dish or a weeknight meal in its own right.

Heat the oven to 180°C/Gas 4 and grease a gratin dish or shallow ovenproof dish with a knob of butter.

Put the cream, milk, bay leaf and garlic into a pan with a generous seasoning of salt and pepper. Slowly bring to a simmer then turn off the heat and leave to steep for 10 minutes.

Peel the potatoes and celeriac and cut the potatoes into 5mm slices and the celeriac into 3mm slices – celeriac cooks more slowly, so by doing this they'll be ready together (a mandolin or food processor is useful here).

Remove the bay leaf from the cream and add the celeriac and potatoes. Mix well then check the seasoning.

Tip the mixture into the gratin dish, spreading it out evenly. Cover tightly with foil and bake until tender to the tip of a knife, about 40 minutes. Remove the foil, sprinkle with the Parmesan and return to the oven for 10 minutes or until nicely browned.

VARIATIONS
* Mix a couple of handfuls of dried breadcrumbs with the Parmesan for a golden crispy topping.
* Mix through some blanched and chopped greens such as kale or spinach before topping with the breadcrumbs.
* Infuse the milk and cream with a sprig or two of a hardy herb, such as sage, rosemary or thyme, along with, or instead of, the bay leaf.
* Stir a tablespoon of both wholegrain and Dijon mustard into the cream before adding the potatoes.

---

roasted celeriac with mustard and bacon

quick & easy

freezable

This is a versatile side dish as it is but you can easily bulk it out and turn it into a main following our suggestion below. Cook the bacon with the celeriac or separately. The former will give the veg a fantastic salty flavour but the latter will ensure a crispier bite to the bacon.

SERVES 4 AS A SIDE

1 medium celeriac (about 800g), peeled, cut into chunks or wedges, and blanched (see page 103)
6 rashers of streaky bacon, rinds removed, diced
light olive oil, to coat
1 heaped tbsp wholegrain mustard
salt and black pepper

Heat the oven to 180°C/Gas 4.

Put the celeriac and bacon into a roasting tin and coat with a generous glug of light olive oil. Season with salt and pepper but go easy on the salt as the bacon will add plenty of its own. Stir so that everything is well coated in oil.

Roast until the celeriac is soft to the tip of a knife and starting to brown, about 20 minutes. Add the mustard and turn again until coated.

VARIATION
* Turn this dish into a main course in its own right: pack the cooked celeriac and bacon into an ovenproof dish, pour over a swirl of cream and grate over a good melting cheese (e.g. Cheddar or Gruyère). Grill until the cheese is bubbling and serve with a dressed salad of bitter leaves.
* Try roasting the celeriac with other cubed root veg – potatoes, carrots or swede would all work well.

smoked mackerel, celeriac and watercress salad

quick & easy

Aromatic and delicate, cooked celeriac works beautifully with fish and seafood - puréed to accompany scallops or roasted in wedges with a meaty fillet of sea bass or skate. Eaten raw, its earthy richness and mineral tang is better balanced as here with the more robust taste of smoked mackerel.

SERVES 4

1 small celeriac (400–500g), peeled and cut into fine matchsticks
1 apple, cored, halved and finely sliced
a good squeeze of lemon juice
2 tbsp cider vinegar
1 tbsp clear honey
2 tsp wholegrain mustard
4 tbsp olive oil
100g watercress, washed and drained
leaves from a small bunch of mixed herbs (e.g. parsley, tarragon, chives), finely chopped
4 smoked mackerel fillets, skinned, bones removed and shredded
salt and black pepper

Toss the celeriac in a large bowl with the apple and lemon juice. Season with salt and pepper.

In a small bowl, whisk together the vinegar, honey, mustard and oil to make a dressing.

Add the watercress, herbs and smoked mackerel to the celeriac. Pour over the dressing and toss to combine. Check the seasoning before serving.

VARIATIONS
* For a heartier salad, add finely sliced fennel, wedges of cooked beetroot, toasted walnuts or slices of cooked, waxy salad potatoes.
* If you don't have watercress, use peppery winter salad leaves such as rocket instead.
* Anything salty and smoked will work here – from trout and hot smoked salmon to smoked chicken breast or ham hock.

celeriac, apple, parsley and walnuts

quick & easy

vegetarian

SERVES 2

1 tbsp crème fraîche
juice of ½ lemon
pinch of sea salt
½ celeriac, grated or cut
   into fine matchsticks
1 apple (crisp and sharp
   is best), diced or cut
   into thin wedges
40g walnuts, toasted
leaves from a small bunch of
   flat-leaf parsley, chopped

Crunchy and sharp, this coleslaw-like salad makes a lovely light lunch, especially alongside slices of ham or other cured meats.

In a small bowl, mix the crème fraîche, lemon juice and sea salt.

Put the celeriac, apple, walnuts and parsley in a salad bowl and pour over the dressing. Toss to combine.

VARIATIONS
* Dress with a swirl of walnut oil.
* Replace the walnuts with hazelnuts.
* Make into a heartier salad by serving with bitter salad leaves, a good crumble of blue cheese and a little olive or hempseed oil.
* For a version that goes well with roast beef, grate rather than chop the apple and combine with a quarter of a grated onion.
* Omit the walnuts and lemon juice, and dress with 100ml crème fraîche mixed with a spoonful of grated or creamed horseradish.

Jerusalem artichokes

october to february

While some people rave about these knobbly tubers, others avoid them like the plague. John Goodyer, the first to plant them in England, didn't enjoy them much himself: 'they stir and cause a filthy loathsome stinking wind, thereby causing the belly to be pained and tormented.' It's true that their nickname - fartichokes - is justly earned. It's also true that peeling them is a bit of a faff. But I think both disadvantages are easily outweighed by their sweet, nutty flavour and versatility in the kitchen: Jerusalem artichokes are delicious roasted, make a fantastic creamy soup and are also pretty good simply boiled and buttered, or even eaten raw in salads.

Jerusalem artichokes are neither artichokes nor from Jerusalem, though their flavour is distinctly artichokey. The first half of their name is thought to be a corruption of *girasole* - 'sunflowers' in Italian - with which they share dramatic yellow flowers.

Beloved of farmers for their extraordinary vigour, Jerusalem artichokes are planted out like potatoes in the spring and can grow over 3 metres tall in a few months, overshadowing even the most competitive weeds. In September they burst into bright sunflower-like flowers, then in the last few weeks of their life in October they fill out into hardy tubers. Like parsnips, they keep best in the soil they grew in, so we lift them with a potato harvester in small quantities as and when they're needed through the winter.

Guy

jerusalem artichokes

storage

Like potatoes, Jerusalem artichokes have a good shelf life and should keep for several weeks in a paper bag at the bottom of your fridge or in a cool veg rack, especially if they're left muddy.

prep

For roasting, frying or gratins it's easiest to keep the skin on – some would argue that this even adds to the flavour. Just give the veg a quick soak in cold water, scrub with a veg brush and trim away any stringy roots. For more delicate dishes, such as soup, risotto and salad – peel the skin with a peeler, using a small sharp knife to skim off any awkward lumps. The exposed flesh discolours quickly, though, so put the pieces in a bowl of cold water acidulated with a little lemon juice or white wine vinegar.

eating Jerusalem artichokes raw

Sweet, nutty and delicately crunchy, raw Jerusalem artichokes make good crudités or additions to salad.

Peel, cut into slender batons and eat dipped into mayonnaise. Or make a lemony dressing (see page 296) and peel and finely slice your artichokes directly into it so they don't discolour. Add toasted hazelnuts, Parmesan shavings and radicchio or watercress.

'FARTICHOKES'

Jerusalem artichokes are nicknamed with good reason! The effect varies from person to person, from light wind to extreme gale. Old wives' tales abound about the best way to minimise the effects, but we've found that in soup, it helps to purée and sieve it; otherwise, pair the artichokes with a second vegetable to dilute the effect – potatoes, celery, celeriac and carrots all work very well. As with most farty food, we should actually be grateful. The bacteria in our guts producing the carbon dioxide and other gases are doing us a favour: they're digesting the fructose chains that we can't.

cooking

Artichokes can be boiled for mash or salads, but roasting or 'stoving' them brings out their sweet, nutty flavour.

roast

Cut all except the small chokes in half lengthways – they roast better that way. Toss in a roasting tray with olive oil and salt, adding bay leaves, thyme sprigs and whole unpeeled garlic cloves too, for more complexity of flavour. Roast in an oven heated to 190°C/Gas 5 for 30–40 minutes, until tender and caramelising around the edges. Give them a shake once or twice to ensure even cooking. Serve hot as a side dish, or leave them to cool and mix into a hearty salad. They go well with cooked spelt or pearl barley, a citrussy dressing, chives and parsley.

boil

For salads: Jerusalem artichokes can be boiled in their skins and peeled afterwards (or left unpeeled). Simmer in salted water for 8–10 minutes, until just tender. Check them with a knife – large tubers may need a few extra minutes. Drain and peel when cool enough to handle, then slice and dress while warm in a simple vinaigrette (see page 296) or three parts olive oil and one part lemon juice.
For mash: peel the chokes first and boil them longer until soft – 10–12 minutes, or more for large tubers. Drain and return to the hob to cook off any excess water as they tend to be watery. Mash with boiled potatoes, butter, cream and chives.

stove

Easy once mastered, this method of steaming then frying Jerusalem artichokes brings out their nutty flavour and gives them a golden crust. It works best with smaller tubers.

Heat a generous glug of oil and a knob of butter in a frying pan (non-stick ideally). Add peeled artichokes in a single layer, cover and cook over a medium heat with the lid on for about 10 minutes, until almost tender, shaking the pan occasionally. Remove the lid and fry for a further 10 minutes or until they are nicely coloured, turning them over frequently so they caramelise evenly.

work well with...

* bacon
* butter and cream
* celery and celeriac
* herbs, especially chives, cress, parsley, bay and thyme
* leeks, garlic and onions
* lemon
* mushrooms, truffles and truffle oil
* nuts, especially hazelnuts and walnuts
* Parmesan
* shellfish – scallops, prawns and crab
* tomato

Jerusalem artichoke and bacon gratin

quick & easy

freezable

This creamy gratin is particularly good for busy weeknights as Jerusalem artichokes cook quickly on the stove, then the dish only needs a blast under a hot grill to finish it off. It still works well if you leave out the bacon.

SERVES 2 AS A SIDE

75g smoked bacon, diced
25g butter
200g Jerusalem artichokes, scrubbed clean
100ml double cream
100ml milk
20g Parmesan, grated
salt and black pepper

Heat the grill to high. Fry the bacon in the butter until crispy. Drain on kitchen paper and set aside.

Peel and slice the artichokes and put them in a small pan with the cream and milk. Bring to a gentle simmer and cook until tender but still holding their shape, about 10 minutes.

Drain the artichokes and put the liquid back on to the stove to reduce. When thickened to a custard consistency, return the artichokes to the pan, add the bacon and season to taste. Tip into a gratin dish and top with the Parmesan. Place under the hot grill until golden, 5–10 minutes.

VARIATIONS

* Substitute half the Jerusalem artichokes for another, less windy, root vegetable such as potato or celeriac. Cut everything into similar-sized slices, but cook the two different vegetables separately, one after the other in the same pan of milk and cream, since they will likely cook at different rates.
* If you have truffle oil, drizzle a little over the gratin just after it comes out from under the grill. As it hits the hot gratin, the aroma will be sensational. Serve a crisp green salad alongside for an elegant supper.

Jerusalem artichoke and leek soup

vegan

freezable

This creamy soup can be dressed with fancy garnishes (see suggestions below), or left plain and eaten with crusty bread for an easy midweek meal.

SERVES 4

2 tbsp sunflower, vegetable or rapeseed oil
2 leeks, washed and sliced
1 onion, sliced
600g Jerusalem artichokes, scrubbed clean, peeled and roughly chopped
1.2 litres vegetable stock, plus a little extra to thin if needed
1 bay leaf
2 rosemary sprigs
pinch of freshly grated nutmeg
salt and black pepper

Heat the oil in large pan. Add the leeks and onion and fry on a very low heat for 10 minutes, until softened, stirring now and then to stop them catching.

Add the artichokes, stock, bay leaf and rosemary and season with the grated nutmeg and salt and pepper. Bring to the boil, reduce the heat and simmer for 25–30 minutes, until the artichokes are very soft.

Remove the bay leaf and rosemary then blitz the soup in a food processor or blender, adding a little more stock or water to thin to your preferred consistency. For an even smoother, creamier texture, pass the soup through a sieve. Reheat gently and check the seasoning before serving.

SERVING SUGGESTIONS
* Swirl a little double cream or crème fraîche on to each bowl of soup just before serving, and garnish with chopped chives or cress.
* Garnish with toasted, chopped hazelnuts and finish with a drizzle of truffle oil.
* Serve the soup in shallow bowls with quick-fried prawns, seared scallops or flaked white crabmeat in the centre.

chicken, Jerusalem artichoke and leek filo pie

a bit fancy

With its crisp ruffled top and rich, flavoursome filling, this is a dish of impressive contrasts; it's good with a simply dressed green salad or with plenty of wilted greens. The filling can be made in advance and frozen. Defrost, top with the pastry and bake as per the recipe.

SERVES 4

500g Jerusalem artichokes, scrubbed clean, unpeeled
squeeze of lemon juice
2 tbsp sunflower, vegetable or olive oil
2 chicken breasts (about 300g), cut into bite-sized pieces
75g butter
2 leeks, washed and sliced
4 sage leaves, finely shredded
3 tbsp plain flour
400ml milk
1 heaped tsp Dijon mustard
leaves from 4 thyme sprigs
1 x 250g pack ready-made filo pastry
50g butter, melted
salt and black pepper

Heat the oven to 180°C/Gas 4.

Cut the Jerusalem artichokes into thin wedges, putting them in a bowl of cold water with a good squeeze of lemon juice to stop them discolouring. Cook in boiling salted water for 8 minutes, until just tender, then drain.

Meanwhile, heat the oil in a heavy-based pan over a medium heat. Add the chicken and fry for a few minutes on each side – just long enough to brown the pieces; they'll finish cooking in the oven. Remove to a plate.

Add the butter, leeks and sage to the same pan. Cook gently for a few minutes to soften the leeks. Add the flour and cook, stirring, for a couple more minutes. Gradually add the milk, stirring continually, until the sauce has started to thicken. Let it bubble for a few minutes to cook out the raw flour flavour.

Stir in the Jerusalem artichokes, chicken, mustard and thyme leaves. Season with salt and pepper and transfer to a pie dish, allowing the mixture to cool.

Lightly brush a sheet of filo pastry with some of the melted butter and place it flat on top of the pie mixture. Trim away any excess, bearing in mind it will shrink very slightly in the oven. Unless you're a very quick pastry worker, lay a lightly dampened clean tea towel over the stack of waiting filo sheets to stop them drying out.

Working with a sheet of filo at a time, brush it with butter, cut it into 5–6cm strips and layer them over the pie to make a ruffled pattern. Keep going until you have created at least a couple of layers of ruffled pastry, tucking it in around the edges and making sure the pie filling is completely covered. Bake for 45 minutes, until the top is golden brown.

VARIATIONS
* You don't have to make ruffles, simply lay six or so sheets of flat buttered filo on top of the pie.
* Use a chilled sheet of shop-bought or home-made puff pastry in place of the filo. Moisten the rim of the pie dish with water and press the pastry on to it to seal. For a golden crust, brush the pastry with beaten egg. Cut a little steam vent in the middle before baking.
* For a vegetarian option, use halved or quartered mushrooms instead of chicken. Or you can use cooked chestnuts (there will be no need to fry them), or chunks of cooked squash or sweet potato.
* You could also add various cooked greens to the pie filling: blanched and chopped spinach, kale, chard or broccoli.

sautéed Jerusalem artichokes

easy

vegetarian

Simplicity is often the best way with vegetables. This dish allows the Jerusalem artichoke's nutty flavour to shine.

SERVES 4 AS A SIDE

600g Jerusalem artichokes,
   scrubbed well
squeeze of lemon juice
40g butter
1 tbsp sunflower or
   vegetable oil
1 or 2 good pinches
   of paprika
leaves from a small bunch of
   parsley, roughly chopped
salt and black pepper

Slice the artichokes into rounds, placing them in a bowl of cold water with a good squeeze of lemon juice as you go to stop them discolouring. Drain and add to a pan of salted boiling water. Cook for 8–10 minutes, until just tender.

Heat the butter and oil in a frying pan over a medium heat. Fry the artichokes, stirring now and then, until nicely browned. Season with salt and pepper.

Sprinkle over the paprika and chopped parsley to serve.

sausage and Jerusalem artichoke bake with cabbage

easy

Assemble a whole meal using just one tray. Ideally your tray should be a roasting tin that can go both on the stove and in the oven. The ones with rims are best since foil crimps tightly over them – the tighter the foil, the quicker the contents will bake.

SERVES 2

rapeseed or sunflower oil,
    for frying
8 pork sausages
1 litre hot chicken stock
600g Jerusalem artichokes,
    scrubbed clean and
    cut in half or in wedges,
    depending on size
80g Puy or dark green lentils,
    rinsed in cold water,
    then drained
leaves from 4 large
    thyme sprigs
1 tsp fennel seeds, crushed
¼ tsp dried chilli flakes
pinch of smoked paprika
    (optional)
1 Savoy or January King
    cabbage, outer leaves
    removed, cut into wedges
    with the root intact
salt and black pepper

Heat the oven to 180°C/Gas 4.

Heat a tablespoon of oil in a flame- and ovenproof roasting tin (or use a frying pan and transfer the cooked sausages to a roasting tin). Fry the sausages, turning now and then to brown them on all sides, for about 10 minutes.

Add 800ml of stock. Cover with foil and bake in the oven for 15 minutes.

Uncover the roasting tin and add the Jerusalem artichokes, lentils, thyme, fennel seeds, chilli flakes and paprika. Season with salt and pepper. Put the tin back into the oven (still uncovered) for 15 minutes or so.

Add the cabbage, wedging it between the other ingredients in the pan. Pour over the rest of stock then return the tin to the oven and cook uncovered for a further 10–15 minutes, until the lentils, artichokes and cabbage are tender.

kale
september to april

Kale was originally grown largely to see cows and sheep through the winter. Given half a chance our cows will eat radicchio, asparagus and grapefruit too - to me they occasionally seem more discerning in their tastes than many human beings.

Like cabbages, kales are members of the brassica family; virtually anywhere in the world, from the tropics to the Arctic circle, you will find varieties that have been bred to suit local conditions and culinary traditions. Their unifying trait is an open growth habit allowing us to pick older leaves over a long season while leaving the central meristem to keep generating new leaves. As with most vegetables, the dark green leaves are richest in nutrition, and, as kale does not have a centre that has been deprived of light, it is among the best sources of vitamins and minerals.

Guy

cavolo nero (black kale)   *curly kale*   *red Russian kale*

identifying

These are the three varieties of kale you are most likely to find in your veg box, each with rather different eating properties. We will also occasionally send out thousand head or 'hungry gap' kale in spring. If you happen to get this, you can use it much like the red Russian variety.

CAVOLO NERO (BLACK KALE) (October–January) is the prince of kales: a slow-growing, dark green plant with elegant, elongated leaves. This is the least hardy of the kales and often we harvest it before Christmas. It's especially good for soups and stews and is generally interchangeable with Savoy cabbage.

CURLY (September–March) is the most ubiquitous kale, the easiest to grow and the least interesting in the kitchen, though it adds a good robust texture and slightly peppery flavour to cooking.

RED RUSSIAN (October–April) has fine-fronded leaves tinged with purple. This is the sweetest and most delicate variety of kale and is best lightly steamed or braised.

storage

Kale is best kept bagged in the fridge. Use red Russian within 2–4 days and curly and cavolo nero within a week. It can be frozen, either as it comes or blanched (see page 128). Curly kale or cavolo nero can also be dried in the oven to make 'crisps' if you wish to keep it for longer (see page 129).

prep

Preparation depends on the type and age of the kale. Generally red Russian needs very little attention; both leaves and stalks should be tender enough to cook together.

For other varieties, as a rule of thumb, if a stem or rib snaps cleanly, include it in your cooking with the leaves. With older, more fibrous specimens, strip the leaves off and discard the stalks or slice finely and cook them for longer. This is almost always required with curly kale and cavolo nero, though you may find a cluster of young tender leaves at the core that doesn't need to be de-ribbed.

To strip the leaves, pinch the base of the stalk at the point where the leaf starts with your thumb and forefinger and then drag towards the tip. The leaf should shear away in a satisfying rip. Leave the leaves whole or slice finely. To slice, pile a few on top of each other, roll them tightly into a cigar, then cut across the roll.

Dirt tends to lurk inside curly kale. The easiest way to get rid of this is to prepare it as above, then swish it in a big bowl or sinkful of cold water. Leave to rest for a few minutes and the dirt will sink to the bottom. Lift out and drain in a colander, then either spin dry in a salad spinner or pat dry with a tea towel.

eating kale raw

De-ribbed and finely shredded kale leaves are good in salads (the tender varieties are best – don't try this with cavolo nero). Massage the leaves together with a little olive oil and sea salt before adding the rest of the ingredients; this softens them by breaking down some of the cellulose structure. Dress in lemon juice, olive oil and grated Parmesan, or in a mustardy dressing (see page 296) with sliced apple, toasted hazelnuts and plumped currants.

cooking

Different methods work best for each variety and cooking times will vary according to how robust the leaves are so check what's best for the type you're using.

blanch and squeeze

Blanching kale before adding it to other dishes is a good way of fixing its colour and ensuring it isn't overcooked. Bring a large pan of salted water to the boil, drop in the kale in small batches and cook for 30 seconds for red Russian, 1–2 minutes for curly and 2–3 minutes for cavolo nero. Remove the blanched kale with a slotted spoon and plunge it straight into a bowl of cold water to stop the cooking and lock in the colour. When cooled, squeeze well to get rid of the water (it's easiest to use your hands), then chop and add where it's needed.

slow braise

This method works best with the more robust leaves of cavolo nero. Cook your kale, partially covered, over a low heat with a little water or stock for about 30 minutes. Add a dash more liquid as necessary to stop it catching. It will retain some bite and the colour should be dark. Let the liquid boil away for the last minutes of cooking so that the edges become very lightly crisped. You can also add flavours or seasonings at the beginning or end of the cooking – see 'works well with…' opposite.

fast cook

Steaming and boiling times depend on the robustness of the leaves and how tender or crisp you would like them: red Russian needs 1–2 minutes; curly and cavolo nero 4–8 minutes. Err on the side of undercooking, as overcooking destroys kale's texture. Alternatively, wilt your kale leaves as follows:

Strip out the stalks and rinse the leaves. Melt some butter in a frying pan and fry a couple of cloves of finely chopped garlic on a low heat for 1–2 minutes, until starting to colour.

Add the kale and cook over a high heat until starting to wilt, about 1–5 minutes, depending on variety. Use tongs to toss the kale around and ensure an even cooking.

When wilted, season with salt, pepper, maybe some chilli flakes and lemon juice.

works well with…

* acid – lemon juice and vinegar
* chilli
* dairy – cream, plus strong, hard cheese
* eggs
* garlic
* mustard
* nutmeg
* nuts – chestnuts and hazelnuts
* pork – particularly bacon, chorizo and sausage meat
* raisins, currants and dried apricots

KALE CRISPS

Heat the oven to 160°C/Gas 3. Wash kale leaves and dry them thoroughly. Trim out and discard the ribs, and cut the leaves into small pieces (about 5cm). Toss the pieces gently in a couple of tablespoons of olive oil, making sure they're well coated. Spread out in a single layer on a baking sheet lined with parchment. Sprinkle with salt and bake for 8–12 minutes, or until just crisp. They go from crisp to burnt very quickly so start checking at 8 minutes.

slow-cooked cavolo nero bruschetta

quick & easy

vegetarian (if using
vegetarian substitute
for Parmesan)

Bursting with flavour and vitamins, this is a favourite with
the Riverford Field Kitchen chefs. It can be eaten as a starter
or dressed up with ham or eggs for a more substantial meal
(also see the variations below).

SERVES 4 AS A STARTER

dash of olive oil

2 red onions, sliced

3 garlic cloves, finely
   chopped

2 heads of cavolo nero,
   leaves stripped from
   the stalks and roughly
   chopped

240ml chicken or vegetable
   stock (or water)

1 tbsp crème fraîche

40g Parmesan
   (or a vegetarian
   equivalent), grated

scant grating of nutmeg

squeeze of lemon juice

salt and black pepper

slices of toasted or griddled
   bread rubbed with
   olive oil, to serve

Heat the olive oil in a pan on a low heat, add the onion and
cook for about 10 minutes, until soft but not coloured.

Add the garlic, cavolo nero, a pinch of salt and half the stock.
Partially cover the pan with a lid and cook slowly on a low
heat for about 30 minutes until the leaves are tender, stirring
occasionally and adding the remaining stock if it starts to dry
out. Let the liquid cook off in the last 5 minutes so that the
edges start to crisp slightly.

Stir in the crème fraîche, Parmesan and nutmeg and add more
salt, some pepper and a squeeze of lemon juice to taste. Heap
on to slices of toasted or griddled bread rubbed with olive oil.

VARIATIONS

* Omit the crème fraîche and instead use ricotta, mozzarella
or burrata.
* Add a pinch of dried chilli and a few sprigs of rosemary
or thyme to the cooking pot for extra punch.
* For a bowl of winter goodness, omit the bread and mix the kale
with cooked white beans or lentils, reheated in a little stock.

kale with raisins and sherry vinegar

quick & easy

vegan

Kale's vibrant, earthy flavour marries well with simple dressings. Often this is just a glug of olive oil and a generous squeeze of lemon. Here though, it's set off by the sweetness of sherry vinegar and raisins.

SERVES 2 AS A SIDE

handful of raisins
200g red Russian
   or curly kale
2 tbsp sherry vinegar
3 tbsp olive oil
salt

Soak the raisins in a cup of boiling water to plump them up while you get everything else ready.

Strip the kale leaves from the stalks if necessary, then shred them, but not too finely.

In a bowl, whisk together the vinegar and olive oil.

Remove the raisins from the water, drain and roughly chop, then mix them into the dressing.

Steam, boil or wilt the kale until just cooked (see page 128) and transfer to a serving bowl.

Spoon over some of the dressing and season with a pinch of salt. Taste, and add more dressing and salt as required.

VARIATIONS
* Instead of vinegar and olive oil, make an Asian-style dressing with 1 chopped red chilli, 1 crushed garlic clove, 2 tablespoons of sunflower or sesame oil and 1 tablespoon of Shaoxing rice wine or sherry vinegar.
* Replace the vinegar with orange or lemon juice for a citrus twist.
* If you want something less sweet, use chopped capers, olives or anchovies in your dressing instead of the raisins.

Guy's kale hash

quick & easy

freezable

This is a real treat on a cold day. You can use any cabbage or sliced Brussels sprouts in place of kale here. To make a complete supper, top with a poached egg.

SERVES 4

300g kale, stripped from its
    stems (cavolo nero or curly
    are best for this recipe,
    but you can use red
    Russian too)
1 tbsp olive oil
300g chorizo, chopped
1 onion, chopped
500g cooked potatoes,
    cut into 2cm dice
2 garlic cloves, crushed
salt and black pepper

Blanch the kale in a large saucepan of boiling water (1–2 minutes for curly, 2–3 minutes for cavolo nero; 30 seconds for red Russian). Drain well, refresh in cold water and drain again. Squeeze out excess water and chop roughly.

Heat the oil in a large frying pan, add the chorizo and cook over a medium heat for 5 minutes, until just starting to brown. Remove the chorizo with a slotted spoon and set aside. Add the onion to the chorizo fat in the pan and cook gently for 10 minutes, until soft.

Add the potatoes and garlic, turn up the heat to get some colour on the potatoes, and cook for 5 minutes, turning the potatoes until browned all over.

Return the chorizo to the pan with the kale, reduce the heat and cook gently for a further 5 minutes, until well mixed and thoroughly heated through. Season and serve.

kale, fruit and nut pilaf

quick & easy

vegan (if you use
a vegan wine)

SERVES 2

150g brown basmati rice

sunflower or light olive oil,
    for frying

1 onion, finely diced

1½ teaspoons garam masala

125ml (a small glass) dry
    white wine

50g dried cranberries

50g raisins

500ml vegetable stock

200g red Russian or curly
    kale, chopped if the
    leaves are large

50g nuts, toasted (see tip
    overleaf) and chopped
    (e.g. hazelnuts, pistachios,
    almonds or walnuts)

a squeeze of lemon juice

salt and black pepper

The kale and cranberries give this spiced rice dish a Christmassy colouring so it's a good one to serve as a healthy meal among all the rich food around. If you've got a large, deep frying pan and want to double the quantities to serve 4, then it should fit, otherwise use a large heavy-based saucepan or flameproof casserole dish. Red Russian and curly kale (leaves stripped from tougher stalks) work best here. It can be made with cavolo nero, but in that case it's best to boil the leaves, refresh, chop and add them at the end of cooking.

Put the rice in a bowl of cold water to soak. Heat 2 tablespoons of oil in a large, deep frying pan or wide saucepan. Add the onion and fry on a low heat for 10–15 minutes, until the onion is soft and translucent. If it looks like catching at any point, add a splash of water.

Drain the rice and add to the onion with the garam masala, then stir. Add the wine and simmer until it's almost all been absorbed by the rice.

Add the dried cranberries, raisins and stock and season with salt and pepper. Simmer on a low boil for 15 minutes, then cover and steam for 5 minutes (if your pan doesn't have a lid, use a large piece of foil). Add the kale, cover again and steam for a further 5 minutes or so, until the kale has gently wilted (not collapsed) and the rice is just tender (brown rice still has a nutty bite once cooked). Stir in the nuts, add a squeeze of lemon juice and more seasoning to taste.

kale, fruit and nut pilaf *continued*

VARIATIONS
* Use shredded cabbage or Brussels sprouts or broccoli florets
in place of the kale.
* Try adding some fresh herbs – chopped parsley or a little
dill or mint.

TIP: TOASTING NUTS
For whole hazelnuts with their skins on, bake in an oven heated
to 200°C/Gas 6 for 8–10 minutes or so, keeping an eye on them,
until the skins turn a dark brown. Transfer to a clean tea towel,
wrap it up and use to rub off the skins. For other shelled nuts, such
as walnuts and almonds, a gentle heat in a dry frying pan or low
oven to warm them through and release their oils is enough.

---

pasta with kale, anchovies and chilli

quick & easy

This simple pasta is a great tonic for a jaded palate. Even if you're not generally a fan, don't leave out the anchovies; they melt into the oil and their flavour is subtle and mellow.

SERVES 2-3

200g kale, stripped from
    its stems if necessary and
    torn into pieces (cavolo
    nero or curly are best for
    this recipe, but you can
    use red Russian too)
250g penne or similar pasta
4 tbsp olive oil
2 garlic cloves, very
    finely sliced
1 large or 1½ small red
    chillies, finely sliced (seeds
    in or out; it's up to you)
6 anchovy fillets, finely
    chopped (see tip)
50g Parmesan, half finely
    grated, half shaved
salt and black pepper

Blanch the kale in a large saucepan of boiling water (2–3 minutes for cavolo nero, 1–2 minutes for curly or 30 seconds for red Russian). Drain well, refresh in cold water and drain again. Squeeze out excess water and chop roughly.

Meanwhile, cook the pasta in salted boiling water according to the packet instructions.

Pour half the olive oil into a large frying pan over a medium heat. Add the garlic and chilli and fry for 1–2 minutes, until the garlic is golden brown. Add the anchovies with a little water and stir until mostly melted. Then add the kale, stir well and season with salt and pepper.

Drain the pasta, reserving a few tablespoons of cooking water. Toss with the kale, the remaining olive oil, reserved water and grated Parmesan. Serve scattered with the Parmesan shavings.

TIP
Many cooks prefer to use salted anchovies. If you're among them, separate the fillets and rinse them well in cold running water before using. Anchovy fillets preserved in oil are also perfectly good and don't need to be rinsed.

baked eggs with kale and cream

quick & easy

vegetarian (if vegetarian
cheese is used)

These ramekins of creamy, vitamin-rich greens topped with an egg make a luxurious (rich!) brunch, lunch or dinner. If you don't have any ramekins, use a small, shallow ovenproof dish and make hollows in the kale mixture for your eggs.

SERVES 4

300g curly kale or cavolo
    nero, stripped from
    its stems
1 tbsp olive oil
2 garlic cloves, very
    finely sliced
300ml double cream
1 pinch chilli flakes
4 eggs
120g Gruyère, grated
salt and black pepper
toast, to serve

Heat the oven to 180°C/Gas 4. Blanch and squeeze your kale as per page 128 (1–2 minutes for curly, 2–3 for cavolo nero).

In a large frying pan over a medium heat, add the oil and garlic and fry for 1–2 minutes. Add the kale and season with salt and pepper. Stir in the cream and chilli and bubble for 3–5 minutes, until thickened slightly.

Divide the kale between four ramekins, making a small well in the centre of each. Break an egg into each well and sprinkle a little of the grated cheese on top. Bake for 8–10 minutes, until golden and bubbling around the edges. Cook for less time if you like your yolk runny. Sprinkle over a little pepper and serve immediately with toast. You can either slide a knife round the edge of the ramekins and turn them out, or eat straight out of them with a teaspoon.

kale and mushroom lasagne

a bit fancy

vegetarian (if using a
vegetarian substitute
for Parmesan)

freezable

SERVES 4

10g dried mushrooms
2 tbsp sunflower or light
  olive oil
1 large or 2 small onions,
  finely chopped
4 garlic cloves,
  finely chopped
4–6 sage leaves, depending
  on size (sage is quite
  strong, so add sparingly)
leaves from 2 thyme sprigs,
  or 1 tsp dried
400g chestnut or other
  closed-cup mushrooms,
  wiped clean, finely chopped
300g curly kale or cavolo
  nero, leaves stripped
  from their stalks
10 pre-cooked lasagne
  sheets (about 200g)
salt and black pepper

For the béchamel sauce
50g butter
50g plain flour
700ml milk
50g Parmesan (or vegetarian
  equivalent), finely grated
1 tbsp Dijon mustard

This calls for quite few steps of preparation, but they can be done well in advance and once the lasagne is in the oven, you can sit back and relax. Red Russian is a little too delicate for this dish; curly kale or cavolo nero are ideal.

Heat the oven to 200°C/Gas 6.

Put the dried mushrooms in a heatproof bowl, pour over 100ml hot water and leave to stand.

Heat the oil in large frying pan. Add the onion and fry on a low heat, stirring occasionally, for 10 minutes, until very soft.

Add the garlic, sage, thyme and fresh mushrooms. Fry, stirring, for 3 minutes more. Season with salt and pepper and set aside.

For the béchamel sauce, melt the butter in a pan, stir in the flour and cook on a low heat, stirring constantly, for 2 minutes. Remove from the heat and add about a quarter of the milk and whisk into a smooth paste. Gradually add the rest of the milk, whisking all the time to avoid lumpiness. Return to the heat, add half the Parmesan, and stir until the sauce starts to thicken. Let it bubble and cook for a further 5 minutes, still stirring. Remove from the heat and stir in the mustard and some salt and pepper.

Blanch and squeeze the kale as per page 128, then finely chop. Drain and finely chop the dried mushrooms, keeping the soaking liquid. Stir the dried mushrooms and reserved liquid into the cooked mushrooms. Add the kale, mix and check the seasoning.

Spread a thin layer of béchamel on the bottom of a baking dish. Add a layer of lasagne, then half the mushroom mixture, then another layer of lasagne, half the béchamel and repeat using up the rest of the mushroom mixture and lasagne, finishing with the rest of the béchamel. Sprinkle over the remaining cheese. Bake for 35–40 minutes, until the top is golden and the pasta is tender.

kale, spelt and chorizo big soup

quick & easy

This 'big soup' is a chunky broth that's almost a stew. It's a great style of dish for using up the last odds and ends in your winter veg box. The basic requirements are onion and garlic, a grain, good stock and lots of veg, but you can liven it up with bacon or chorizo, by stirring in pesto or by sprinkling over gremolata (see page 214). It also reheats well.

SERVES 4

2 tbsp rapeseed or
    sunflower oil
1 onion, chopped
2 cooking chorizo sausages,
    skins removed, crumbled
    into small pieces
1 dried red chilli or a good
    pinch of chilli flakes,
    to taste
4 tomatoes (peeled if you
    have time), finely chopped,
    or 1 tbsp tomato purée
150g pearled spelt, rinsed
    well and drained
1.5 litres chicken or good
    vegetable stock
200g curly kale or cavolo
    nero, leaves stripped
    from their stalks and
    roughly chopped
salt and black pepper

Heat the oil in a pan over a low heat, add the onion and fry gently for 10 minutes, stirring now and then to stop it catching, until soft and translucent.

Add the chorizo and fry, stirring occasionally, for a few minutes more. Stir in the chilli, tomatoes, spelt and stock and season with salt and pepper. Bring to the boil, reduce the heat and simmer for 20 minutes.

Meanwhile, blanch and squeeze the kale, as instructed on page 128. Add the kale to the pan and cook for a further 15 minutes or until the spelt is tender. Keep an eye on the liquid and top up a little if needed. Check the seasoning before serving.

TIP: PEELING TOMATOES
To skin tomatoes easily, cut a little cross in the base then lower them in a bowl of boiling water. Leave for about 45 seconds until you can see the skins just starting to furl away at the base, then transfer them to a bowl of cold water and peel off the skins. A good tomato purée (containing only tomato) is often a better alternative in winter.

leeks
october to january

Our leeks are pulled, stripped and trimmed by hand. Surviving the grim hardship of a January day spent bent over in a windswept field with 5 kilos of mud clinging to each boot also requires a zen-like quality possessed by only a small minority. I reckon the pickers deserve to be paid more than bankers but I'm not sure we would sell many leeks if they were.

If you were to judge by supermarket availability, you'd be forgiven for thinking the leek season runs from July to mid April. Early plantings can be harvested from late July but with so many other veg in season through the summer, we save leeks for the autumn and winter with harvest starting in earnest in September or October. Later, winter-hardy varieties tend to be shorter and stouter with darker leaves, and arguably they taste better. By March, the spring warmth encourages them to bolt – if you dissect one you might see the bolt thrusting up through the centre. Initially this is tender and edible, but by May you should be wary of buying them as they become hard, yellow and bitter. Leeks are a winter vegetable and should be kept that way.

Along with onions, garlic and chives, leeks belong to the genus *Allium*. Pungent and potent when raw, leeks turn gorgeously sweet when cooked, and though they're not the star of many dishes they are an important ingredient of many.

Guy

leeks

storage

Leeks will be fine in the bottom drawer of the fridge for a week or more. Chop off and compost the very tops if they're too long to fit, or keep them for making stock (see page 290).

prep

Leeks tend to harbour a bit of mud. If you have only one to clean, cut it in half lengthways, leaving the root base intact. Hold each half under the cold tap, root end up, fanning out the leaves with your fingers. For a bigger batch, it's easier to slice the leeks first: cut off the root base and the dark green top and use the white and paler green section. Let the rings soak for a few minutes in a bowl of cold water so the dirt sinks, then drain in a colander.

eating leeks raw

Slender young leeks are delicate enough to be used raw. Halve lengthways and slice the tender white and pale green sections into fine half moons. Dress with a little vinegar and salt, or a light vinaigrette (see page 296). Use in salads, as a garnish for fish, or in sandwiches; the zingy effect is like adding capers or pickles. For a milder flavour, soak them in cold water for an hour or so first.

WASTE NOT, WANT NOT
The dark green part of a leek is less tender but full of flavour and nutrients. Discard any discoloured bits, then keep the rest for the stockpot.

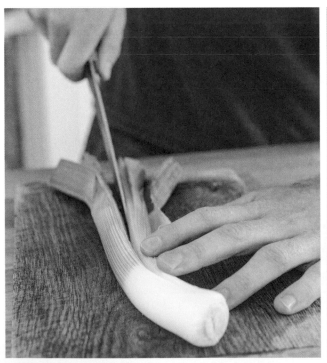

cooking

If a recipe calls for onions you can use leeks instead or as well. They are a good base for stocks, braises and soups and give a more refined flavour than onions alone. If you have larger leeks, they're best slow-fried or braised; steaming and griddling is better suited to smaller, younger leeks.

griddle

Steam or simmer your leeks (see overleaf), either in 5–10cm chunks, left whole (if small), or halved lengthways with the root base intact to hold them together. Drain well and gently squeeze out any excess water. Heat a griddle pan or barbecue. Brush the leeks with olive oil, sprinkle with salt and then sear until charred with brown ridge marks, 3–4 minutes on each side.

slow-fry

Slow-frying leeks in butter or oil brings out their silky sweetness. They're good alone, or as an unctuous base to other recipes. The key is patience and a low heat, to avoid ending up with a nasty mixture of burnt and raw leeks.

Sweat sliced leeks on a medium–low heat, stirring frequently, until they are completely tender but not coloured – they need a good 10–15 minutes. To be sure they're done, taste a piece – it should be sweet and soft. Season with a little salt and pepper and a tiny dash of vinegar if you need to balance the sweetness.

IDEAS FOR USING SLOW-FRIED LEEKS

* Creamy leeks: add a dash of cream to the cooked leeks and simmer gently for a few minutes until reduced to a thick, glossy coating. To brighten, add a scattering of chopped parsley or chervil, or grated lemon zest. This makes a lovely pasta sauce or a topping for sourdough toast.

* Make a simple soup: after 5 minutes of cooking the leeks, add thinly sliced garlic, diced potatoes, a bouquet garni (bay leaves, thyme and parsley tied together in a bunch) and enough stock to cover and cook until the potatoes are completely tender, about 20 minutes.

steam or simmer

Cut your leeks into large chunks and steam for 5–10 minutes, until just tender. Test by piercing with a knife or eating a piece – any hint of raw crunch should have disappeared. Alternatively, simmer the chunks in salted water, testing in the same way. To preserve their colour, plunge them into cold water as soon as they're done, then drain well to avoid any risk of sliminess.

work well with...

* cheese – blue cheeses, Cheddar, feta, goat's cheese, Gruyère, mozzarella, Parmesan and smoked cheeses
* cured meat – bacon, ham, pancetta
* chicken
* cream, crème fraîche, sour cream and yoghurt
* fish – salmon, white fish, mussels
* herbs – chives, chervil, mint, parsley, tarragon and thyme
* lemon
* white wine

IDEAS FOR USING STEAMED OR SIMMERED LEEKS

* Leek vinaigrette: while your leeks are still warm, spoon over a simple vinaigrette (see page 296). Top with chopped hard-boiled eggs, and perhaps some chopped capers and parsley. Serve warm or at room temperature. (This also works well with griddled leeks.)

* Pasta sauce: for an easy supper, warm your leeks with plenty of melted butter and toss with cooked pasta (pappardelle or penne are good), black pepper and grated Parmesan or Cheddar.

* Leek gratin: nestle the cooked leeks in a buttered gratin dish, adding thyme leaves if you have any. Pour over cream, stock or a mixture, top with breadcrumbs and/or grated cheese and dot with butter. Bake at 190°C/Gas 5 for about 30 minutes, until the cream has bubbled and reduced and the top has browned. Serve warm rather than piping hot for the best flavour.

griddled leeks, wild rice and quinoa with chervil

a bit fancy

vegan

**SERVES 4-6 AS A SIDE
OR 2-3 AS A MAIN**

75g wild rice
3 medium or 2 large leeks,
    washed and cut into
    5cm lengths
50g quinoa (a mixture of
    red and white is prettiest
    if you can get it)
good olive oil, for drizzling
15g fresh chervil, leaves
    picked off their stalks
salt and black pepper

For the dressing
3 tbsp extra virgin olive oil
1 tbsp vinegar (white wine,
    balsamic or cider)
2 tsp Dijon mustard
juice of ½ lemon, or to taste

Packed with nutrients from the wild rice and protein from the quinoa, this is a nourishing and really flavoursome meal on its own or is also a good side dish for chicken or pork. Chervil has bright green leaves a bit like carrot tops and a mild, sweet aniseed flavour. Use parsley if you can't get hold of it; it will give a more robust finish.

Put the wild rice in a pan of lightly salted boiling water and cook for 35–40 minutes, until tender.

Meanwhile, simmer the leeks in another pan of lightly salted water for about 8 minutes, until tender. Lift out with a slotted spoon, reserving the cooking water, and gently squeeze out any excess water. Add the quinoa to the pan and boil for 15 minutes.

To make the dressing, whisk the oil, vinegar, mustard and lemon juice in a big bowl. Season with salt and pepper.

Heat a griddle pan until really hot. Drizzle the leeks with a little oil and grill for 3–4 minutes on each side, until branded with brown ridge marks.

Drain the rice and quinoa and add to the bowl of dressing along with most of the chervil. Toss to dress and check the seasoning. Top with the leeks and sprinkle over the remaining chervil.

leek and feta fritters

quick & easy

vegetarian

A very moreish starter or light lunch with a bitter leaf salad. The dip includes sumac, a deep-red, lemony spice used a lot in Middle Eastern cuisine. It's increasingly available in supermarkets, but if you can't find it, use a little extra lemon juice and a couple of grinds of pepper instead.

SERVES 4

For the fritters
3 leeks, washed, trimmed
    and finely sliced
25g butter
2 tbsp olive oil
2 large eggs
50g crème fraîche
70g self-raising flour
30g gram (chickpea) flour
    (or just use a total of
    100g self-raising flour)
1 tsp baking powder
80g feta, crumbled
small bunch of tarragon,
    leaves chopped
cayenne pepper
dash of milk (if necessary)
sunflower oil, for frying
salt and black pepper

For the dip
zest and juice of ½ lemon
150g crème fraîche
sumac (or see introduction
    for alternative)
lemon wedges, to serve

Heat the oven to 180°C/Gas 4.

Lightly fry the leeks in the butter and oil in a frying pan over a medium heat until starting to soften, about 7 minutes.

Whisk the eggs and crème fraîche until light and starting to increase in volume. Sift in the self-raising flour, gram flour, if using, and baking powder and gently mix into a batter. Fold in the leeks, feta and tarragon. Add a pinch of cayenne and some salt and pepper. You should have a consistency that will drop slowly from a spoon. If too dry, add a dash of milk; too wet, add a pinch of flour.

Pour oil into a frying pan to a depth of about 5mm and heat until a test teaspoonful of batter sizzles immediately. Using a spoon, add three or four separate dollops of batter to the pan. Push each one with the back of the spoon until you have small patties about 8cm across. Cook until golden, about 3–4 minutes on each side.

Remove the cooked fritters to a baking tray and repeat until you have used up the batter. You may need to heat up fresh oil between batches if it starts to run dry. When all are done, place the fritters in the oven for 10–12 minutes to warm through.

Meanwhile, make the dip. Mix the lemon zest into the crème fraîche with a pinch of salt and add the lemon juice to taste. Sprinkle liberally with sumac and serve with the lemon wedges.

VARIATIONS
* Add chopped, fried crispy bacon to the batter, or replace the feta with cooked, shredded chicken.
* Instead of tarragon use dill or mint.

leek and Parmesan tart

quick & easy

vegetarian (if using a
vegetarian substitute
for Parmesan)

SERVES 4-6

3–4 tbsp olive oil,
    or 50g butter
6 large leeks, washed,
    dried and thinly sliced
bunch of thyme, tied
    with string
1 x 300g ready-rolled sheet
    all-butter puff pastry
25g Parmesan (or vegetarian
    equivalent), finely grated
salt and black pepper

The secret of this recipe lies in cooking the leeks long and slow,
so that they become sweetly caramelised. The rest takes no time at
all and you can exercise your imagination adding extra toppings.

Heat the oven to 200°C/Gas 6.

Heat the oil or butter in a heavy-bottomed saucepan and add the
leeks and thyme. Slow-fry the leeks as described on page 145 until
they are very soft and starting to brown, a good 10–15 minutes.
Cover the pan initially to help them sweat, then take off the lid
halfway through so the liquid evaporates. Stir at intervals to stop
them catching. Season with salt and pepper then cool.

Meanwhile, lay out your pastry flat on a lightly greased non-stick
baking sheet and bake for about 10 minutes until it has completely
puffed up and is golden brown. (Check the bottom of the pastry
is cooked too.)

Flatten the pastry back down by covering it evenly with the
leek mixture, leaving 5mm around the edge. Sprinkle with the
Parmesan and any other toppings (see suggestions below) and
return to the oven for a further 5 minutes, until the cheese
has melted. Serve warm.

VARIATIONS
* Onions work as a replacement for or combined with the leeks.
* Experiment with extra toppings, just like a pizza: try anchovies,
olives or different cheeses, such as mozzarella or goat's cheese.

leeks 151

chicken, leek and tarragon pasta

quick & easy

Chicken and tarragon's lemon-aniseed flavour is a time-honoured combination with good reason and makes this a beautifully balanced, simple dish. Stir a spoonful of wholegrain mustard into the sauce if you want more of a kick.

SERVES 2

3 tbsp olive or vegetable oil

2 medium leeks, trimmed and finely sliced

200g ribbon pasta (e.g. pappardelle, fettuccine, tagliatelle)

2 chicken breasts, cut into thin strips

1 small glass (about 125ml) of white wine

2 tbsp chopped tarragon leaves or 1 tsp dried tarragon

100g cream cheese or double cream

25g Parmesan, finely grated

salt and black pepper

Heat 2 tablespoons of the oil in a large pan on a low heat. Add the leeks and cook very gently for 10 minutes or until soft, stirring now and then to stop them catching.

Cook the pasta in a large pan of salted boiling water according to the packet instructions. When cooked, reserve a ladleful of the cooking water and drain.

When the leeks are done set them aside. Increase the heat to medium–high and add the remaining tablespoon of oil to the same pan. Add the chicken and fry until browned and cooked through, about 5 minutes. You don't want to overcrowd the pan or it will sweat rather than fry, so you may need to cook it in batches.

Return the leeks to the pan with the chicken, add the wine and cook for about 2 minutes, until it has reduced by half, then add the tarragon, the reserved pasta water, the cream cheese and half the Parmesan. Season well with salt and pepper, stir to combine, then toss with the cooked pasta. Serve sprinkled with the rest of the Parmesan.

VARIATION
Replace the leeks with finely shredded Brussels sprouts or cabbage.

simple mussels with leeks

quick & easy

A favourite recipe of Riverford Cook Anna Colquhoun, this cooks quickly and is delicate and light. Mussels are a seasonal food: they're at their best in the winter, when they are plump and tasty, so, as the old saying goes, only eat mussels in months with an 'r' in them.

SERVES 2

2kg live mussels
2 tbsp olive or sunflower oil or 25g butter
1 large or 2 small leeks, washed, trimmed and finely sliced into half-moons
2 garlic cloves, finely chopped
1 or 2 pinches of red chilli flakes
175ml white wine (or cider)
handful of parsley leaves, finely chopped
salt

Scrub the mussels under cold running water, pulling off the beards and discarding any that are cracked or don't close when tapped sharply.

In a large, lidded pan, heat the oil or butter on a low heat then add the leeks and fry slowly until they start to soften, about 7 minutes. Add the garlic, chilli flakes and a good pinch of salt, and cook for a further 3 minutes.

Turn the heat up high, add the wine and wait until it starts to boil. Wait 1 minute and then add the mussels. Cover the pan immediately and cook on a high heat for 2–3 minutes, giving the pan a shake now and then. The mussels are ready when they are gaping open (discard any that aren't).

Stir in the parsley then tip into a large bowl and serve with bread to mop up the juices. You'll also need napkins and a big bowl for your empty shells.

leek and smoked cheese macaroni

quick & easy

freezable

An invigorating winter dinner, this goes well with salad or a generous helping of wilted greens. Make more than you need, as this freezes well either before or after it is baked.

SERVES 4

400g macaroni
drizzle of olive oil
40g butter
4 small leeks (about 400g),
    washed and shredded
4 heaped tbsp plain flour
800ml milk
200g smoked Cheddar,
    grated, plus extra
    for topping
2 tsp Dijon mustard,
    or to taste
4 tbsp breadcrumbs
    (optional)
salt and pepper

Heat the oven to 200°C/Gas 6.

Boil the macaroni in a pan of salted water until nearly cooked, about 8 minutes. It should be slightly too al dente to eat. Drain and toss in a little olive oil to stop it sticking together.

While the pasta is cooking, melt the butter in a small pan on a low heat. Add the leeks and cook gently until soft, about 7 minutes, stirring now and then.

Add the flour and stir over a low heat for 2 minutes, then gradually stir in the milk (a whisk helps avoid lumps). Add the cheese and heat gently, stirring, to thicken the sauce and melt the cheese. Season to taste with mustard, salt and pepper.

Combine the pasta with the leek mixture and transfer to a baking dish. Sprinkle over a little more cheese and the breadcrumbs, if using, and bake for about 20 minutes, until golden on top.

VARIATIONS
* Add some leftover cooked chicken or fried bacon pieces to the leek mixture before baking.
* For extra veg, stir through some blanched and chopped kale, cabbage, spinach, chard or broccoli.

onions
and
shallots
july to march

A humble vegetable but crucial in kitchens all round the world. Much as my mother tried to keep the five of us from creating chaos into her kitchen I was around enough to remember her forever chopping and gently frying onions in thick aluminium pans on the ancient Aga; when asked what was for lunch she would as often as not reply that she 'hadn't decided yet'.

Many meals start with frying an onion so we provide a year-round supply in our veg boxes, in various forms, starting the season with bunched green onions in May and moving on to a succession of yellow and red onions and shallots. We grow the early crop in Devon but the south west is too damp to reliably produce a mature crop which stores without rotting, so we look to our grower group in the drier east of England for most winter onions. The only break you may get in onion supply is March and April when the stored crop is starting to sprout and even autumn-planted onions are not yet ready, making the only option importing from the southern hemisphere. At this time we risk a week or two without onions and encourage our customers to substitute with a leek, which are normally in good supply as they make a last push before running to seed; this works pretty well in most recipes: leeks share the onion's harsh pungency in its raw state, giving way to a savoury sweetness on cooking.

Guy

identifying

These are the main onions you will get with your veg box over the autumn and winter months.

YELLOW ONIONS (aka brown or white onions) are your regular, all-purpose onions. Their pungency depends on variety, growing conditions and length of storage. Enjoy them sharp and punchy when eaten raw, or mellow and caramelised after a long, slow cook.

RED ONIONS arc slightly sweeter than regular onions. The maroon-skinned bulbs are good raw in salads or roasted, whole or in wedges, with a little sugar or honey. They can stand in for yellow onions in most recipes.

SHALLOTS are milder and sweeter than onions. They require more effort to grow and dry (and peel) but are worth it for recipes calling for a less astringent taste. Use them finely diced in dressings, salsas and garnishes, roast them whole, or substitute them for onions as the base of risottos or sauces.

storage

As long as they are firm and not about to sprout, onions last well for several weeks anywhere cool, dry and dark. They don't need to be in the fridge and like a bit of air movement.

prep

Shallots have a slightly different anatomy to onions, but the same methods work for both. Unless you're planning to bake onions whole, pickle them or cut them into rings, it's generally easiest to halve them before peeling; cut the onion in half directly through the root base, so that each half is held together at the bottom, then peel.

slice

Place the onion half flat-side down and cut into half-moons, stopping just short of the root end. Alternatively, remove the root end with a little wedge-cut then cut the onion lengthways into strips. Half-moons seem to work best for salads and quick-frying; slice lengthways for slow-frying.

dice

Place the onion half on its flat side. Leaving the root end intact so that it holds everything together, first cut it lengthways, tip to root, with each cut following the curve of the onion, so those at the sides will be at an angle to the board and those on the top will be vertical. You should end up with a fan of sliced onion, all held together by the root base. Now cut the onion crossways, perpendicular to the first set of cuts. As you slice, the onion will fall apart into dice. You'll be left with a little stump of root base.

eating onion raw

A little raw onion can really brighten a dish, but slice finely and don't be overgenerous as a little goes a long way. Milder and sweeter, shallots and red onions are better for this than yellow. For a milder flavour, soak sliced onions in cold water for an hour or so. To accentuate the sweetness of red onions and shallots, slice or dice them finely then soak in red wine vinegar with a good pinch of salt and sugar. Even leaving them for half an hour makes a big difference, although a couple of hours is even better.

cooking

Onions are stalwarts of the vegetable world with an incredible versatility of flavour. Sweated down, they're the base for any number of stews, sauces and soups, but they can also be placed centre stage – baked whole until tender, caramelised and sticky, or used as a sweet-savoury filling for a tart.

slow-fry

Recipes tend to be optimistic about how long it takes to sweat an onion, often specifying 3–5 minutes. For sweet, soft, juicy onions, you will need to cook them for anywhere between 10 and 20 minutes on a low–medium heat,

onions and shallots

stirring frequently. A pinch of salt draws out some moisture, making them less likely to dry out and burn. If they look like doing so, add a dash of water. Use enough fat to keep the onions moist. Butter tastes great but browns easily, so a combination of butter and oil is best, or for curries and stir-fries, try coconut oil. The onions are done when transparent and very tender. Completely caramelised onions, needed for French onion soup (see page 162), onion gravy or onion jam, require an extra 20 minutes or so to allow them to brown gently and evenly.

quick-fry

Briskly sautéeing your onions on a high heat is good if you're after some caramelisation and don't mind leaving the centres of the onion pieces a little raw. This gives a contrast of flavours that works well for stir-fries and some strongly spiced Indian dishes. Burnt is never good though, so stir diligently, catching the bits that stick to the side of the pan.

bake/roast

Onions and shallots roast brilliantly; their sugars caramelise to an almost toffee-like sweetness. All that's needed is a bit of time.

Put them whole, skins on or off, drizzled with oil, in an oven tray and bake at 200°C/Gas 6 for 45–60 minutes (depending on size), until tender.

Alternatively peel, drizzle with olive oil, and start them off with foil on top for the first 30 minutes to trap the steam, then remove the foil and continue roasting for a further 30–45 minutes to caramelise.

CRISPY FRIED ONIONS

One of the best ways to enjoy a glut of onions is to deep-fry them until crispy. The chopping will be a bit time-consuming unless you have a food processor or a mandolin but the onions will keep in an airtight container for five days and are good for perking up salads, sprinkling over meat, fish and roasted veg, or scattering on mash.

Very finely slice your onions. Pour sunflower or vegetable oil into a large, deep pan to about 5cm depth (or use a fat fryer) and heat to 180°C. Use a thermometer to check (see page 88 for tips on deep-frying). Add a handful or two of onions to the hot oil. Don't overcrowd or you risk the temperature dropping or the oil overflowing. Fry the onions until golden brown, keeping the oil temperature steady. Remove with a slotted spoon to a colander lined with kitchen paper. Once cool, spread them out and sprinkle lightly with sea salt.

For a quicker cook, peel, slice into wedges, toss with oil, salt and pepper, and roast for 45 minutes at 190°C/Gas 5, turning them over once. Experiment with different fats, vinegars and herbs, or a little sugar or honey. For more ideas, see Whole Roasted Onions with Thyme, page 165.

slow-fried onions with rosemary and cream

quick & easy

vegetarian

This is a lesson in the transformative power of time and heat. Even before you add wine, cream or herbs, you'll have a wonderful foundation of melted onions. Eat spooned over cooked grains or toast, or with fried sausages, liver and crispy bacon, or alongside roast lamb.

**SERVES 4 AS A
SIDE OR GARNISH**

40g butter

2 tbsp light olive or other
mild oil

4 large yellow onions,
finely sliced

1 small glass of white wine or
sherry or a tot of brandy

100ml double cream

leaves from a rosemary sprig,
finely chopped

salt

Melt the butter and oil together in a pan on a low heat. Add the onion, along with a pinch of salt, and cook, stirring frequently, for about 20 minutes, until the onion is totally transparent and meltingly tender.

Add the wine, sherry or brandy and allow it to bubble away until most of the liquid has evaporated and you have a golden, buttery tangle. Season well with salt.

Add the cream and rosemary and simmer for a further 10 minutes to reduce the mixture slightly.

VARIATIONS

* For an onion sauce (a good vegetarian alternative to gravy), omit the rosemary and blend it all with a squeeze of lemon juice or white wine vinegar.

* These onions also make the beginnings of very good classic onion gravy: add a tablespoon of plain flour in place of the cream and herbs and cook for a few minutes, then add 300ml of good-quality stock and any scrapings from your meat roasting pan. Simmer for 10 minutes then add a teaspoon of mustard and a dash of Worcestershire sauce.

French onion soup

long slow cook

freezable

There's only one trick to this sumptuous classic: time. Riverford Cook Anna advises cooking the onions for up to an hour to achieve melting, caramel perfection, and once you've added the stock, they need to simmer for another hour. The taste will prove that it's not time wasted. Fresh beef stock really does make a difference.

SERVES 4

35g unsalted butter
1 ½ tbsp olive oil
500g yellow onions,
   thinly sliced
½ scant tsp caster sugar
1 ¼ litres good-quality beef
   stock (preferably not
   a stock cube)
1 tbsp plain flour
120ml dry white wine
4 slices of crusty bread
   or baguette
1 garlic clove
1 ½ tbsp brandy, or to taste
   (optional)
150g Gruyère or Emmental
   cheese, thinly sliced or
   coarsely grated
salt and black pepper

Melt the butter and olive oil in a heavy-bottomed pan or casserole on a low heat. Add the onion, a good pinch of salt and the sugar and cook on a low heat, stirring often, for 45 minutes to 1 hour, until the onion is very soft, golden brown and sweet.

Pour the stock into another pan and bring to a boil. Add the flour to the caramelised onions and cook, stirring, for another few minutes. Add the hot stock and the wine, season with salt and pepper and bring back to a boil.

Reduce the heat and simmer gently for at least 45 minutes, preferably an hour, stirring occasionally to check it's not catching.

Toast the bread and then rub with the garlic clove on both sides while still warm, then cover each with cheese. Preheat the grill.

Add the brandy to the soup, if using, and check the seasoning. Ladle into ovenproof soup bowls and top each one with a piece of toast. Place under the grill until the cheese is bubbling. If this manoeuvre seems risky, grill the cheese toasts on a baking tray separately then serve them on top of your soup bowls.

VARIATIONS
* For a lighter soup, use chicken instead of beef stock.
* Play with the booze: replace the white wine with red or even port; instead of brandy, use Madeira or Marsala (the latter's good with chicken stock); or add an apple note by using a strong cider in place of the wine and finishing the soup with Calvados or cider brandy.
* Throw in a handful of sage or thyme leaves or chopped rosemary along with the onions.

whole roasted onions with thyme

vegetarian

Roasted onions are rich enough for a dinner-table centrepiece. They're also particularly good with Sunday roasts and sausages, or broken up and spread on toast, topped with slices of goat's cheese or brie, and grilled until golden. They reheat very well, so you can make more than you need for one meal.

SERVES 4-8 AS A SIDE

8 red or yellow onions,
    peeled but roots left intact
about 50g butter
1 tbsp soft light brown sugar
2 tbsp vinegar (balsamic,
    sherry or red – whatever
    you have to hand)
100ml vegetable stock
    (or water)
4 thyme sprigs
salt and black pepper

Heat the oven to 200°C/Gas 6.

Put the onions into a baking dish, packed in fairly tightly.

Melt the butter in a pan, then add the sugar, vinegar, stock and thyme and mix everything together. Pour the mix over the onions and season well with salt and pepper. Cover the dish tightly with foil and roast in the oven for 45 minutes.

Remove the foil and roast for a further 45 minutes or so, until the onions are sticky and starting to caramelise.

shallot tarte Tatin

quick & easy

vegetarian

A savoury twist on the classic French apple tart, this makes an excellent lunch or supper with a simple green salad and some good sharp cheese (goat's or other). If you don't have the right-sized ovenproof frying pan, transfer the cooked shallots to a small greased pie dish or shallow cake tin before topping with the pastry.

SERVES 4

50g butter
500g shallots, peeled
120ml good-quality
   balsamic vinegar
small bunch of thyme, tied
   together tightly with string
1 x 300g ready-rolled sheet
   all-butter puff pastry
salt and black pepper

Heat the oven to 200°C/Gas 6.

Heat the butter in a heavy-bottomed ovenproof frying pan (beware wooden and plastic handles!). The shallots will shrink a lot, so the pan might need to be smaller than you'd imagine. Add the shallots and cook on a medium heat until they start to brown, turning occasionally, about 8 minutes.

Add the balsamic vinegar, thyme, a teaspoon of salt, some pepper and enough water to cover. Poach the shallots until they are cooked through and completely soft, about 10 minutes, adding more water if necessary.

Remove the thyme, then bubble the liquid and reduce it until the balsamic vinegar becomes syrupy. Remove from the heat and check the seasoning.

Cut a circle of pastry a little larger than the pan, then lay it over the shallots and quickly tuck down the sides (without burning your fingers). Cut a small slit in the centre for a steam vent.

Immediately place the pan in the oven and bake for 20–30 minutes until the pastry is puffed and golden. Leave to cool for 5 minutes, and then invert on to a large flat plate or wooden board, cut into wedges and serve warm.

november to march

parsnips

Before the arrival of cane sugar in Europe, parsnips were used as a sweetener for jams and cakes. Once sugar was introduced along with potatoes, some countries were pretty quick to relegate them to the category of cattle fodder. But the Brits kept them on as a significant commercial crop, and they are still one of the joys of winter: sweet, cheap and easy to cook. They are of course wonderful roasted but also make a soothing soup, add a sweet crunch to raw winter salads, and work very well with all sorts of spices. They are an even better source of vitamins and minerals than the more highly bred carrot.

Parsnips are notoriously fickle in their germination, with seeds taking anywhere between 10 and 30 days to emerge. This makes it difficult to achieve a uniform crop; it used to be a problem when I started off supplying supermarkets, but our box customers are, happily, a lot more accommodating of oversized and oddly shaped veg. A giant parsnip whose neighbours have failed will be just as good as its smaller neighbour who has been cramped by a crowd, and much easier to prepare.

Parsnips are also slow to grow, which is good because their best flavour comes once we've had a few hard frosts – these unquestionably improve their sweetness, as part of the starch converts to sugar. We generally wait until November to start harvesting and keep going until late March; avoid buying them any later in the year, when they'll either be tough and woody or have been shipped from afar.

Guy

RIVERFORD SACREWELL

storage

Parsnips have soft, porous skins and lose
moisture faster than most other root veg.
It's best to leave the mud on as a protective
coat. Store them somewhere cool and dark,
or in a paper bag in the bottom of the fridge,
and they'll keep for a good 2–3 weeks. Even
if they've gone a bit floppy, their flavour
is generally still fine.

prep

Soak your parsnips for a couple of minutes
in cold water then give them a scrub or peel.
Cut off the top and any spindly root ends.
Usually you can use the whole vegetable,
though late in the season (late February)

the core might start getting a little tough, in
which case quarter the parsnip lengthways
and cut it out. Parsnip scraps are good for the
stockpot – though not too many as they can
dominate other flavours.

eating parsnips raw

Like raw celeriac, raw parsnip has earthy
sweetness and crisp texture that's good in
salads. As the weather gets colder the starches
in the root turn to sugar, so they'll be at their
best after the first frosts. Choose small ones
and cut them into fine matchsticks, grate on
a box grater or shave using a vegetable peeler.
Combine with carrot, beetroot, apple, dried
fruit, nuts and parsley. Dress in lemon juice,
honey, salt, pepper and a dollop of yoghurt.

cooking

Roast parsnips are a staple of many a Sunday roast, but boiled or steamed they provide a good base for mash and salads, or a component of curries and stews.

roast

Chop into even batons, toss with oil and salt and roast at 180°C/Gas 4 for about 40 minutes, turning them over once or twice as needed. You can add flavourings to the oil such as honey, maple syrup and/or wholegrain mustard.

Alternatively, for a slightly fluffier centre and crisper outside, steam or boil your batons for 10 minutes then roast at 200°C/Gas 6 in a preheated roasting tin stirred into a generous layer of oil or duck fat. Don't crowd the tray or they will end up steaming rather than roasting. Turn them over in the fat once or twice during cooking. They're done when tender to the core and caramelised on the outside, anything from 20–40 minutes, depending on the size of your parsnip pieces.

boiled/steamed

Boiled or steamed parsnips are a versatile base for a meal. Cut them into even-sized pieces and cook for 10–15 minutes in boiling salted water or a double boiler. They're done when tender to the tip of a knife. Then you can:

* Toss with melted butter, pepper and chopped herbs such as parsley, chives and tarragon.

* Cool, dress and serve as a simple salad with 1–2 tablespoons of yoghurt per person, a good squeeze of lemon and ½ teaspoon of harissa (or more to get the heat right for you).

* Mash or purée them – they're good with white fish or poached eggs.

* Use to make parsnip cakes (see page 174).

* Deep-fry them as chips: roll them in flour, egg and breadcrumbs before frying, including a generous handful of grated Parmesan in with the breadcrumbs (see page 88 for notes on deep-frying).

work well with...

* apple
* butter and cream
* cheese, especially Cheddar and Parmesan
* herbs – thyme, rosemary, parsley, chives, tarragon and coriander
* honey and maple syrup
* mustard
* nuts, especially hazelnuts and almonds
* spices – nutmeg, cumin, coriander, turmeric and other Indian spices
* sweet dried fruits, such as dates

LEFTOVER COOKED PARSNIPS

Throw boiled, steamed or roasted parsnips into curries and stews; combine with fried onions and stock to make a soup; or use in a hearty salad – they're good with other roast veg and couscous, or tossed with spelt, chopped walnuts and dates, watercress and feta. Another home for leftovers is Parsnip, Brussels Sprout and Bacon Potato Cakes (see page 174).

North African spiced beef and root vegetable stew

freezable

long, slow cook

Ras el hanout is a complex North African spice mix. If you can't get hold of it, mix a large pinch each of cumin, coriander, cinnamon, ginger, turmeric, cardamom, chilli or cayenne and black pepper.

Cinnamon sticks can vary in strength, so taste at intervals and remove when the flavour reaches your liking. Serve this stew with couscous or bread to soak up the juices.

SERVES 4

3 tbsp olive, sunflower or vegetable oil

450g beef braising steak, cut into 4 similar-sized pieces

1 large onion, sliced

2 garlic cloves, crushed or finely chopped

2cm piece of fresh ginger, peeled and grated (or add 1 rounded tsp dried ginger to the ras el hanout)

1 rounded tbsp ras el hanout (or see above for alternative)

800g mixed root veg (e.g. parsnips, carrots, celeriac and swede), peeled and chopped into large chunks

1 large glass of red wine (optional; you can use more stock instead)

400ml beef stock

1 cinnamon stick

1 x 400g can chickpeas, drained

100g pitted prunes

leaves from a small bunch of parsley and/or coriander, roughly chopped

seeds from 1 pomegranate (optional)

salt and black pepper

Heat a tablespoon of the oil in a heavy-based pot or casserole and fry the beef over a medium–high heat, turning it over so it browns on both sides. Remove to a plate.

Add the remaining oil to the pot, turn the heat right down and add the onion. Fry gently, stirring often, for 10 minutes to soften without colouring. Add the garlic, ginger and ras el hanout and cook, stirring, for a couple more minutes.

Return the beef and add the vegetables and wine (if using). Bring to a simmer and bubble for a couple of minutes. Then add the stock and cinnamon stick, cover and simmer gently for an hour.

Stir in the chickpeas and prunes, re-cover the pot and simmer for a further 15 minutes, until the meat is totally tender. Sprinkle over the herbs and pomegranate seeds if using.

VARIATION
Replace the beef with diced lamb shoulder or lamb leg steaks. In this case, add a half teaspoon of turmeric and/or a pinch of saffron along with the ras el hanout and substitute dried apricots for the prunes.

parsnip, Brussels sprout and bacon potato cakes

a bit fancy

This is a jazzed-up version of bubble and squeak and can be adapted to finish up all sorts of leftover vegetables, though parsnips, sprouts and bacon is a particularly satisfying combination. A poached or fried egg or sausages would be a good addition.

SERVES 4

200g parsnips, peeled and
 cut into even-sized pieces
 (alternatively, you could
 use leftover boiled, steamed
 or roasted parsnips)
3 tbsp olive oil
300–400g potatoes,
 peeled and cut into
 even-sized pieces
200g Brussels sprouts,
 outer leaves removed
8 rashers smoked streaky
 bacon, finely sliced
polenta flour (or use ordinary
 plain flour), for dusting
salt and black pepper

Heat the oven to 200°C/Gas 6. Toss the parsnips with salt, pepper and about a tablespoon of the oil. Spread over an oven tray and roast for about 40 minutes, until soft and beginning to caramelise. Remove, allow to cool then roughly chop.

While the parsnips are roasting, boil the potatoes in salted water until soft, about 20 minutes. Drain well and mash while warm. Keep your mash as dry as possible so that the cakes hold together; if it seems wet stir it over a low heat for a few minutes.

Cook the sprouts in plenty of salted boiling water until tender, about 5 minutes. Drain well and cut into quarters. Fry the bacon over a medium–high heat with a drizzle of oil in a large frying pan (preferably non-stick) until really crispy. Remove with a slotted spoon and drain on kitchen paper. Keep the oil left in the pan to fry the cakes.

Mix all the veg with the bacon and season with salt and pepper. Dust your hands with flour then mould the mixture into burger-sized patties.

Add the remaining oil to the frying pan, place over a medium heat and fry the cakes in batches until they are golden brown, about 5 minutes per side. Add more oil to the pan if you need it. If the first cakes have cooled down by the time you have fried the last, you can reheat them all in the oven for 5–10 minutes, until piping hot.

VARIATIONS
* Replace the parsnips with roasted beetroot or squash for striking coloured alternatives.
* Use raw grated apples instead of bacon for a vegetarian option.
* Experiment with your greens: try cabbage or kale.

parsnips Molly Parkin

quick & easy

vegetarian (if vegetarian
cheese is used)

Browned parsnips layered with tomatoes and baked in a rich sauce.
Parsnips Molly Parkin (named after a flamboyant fashion writer
of the 1960s and 70s) is a satisfying old-fashioned British dish
that's well worth reviving. A fresh green salad will cut through
the richness and warm crusty bread will mop up the juices.

SERVES 2 AS A MAIN
OR 4 AS A SIDE

sunflower or light olive oil,
   for frying
25g butter, plus extra for
   greasing the dish and
   dotting over the top
1 tbsp soft light brown sugar
350g parsnips, peeled and
   thinly sliced into rounds
250g tomatoes, thinly sliced
75g Gruyère or
   Emmental, grated
125ml double cream
2 tbsp dried breadcrumbs
salt and black pepper

Heat the oven to 180°C/Gas 4.

Heat a tablespoon of oil and the butter in a large frying pan.
Sprinkle in the sugar and lay the parsnips over the top. If you can't
fit them all in, divide the parsnips, sugar, butter and oil in half and
fry in two batches. Fry for 3–4 minutes, then turn them over and
fry for a further 3 minutes or so, until they are just starting to
caramelise. Remove from the heat.

Grease a casserole or baking dish with a little butter, then start
to add the parsnips, tomatoes and cheese in layers, seasoning with
salt and pepper as you go, and finishing with a layer of cheese.

Pour over the cream, then cover with the breadcrumbs and dot
with butter. Bake for 40–45 minutes, until the top is golden and
the parsnips tender.

VARIATIONS
* Thyme and mustard go very well in this recipe if you have
them to hand: add the leaves from a couple of sprigs of thyme
(or a good pinch of dried thyme) to the parsnips halfway through
cooking them and mix a tablespoon of smooth Dijon mustard
into the cream before you pour it over.
* Use Cheddar in place of Gruyère or Emmental for
a milder flavour.

parsnip, apple and ginger soup

easy

vegetarian

freezable

SERVES 4-6

knob of butter
2 tbsp olive oil
2 large onions, diced
2 medium leeks, washed,
    white part only,
    finely sliced
2–3 garlic cloves,
    finely chopped
2–3cm piece of ginger,
    peeled and finely grated
3 medium parsnips, peeled
    and roughly chopped
3 apples, peeled, cored and
    roughly chopped
2 medium potatoes, peeled
    and roughly chopped
1 bay leaf
1 litre vegetable stock
soft light brown sugar,
    to taste
juice of ½ lemon
salt and black pepper
cream or crème fraîche,
    to serve (optional)

Parsnip, apple and ginger make a fantastic trio. The ginger brings out the warmth of the parsnip, and the apple cuts its earthy flavour with its sharp fruitiness. You could use eating or cooking apples; the latter will be more acidic so you may not need much lemon juice at the end.

Melt the butter with the olive oil in a large pan, then add the onions and leeks and fry over a medium–low heat, stirring now and then, for about 10 minutes, until softened.

Add the garlic and ginger and cook gently for a further 5 minutes, making sure the garlic doesn't burn.

Add the parsnips, apples, potatoes, bay leaf and just enough stock to cover the veg. Top up with some water if necessary. Simmer for 40 minutes, or until everything in the pan is soft and falling apart.

Remove the bay leaf and blend well until smooth (use a hand blender or food processor), adding more water or stock if it feels too thick. Taste, then season with salt and pepper and add a good pinch of sugar if needed. Finish with a squeeze of lemon juice and a good swirl of cream or crème fraîche, if using.

parsnip, cauliflower and chickpea korma

easy

vegan

freezable

Curries are a really good way to use up vegetables. This mild, warming spicy curry transforms parsnips into a creamy, comforting cold-weather dinner in less than half an hour. The Indian flavours of ginger, coconut and fresh coriander work beautifully with parsnips. Eat with boiled rice or warm naan bread, and pickle or chutney.

SERVES 2-3

2 tbsp sunflower or
   coconut oil
1 onion, finely chopped
2 garlic cloves, very
   finely chopped
2.5cm piece of fresh ginger,
   peeled and finely grated
2 tsp medium-hot
   curry powder
2 tsp ground cumin
2 parsnips (about 300g),
   peeled and cut into
   1cm chunks
400ml can coconut milk
400ml can chickpeas,
   drained
50g ground almonds
1 cauliflower (about 850g),
   cut into large florets
juice of 1 lime
1 bunch fresh coriander,
   roughly chopped
salt and black pepper

Heat the oil in large heavy-bottomed pan then add the onion and fry, stirring occasionally. over a medium–low heat for about 10 minutes, until soft and translucent.

Add the garlic and ginger and cook for a minute then add the curry powder, cumin and a good pinch of salt. Gently stir in the parsnips and cook for a further minute.

Add the coconut milk, chickpeas and ground almonds, cover with a lid and cook at a gentle boil for 10 minutes. Check the seasoning, adding more salt and pepper if needed. Add the cauliflower, then cover again and cook for a further 5 minutes or so, until the cauliflower is just tender. Sprinkle the lime juice over the curry and stir in the coriander.

parsnip skordalia

easy

vegetarian

freezable

SERVES 4-6 AS
A SIDE OR DIP

1kg parsnips, peeled and
    chopped into even-
    sized chunks
1 bay leaf
400ml milk
60g fresh breadcrumbs
80g flaked almonds,
    lightly toasted
3–4 garlic cloves, crushed
80ml good olive oil
juice of 1 lemon
salt

Skordalia is a Greek side dish of potatoes and garlic whipped into
a dip, thickened with stale bread or nuts and spiked with lemon.
This parsnip version is good warm with lamb or mushrooms, or at
room temperature as a dip for pitta bread. Parsnips are less likely
to go gluey than potatoes when blended. The pungency of raw
garlic is all part of the appeal in the original dish, but we
recommend you add it a little at a time and taste.

Put the parsnips into a pan with the bay leaf and cover with the
milk. Bring gently to the boil and simmer for 15–20 minutes, until
very soft.

Strain the parsnips, reserving the milk. Put the parsnips into a food
processor with a dash of the milk and blend until smooth. Add the
breadcrumbs, almonds and half the garlic and blend while adding
the olive oil in a steady stream. Add half the lemon juice and
a good pinch of salt. Check the seasoning and add more garlic,
lemon juice and salt as you wish. If the mix is stiffer than you
want, add a little more of the warm milk to loosen it.

VARIATIONS
* This dish can be warmed up with a little bit of spice. A clove
or two added to the milk when you cook the parsnips works
well (remove before you blend), as does a teaspoon of freshly
ground cumin.
* If the punch of raw garlic is too much for you, take the edge
off by adding the peeled garlic cloves to the milk and simmering
them with the parsnips.
* Replace the almonds with toasted and skinned hazelnuts.

potatoes

september to january

Modern farming methods have not been kind to the humble potato. Intensively cultivated for high yield and fast growth, it's been bred into staggering blandness, with generic offerings of 'red' and 'white' potatoes.

But this is not an irreversible trend and potatoes really do not have to be either bland or homogeneous. We grow our potatoes slowly, choose our varieties judiciously and encourage you to savour their flavour and not consign them to use as a bulking item on your plate. We work our way through a few different varieties as the season progresses, so look out for the name on your paper bag; consider their qualities and play to their strengths in how you cook them (see 'identifying'). This book in the series focuses on the autumn and winter varieties; new and salad potatoes are covered in *Spring and Summer Veg*.

Despite their ubiquity, potatoes are a tender and demanding crop, susceptible in particular to frost and blight. We grow our earliest on the warmer fields by the coast, planting in February for digging up in June, then the main crop is harvested in September and October and gently stored in wooden bins to tide us through the winter.

Guy

potatoes

identifying

All potatoes were not created equal. There are the waxy kinds, which have a high water content and hold their shape well when boiled. Then there are the floury kinds – fluffy, with a low water content, and better suited to baking, roasting, mash and chips. All-rounders lie somewhere in between. And there are huge variations in flavour. In the autumn and early winter our preferred varieties are:

COSMOS (floury) have an excellent flavour and are very good for roasting.

DESIREE (floury) are a good, red-skinned all-rounder, but particularly good for baking.

KING EDWARD (floury) have a good flavour but are hard to grow.

MARFONA (between floury and waxy) are very smooth-textured, which suits boiling, mashing and roasting.

ORLA AND TRIPLO (between waxy and floury) are easy to grow and very versatile.

PINK FIR APPLE (waxy) are hard to grow but have a fantastic nutty flavour and waxy texture, which is great boiled.

storage

Unlike spring's loose-skinned new potatoes, set-skinned maincrop potatoes keep well for weeks, sometimes even months. For the best shelf life, leave them muddy in a paper bag somewhere dark and cool (there's no need to store them in the fridge). By late winter they may start to sprout in anticipation of spring, but provided they haven't turned green, it's fine to knock off the chits and eat them. The flavour can even become sweeter as they start turning their energy store of starch to sugar. Extensive greening is a sign of the toxin solanine and green potatoes are best discarded.

prep

Remove any sprouts, green patches or gnarly bits, then either peel or soak for a few minutes in cold water before scrubbing clean with a veg brush. Peeling has become more common practice where spraying pesticides is the norm, but remove the pesticides and it becomes less critical – especially since there are so many nutrients in the skin. If you do peel them, put your potatoes in a bowl of cold water as you go to prevent discolouration.

cooking

A good starting point in deciding how to cook your potatoes is to work out whether your chosen variety is waxy, floury or somewhere in between. Results will be more satisfying if you work with your potatoes' natural character (see above).

roast

The very best roasties are made with floury potatoes, although all-rounders are fine. There are two methods: the long way round, boiling first, gives the crispiest, crunchiest results; the second option, cutting them into wedges and roasting from raw, is also pretty good and a bit simpler.

To boil first, heat the oven to 210°C/Gas 7 and put in a baking tray with a thin layer of light olive or sunflower oil or duck or goose fat. Halve peeled potatoes and place them in cold, well-salted water. Bring to the boil, then simmer for a further 10 minutes, until almost cooked through. Drain, leave to dry for a few minutes, then toss them in the colander to roughen their surfaces. Carefully add the potatoes to the preheated baking tray, turning to coat in fat, then immediately return to the oven and roast for 30–40 minutes, until cooked through and golden. Turn them over once or twice during roasting for even results. For variations, see Roast Potatoes with Lemon, Rosemary and Thyme on page 188.

To roast from raw, heat the oven to 200°C/Gas 6. Scrub the potatoes, but do not peel them, and pat them dry. Cut into wedges and toss with a generous amount of olive oil, salt and pepper. Spread on a lined baking sheet, making sure they aren't too crowded, and roast for 35–45 minutes, until tender in the middle and golden on the outside, turning them over halfway through. Serve hot with a sprinkling of salt.

boil

Waxy potatoes don't collapse when boiled, so are best used for eating whole or making potato salad. Place them in cold, well-salted water and bring to the boil. Reduce the heat and simmer until tender, about 15 minutes, depending on size.

bake whole

Baked potatoes are an inexpensive and comforting meal that can be adapted to your kitchen contents. Rub the skins of big, floury potatoes with oil and salt and cut a cross in the top of each. Bake for an hour or so at 190–200°C/Gas 5 or 6), until cooked all the way through. Cut in half and either pile on your topping or scoop out some of the flesh and mix it with a filling then scoop back into the skin. Good fillings include Bolognese sauce, grated cheese and cooked greens, pesto and crème fraîche or that old standby, baked beans. See Baked Potatoes with Cheesy Kale filling, page 193.

POTATOES LOVE SALT
Without salt, potatoes can be bland, so your boiling water should be salty as the sea. Simmering starches absorb salt well, so your potatoes get seasoned from the inside.

gratins

All-rounder potatoes are best for gratins,
but any variety can work. Slice peeled
potatoes into 2–3mm rounds, place in a pan
and just cover with stock or milk then bring
to the boil. Simmer for 5 minutes, season
well and transfer to a gratin dish, spreading
everything so there's an even distribution of
potatoes and liquid. Cover with foil and bake
at 180°C/Gas 4 until the potatoes are tender,
about 50 minutes. Take off the foil and cook
for 10 minutes more so that the top turns
golden. For more variations, have a look at
Gratin Dauphinois (page 195), Beetroot and
Pink Peppercorn Gratin (page 30), Potato
and Celeriac Gratin (page 108), Jerusalem
Artichoke and Bacon Gratin (page 116) and
Swede, Leek and Bacon Gratin (page 281).

MASTERING PERFECT MASH

The smoothest mash calls for a potato
ricer, which you can pick up cheaply
in most kitchen shops or online, but
an ordinary potato masher comes in
a close second. For mashed potatoes,
choose floury or all-rounders, and
make sure they are well and truly
cooked through before draining, or
you will end up with bullet hard pieces
in your mash. Use about 250g potatoes
per person. Peel and chop into even-
sized chunks (not too small or they'll
be watery) and place in a pan of cold,
well-salted water. Bring to the boil and
simmer for 12–15 minutes, depending
on size, until tender. Drain in a
colander, leave the excess water to
evaporate for a minute, then return
to the pan.

Don't be afraid of adding the good
stuff; all things dairy make deliciously
unctuous mash. Start with a large
knob of butter and a glug of milk for
everyday mash or double cream or
crème fraîche for feast days. Then
mash, adding a little more milk or
cream to get a good consistency.
Season well with salt and pepper.

Good additions include a little freshly
grated nutmeg, lots of wholegrain
mustard, a handful of chopped fresh
herbs, grated Parmesan, Cheddar or
blue cheese. You can also add cooked
greens – anything from broccoli to
cabbage, kale and shredded sprouts.

fry

Here are two fried potato methods, the first is a little easier but requires more pans:

BOIL FIRST: You can use waxy or floury potatoes for this. Peel and boil (see page 185) until just tender, then cut into cubes or slices and fry in a single layer in a wide frying pan of preheated sunflower or light olive oil, or lard, duck or goose fat. You need a generous amount – 2 tablespoons per 500g of potatoes – and it needs to be very hot. Flip the potatoes after a few minutes so that they colour and crisp on both sides. They should become very crisp on the outside with perfectly fluffy insides. Add extra fat if cooking in batches.

FRY FROM RAW: Waxy potatoes are best for this since they hold their shape while being sautéed. Don't bother peeling them; just cut into thin slices or 2cm cubes. Fry in fairly hot oil – again about 2 tablespoons per 500g of potatoes, stirring and tossing frequently, until the potatoes are cooked through and crisp on the outside, about 20 minutes. Test by eating a piece. They'll need more or less constant attention to prevent burning; a non-stick pan makes this easier. Throw in a knob of butter and some finely diced garlic a couple of minutes before they're done, then serve with chopped parsley and a sprinkle of sea salt.

work well with...

* anchovies
* all meat and fish
* capers
* dairy – especially hard cheeses, butter and cream
* eggs
* garlic and onion
* herbs – especially chives, dill, lovage, parsley, rosemary and tarragon
* lemon
* mustard
* spices – caraway, cayenne, cumin, nutmeg and saffron

roast potatoes with lemon, rosemary and thyme

quick & easy

vegan

Crisp and caramelised from roasting, tart and tangy from the lemons, this variation on traditional roast potatoes makes a particularly good side for chicken or fish, accompanied by a bitter leaf salad.

SERVES 6 AS A SIDE

1.5kg fairly waxy potatoes (such as Marfona, Orla or Triplo), washed but not peeled, cut into halves or quarters, depending on size
2 lemons, cut into thick slices, plus an extra ½ lemon to finish
7–8 garlic cloves, unpeeled, lightly smashed
4 rosemary sprigs
6 thyme sprigs
4 tbsp olive oil
salt and black pepper

Heat the oven to 180°C/Gas 4.

Put the potatoes into a pan of cold salted water, bring to a boil, then simmer for 10 minutes. Drain and let dry in a colander for a few minutes.

Transfer to a roasting pan and scatter over the lemon slices, garlic, rosemary and thyme. Drizzle over the oil and toss together with your hands, making sure each potato is coated in oil. Season well with salt and pepper.

Roast for 35–40 minutes, turning everything once or twice, until the lemons are starting to caramelise and the potatoes are golden brown. Squeeze over the extra lemon half, sprinkle with a little more salt and serve immediately.

VARIATIONS
* Small waxy potatoes such as pink fir apples and Charlottes can be halved lengthways, tossed with oil and salt and roasted from raw at 180°C/Gas 4.
* Toss the potatoes with a tablespoon of wholegrain mustard before roasting for more of a zing.

potato latkes with smoked fish and sour cream

a bit fancy

These crispy potato pancakes are traditionally eaten with apple sauce and soured cream for Hanukkah. Smoked fish makes an excellent topping, but they're equally good topped with a fried or poached egg.

SERVES 4-6

1kg potatoes, peeled and left in cold water until needed
1 onion, peeled
25g plain flour or fine matzo meal
1 egg, beaten
light olive or vegetable oil, for frying
salt and black pepper

To serve
400g cured or smoked fish, such as gravadlax or smoked mackerel
300ml soured cream
a small bunch of chives, snipped
lemon wedges, to serve

Finely grate the potatoes and onion and mix together. Squeeze out as much moisture as you can by pressing them down in a colander or rolling them in a tea towel and wringing tightly.

Put the potato and onion into a bowl with the flour and beaten egg, then season with salt and pepper and mix well.

Heat the oil in a frying pan over a medium–high heat until hot, then, working in batches, heap a few tablespoons of mixture into the pan. Flatten each heap with a spatula and shallow-fry for about 5 minutes on each side, until golden.

Remove the latkes from the pan and drain on kitchen paper then continue frying them in batches, adding more oil if the pan is getting dry. If the first ones have cooled too much, reheat them on a baking tray in an oven set at 180°C/Gas 4 for about 5 minutes. Serve topped with the smoked fish, soured cream and chives, finishing with a squeeze of lemon juice.

VARIATION
Add a tablespoon of horseradish sauce or a couple of tablespoons of freshly grated horseradish to the soured cream for more of a spicy kick.

creamy tartiflette

a bit fancy

SERVES 4

1.2kg potatoes, peeled
   and cut into thick slices
1 tbsp sunflower or
   rapeseed oil
50g butter
200g smoked streaky
   bacon, diced
2 large onions, diced
2 large garlic cloves,
   crushed or grated
250ml double cream
300g Camembert or Brie
salt and black pepper

A glorious, bubbling combination of potatoes, onion, bacon and cheese, this dish is traditionally the preserve of the ski resort but is just as good for Sunday lunch after a winter's walk. It's usually made with reblochon, but Camembert or another soft, thick-rinded cheese also work. Serve it with a bowl of bitter winter leaves to help cut through the richness.

Bring a large pan of salted water to the boil and cook the potatoes for 10 minutes, until just tender. Drain in a colander and set aside.

Meanwhile, heat the oil and half the butter in a frying pan. Add the bacon and fry on a medium heat until browned and starting to crisp, about 5 minutes. Remove to a plate.

Add the remaining butter and the onion to the same pan and fry on a low heat, stirring occasionally, for about 10 minutes, until the onion is soft and translucent. If it looks like catching, add a splash of water, stir well and turn the heat down.

Add the garlic and bacon and cook for a further 2 minutes.

Preheat the grill to a medium heat.

Add the drained potatoes to the frying pan and pour in the cream. Season with salt and pepper. Let the mixture bubble gently for a couple of minutes, just enough to thicken the cream slightly.

Cut the cheese into 0.5cm slices and arrange it over the potato mixture. Grill until the cheese has just started to melt.

baked potatoes with cheesy kale filling

quick & easy

vegetarian (if a
vegetarian cheese is used)

Baking potatoes aren't, as some people believe, a type – the name refers to the size. Floury potatoes give the fluffiest insides when baked, but all varieties work for this comforting, low-effort meal.

SERVES 4

4 baking potatoes
(250–300g each)
olive oil
2 good handfuls (about 50g)
curly kale leaves, stripped
from their stems
150g mature Cheddar, grated
salt and black pepper

Heat the oven to 190°C/Gas 5.

Put the potatoes in a baking dish and prick them a few times with a sharp knife. Rub the skins all over with a little olive oil and sprinkle with sea salt. Bake for 1–1½ hours, depending on size, until the insides are tender and the outsides crisp.

Meanwhile, boil the kale for 4 minutes in salted water. Refresh in cold water, drain well, chop and set aside.

When the potatoes are ready, remove them from the oven and leave until just cool enough to handle. Slice off the tops (serve them with the potatoes), and use a teaspoon to scoop out most of the insides, being careful not to break the skin. Put the flesh in a bowl and mash with the kale and three quarters of the cheese. Season with salt and pepper to taste.

Spoon the mixture back into the skins, scatter over the remaining cheese and return to the oven for about 15 minutes, until the cheese is golden and bubbling.

VARIATIONS
* Replace the kale with chard, spinach, mashed broccoli, sliced leeks, shredded cabbage or Brussels sprouts.
* Mash a dash of soured cream or crème fraîche or a scoop of cream cheese in with the filling.
* Try a goat's cheese or a blue cheese instead of the Cheddar.
* Swap the potatoes for sweet potatoes; they don't take as long to cook – about 40 minutes for small ones and up to an hour or more for really large ones.

venison (or beef) cottage pie

a bit fancy

freezable

This requires a few preparatory steps, but they're all easy and the results are really sumptuous. Use venison or beef and any mix of root veg for the topping in place of celeriac and potatoes: parsnip, swede, carrot and/or beetroot (though you'll get pink mash!). Good with piles of buttery cabbage or kale.

SERVES 4

800g potatoes, peeled and
  cut into 2–3cm chunks
400g celeriac, peeled and
  cut into 2–3cm chunks
75g butter
about 125ml milk or cream
  (you may need less
  depending on the
  potato variety)
3 tbsp sunflower or light
  olive oil
700g venison or beef mince
2 smoked streaky bacon
  rashers, finely chopped
1 large onion, finely chopped
2 carrots, peeled and diced
2 garlic cloves, crushed
  or finely chopped
4 mushrooms, chopped
  into small pieces
2 tbsp tomato purée
about 175ml red wine
splash of Worcestershire
  sauce
½ tsp dried thyme or leaves
  from 2 thyme sprigs
200ml beef stock (or water)
1 heaped tsp cornflour
salt and black pepper

For the mash, put the potatoes and celeriac in a large pan of cold salted water, bring to the boil and simmer for about 12 minutes, or until very tender. Drain, return to the hot pan for 2 minutes to allow excess water to evaporate, then mash with the butter and as much of the milk or cream as you need to give you a firmish consistency, seasoning well with salt and pepper.

Heat the oven to 200°C/Gas 6.

Heat 2 tablespoons of the oil in a frying pan (non-stick is best) over a high heat. Brown the mince, breaking up larger bits, then tip on to a plate.

Reduce the heat to medium, then add the bacon, onion and carrot with a splash more oil if needed. Cook until the onion is soft, around 10 minutes, stirring now and then. Add the garlic, mushrooms and tomato purée and cook for a further 2 minutes.

Return the mince to the pan, pour in the wine and simmer for 2 minutes, or until the wine has almost all evaporated. Add the Worcestershire sauce, thyme and stock, season with salt and pepper and bring to the boil. Reduce the heat and simmer for 10 minutes.

Put the cornflour into a small bowl with a splash of cold water and stir to make a paste. Stir into the mince and cook for another 5 minutes or so to thicken it slightly. Taste and check the seasoning.

Tip into an ovenproof dish and level out. Spoon the mash over the top, making sure the meat is covered. Spike the mash up a little using a fork – this helps it crisp. Bake for 20–30 minutes, until golden on top.

gratin dauphinois

long slow cook

vegetarian

freezable

Creamy or crusty? Waxy or floury potatoes? Everyone has their personal preference and there is certainly more than one way to make gratin dauphinois. The question of how to cook an authentic version was apparently so aggressively contested that Charles de Gaulle held a competition to determine the definitive recipe. Riverford Cook Anna learned this method from a Parisian chef, who assured her it was the real deal!

SERVES 6 AS A SIDE

50g butter
700ml whole milk
2 garlic cloves, peeled and
    smashed
1 tsp fine salt
1 tsp ground black pepper
1 tsp grated nutmeg
1kg medium all-rounder
    potatoes (see page 184),
    peeled and cut lengthways
    into 4–5mm thick slices
200ml double cream

Heat the oven to 180°C/Gas 4 and grease a gratin or shallow ovenproof dish (about 15 x 20cm) with half the butter.

Put the milk, garlic, salt, pepper and nutmeg in a large pan and slowly bring to the boil. Add the potatoes, return to the boil and simmer for 10 minutes, until half cooked.

Using a slotted spoon, lift the potatoes from the milk into the dish. Discard the milk (or save it for another purpose). Shake the dish to distribute the potatoes evenly. Pour the cream over the potatoes and dot with the remaining butter. Bake uncovered for about an hour, until the potatoes are tender and a golden crust has formed. To make it easier to cut, let the gratin cool slightly before serving.

VARIATION
For something slightly less rich, layer the potatoes with 1 very finely sliced onion or leek and a few thyme leaves in a well-buttered gratin dish, seasoning each layer. Pour over 300ml chicken or veg stock (or a mix of half milk and half stock), dot with a little butter and bake for about 1 hour, or until the potatoes are cooked through. The top should be a little crispy, but if it is getting too brown before the potatoes are cooked, cover it loosely with foil.

pumpkin
and
squash
october to january

Pumpkins and, in particular, squash are heat, sun and muck lovers and can struggle in a dull and damp UK summer. In a halfway decent year though, planted in a favourable position, they are a very rewarding crop. Given sunshine, plenty of manure and careful early weeding, by mid-summer they go rampant, climbing over bushes, fences, and even, given a leg up, trees. The big challenge in the UK is to get them ripe before the first frosts so they develop their full flavour and the hard skins that allow some varieties to keep for 6 months or more.

Winter squash and pumpkin, like all cucurbits (such as melon and cucumber) originate in the Americas but are grown around the globe just about anywhere where the summers are good enough. Pumpkins have a higher water content and more limited potential. The smaller ones can be okay for soup, stuffing or pumpkin pie, for those with a taste for it, but in my view they are best used for Jack-o'-lanterns. Denser-fleshed squash are another matter. They vary hugely in shape, size, colour, the percentage given over to seeds and cavity rather than to edible flesh, and ease of peeling. We go for varieties that are sweetly nutty and full-flavoured. A tray of slow-roasted squash is one of the most versatile bases out there are for a hearty meal. They are also a rich source of beta-carotene, a welcome addition to the immunity arsenal during the colder months.

Guy

pumpkin and squash

identifying

Squashes and pumpkins come in a fantastic range of shapes and sizes, and with different varieties come different tastes, textures and cooking properties. Other than for decoration, we tend to favour butternut or crown prince, but many of those below can be used interchangeably.

ACORN is a small squash that comes in a variety of colours and serves only one or two people. Its ridges make it a little irksome to peel, but it is ideal for stuffing or using as a vessel for squash soup (see page 208).

BUTTERNUT is one of the few squash that can be peeled with a veg peeler. It also has the highest proportion of edible flesh to seed and cavity and a clean, creamy taste. The flip side is that it is a poor keeper, lasting 1–3 months, particularly when grown in the UK, where it is hard to get it fully ripe.

CROWN PRINCE is a type of hubbard squash, which is at the other end of the spectrum from butternut: large with a very hard skin. This means that it's a brute to get into but it also has an excellent shelf life of up to a year. You could commit heinous crimes with a crown prince without leaving a blemish on the squash. It also has consistently good flavour.

KABOCHA (GREEN AND ORANGE), also known as Japanese squash, is a beautiful squash with a particularly sweet, firm and dense orange flesh that is good simmered, steamed and mashed, or roasted in wedges with the skin left on.

ONION, also known as red kuri, is a bright orange, onion-shaped squash with a soft, sweet flesh that is versatile but perhaps best used for mash and risottos. Its large seed cavity is also ideal for stuffing.

SPAGHETTI SQUASH stays true to its name and the flesh of this bizarre variety falls into spaghetti-like strands as it cooks. It's no good for recipes that call for chunks of squash, but good if treated like spaghetti and served with sauce. It also works served cold and dressed as a salad (see box below).

SUGAR PUMPKIN is the best culinary pumpkin grown in the UK, but still not quite as tasty as squash. If you get one of these in your squash box, use it first, as it will only keep for 1 month . It has a mild flavour and is good for soup, mash and pumpkin pie.

SQUASH SPAGHETTI
Cooked spaghetti squash can be separated out into noodle-like strands, which is a good kitchen project for children. Heat your oven to 200°C/ Gas 6. Cut the squash in half lengthways, place cut-side up on a baking tray and drizzle with oil, salt and pepper. Turn it over and roast for about 1 hour, depending on size, until completely tender. Let cool a little then scrape across the squash with a fork.

Spaghetti

Red kabocha

Crown prince

Green kabocha

Harlequin

Red onion

storage

Squash and pumpkin like to be kept dry
and warm, ideally above 14°C. A kitchen
shelf is ideal – our mixed squash box makes
a colourful rustic autumn display along the
kitchen shelf or windowsill. Thin-skinned
varieties such as butternut will store well for
up to three months; the harder-skinned types
like crown prince can last up to 12 months.
Once you've cut them, keep the remainder
in the fridge and use within a week.

SNACK ON SEEDS
Rich in good oils, roasted pumpkin
seeds make an excellent healthy snack,
salad ingredient or garnish. Separate
the seeds from the pulp and toss them
with a little oil and salt or soy sauce.
You can add flavours to the oil, such
as spices, honey or dried herbs. Spread
over a baking sheet and roast at
160°C/Gas 3 for 10–15 minutes,
until crisp and lightly golden. Once
cool, the roasted seeds will keep in
an airtight container for a week or so.

prep

Squash and pumpkins call for a bit of work. First there's making the initial breach in the tough skin (a heavy, very sharp knife is essential). Then there's the peeling, deseeding and chopping. It's worth it, though, for the sweet, velvety flesh within. There are two methods to try:

FOR THIN-SKINNED VARIETIES, such as butternut, peel the whole thing using a veg peeler. With butternut, you may find it easier to first cut it crossways into two sections, dividing the bulbous bottom half from the neck. Rest the squash on its flat bottom and cut in half lengthways. Scoop out the seeds with a spoon. To cut each piece of squash into smaller pieces, rest it on its flat side to prevent it rolling around. Chunks or wedges about 2.5cm wide work well for roasting.

FOR TOUGH-SKINNED VARIETIES, cut the squash in half first, then rest each half on its cut face and peel it with a small, sharp serrated knife, following the natural curve of the squash and always cutting away from your hand. Scoop out the seeds, then cut the rest into wedges or chunks. You can also roast squash with its skin on – cut it in half first, though, or it may explode!

cooking

Roasting produces a dish of glorious colours and deep, sweet flavours, with a pleasingly sticky caramelised surface. Alternatively, squash can be stuffed and baked, or simmered for stews, curries or soups.

roast

Heat the oven to 200°C/Gas 6; lower and the squash will still cook but won't colour. Rub your squash pieces with a generous amount of olive oil, season well and spread them across a baking tray so they're not crowded. Add a sprinkling of chilli or ground spice if you like, but if you are using herbs such as thyme or rosemary add them 5–10 minutes before the end of the cooking time as they burn easily. Squash will take 20–40 minutes, depending on size of the pieces, type of squash, time of year, water content and how caramelised you want it. A light squeeze will tell you if it's cooked; you don't want to roast it to a pulp, so if it yields to pressure it is done. See overleaf for ideas on how to use your roasted squash.

FEED THE STOCKPOT!

Save the skin, pulp and other trimmings for making veg stock (see page 290). This is especially good for making a squash risotto: let the squash stock simmer for half an hour or so while you roast chunks of squash and fry the onions. Pop your onion ends and the Parmesan rind into the pot, too, for extra flavour.

bake whole or stuffed

Baking whole can be achieved either by slicing off the top, scooping out the pulp and seeds and stuffing the cavity, or by cutting your squash into two and stuffing the halves. Smaller varieties of squash are the most practical for stuffing – onion squash in particular are easy to handle and hold their shape well. It's best if the stuffing ingredients contain a reasonable amount of moisture for tender results – a leftover Bolognese-style sauce would work well.

Once stuffed, bake on a roasting tray in an oven heated to 180°C/Gas 4 for 30–45 minutes, depending on the filling and type of squash. Alternatively, roast squash halves empty until tender (again, 30–45 minutes), then stuff them with a precooked filling and finish them under the grill for a few minutes until golden and bubbling.

simmer

Squash lends flavour and toothsomeness to curries, stews and soups and is a good alternative to meat. The trick is to add it at the right time, so it retains its structure and doesn't turn to pulp. For a thick, slow-cooked stew, add 30–40 minutes before the end of cooking; for something quicker-cooked and with more liquid, add only 10–15 minutes before the end of cooking.

Chunks of squash can also be simmered on their own. A classic Japanese way to prepare kabocha squash is to cut it into large chunks (around 6cm long), leaving the skin on to help the pieces keep their shape, and simmer it in dashi (a fish stock used in Japanese cooking) with other seasonings,

* Serve as a starter or side, warm or at room temperature, with a drizzle of chilli oil, dollops of yoghurt or hummus and a scattering of toasted pumpkin seeds.

* Mash with a fork or purée in a food processor and serve in place of mashed potato. A little grated nutmeg, salt and pepper and a dash of cream or butter work a treat here.

* Stir into a risotto a few minutes before the rice is cooked. See page 294 for a basic risotto method that also works with pearled spelt and pearled barley. Add sage for a lovely combination.

* Fold into a salad with cooked lentil or couscous, other roasted veg and some crumbled feta.

but you could simmer yours gently in veg stock or water. Season the cooking liquid with Japanese flavourings such as soy sauce (1–2 tablespoons per squash), sugar (a teaspoon), and mirin (1–2 tablespoons) for about 30 minutes until tender. Remove from the heat and let steep in the liquid for another 30 minutes or so. Serve warm or cold with some of the cooking liquor poured over.

work well with...

* Asian flavourings, including soy sauce, fish sauce, coconut, lime and lemongrass
* cheese, especially strong hard cheeses, feta, goat's cheese and blue cheese
* dairy - butter, cream, crème fraîche, sour cream and yoghurt
* garlic and onion, especially roasted red onions
* nuts – almonds, hazelnuts, pecans, pistachios and walnuts
* pork
* sesame seeds, including tahini
* spices, especially chilli, cinnamon, coriander, cumin, nutmeg and star anise
* strong herbs such as rosemary, sage and thyme

spaghetti squash spaghetti, with chilli, parsley and lemon

easy

vegetarian (if a vegetarian cheese is used)

Spaghetti squash generally has a fairly mild flavour but is fun to cook and shred into noodle-like strands. You could omit the pasta from this recipe and serve it as a side with some grated Parmesan.

SERVES 2

1 spaghetti squash
sunflower or light olive oil, for roasting and frying
50g pine nuts
150g spaghetti
1 onion, finely diced
2 garlic cloves, finely chopped or crushed
1 red chilli, deseeded and finely chopped (or leave the seeds in for more heat) or a crumbled dried chilli or chilli flakes
extra virgin olive oil, for seasoning
1 tsp finely grated lemon zest
50g Parmesan or similar hard cheese, finely grated
leaves from a small bunch of parsley, roughly chopped
salt and black pepper

Heat your oven to 220°C/Gas 7. Cut the spaghetti squash in half lengthways. Lay the two long halves cut-side up on a baking tray, drizzle with oil and season with salt and pepper. Roast in the oven for about 1 hour, until tender.

Toast the pine nuts in a dry frying pan over a low–medium heat, stirring and keeping an eye on them as they can easily burn. Tip them into a small bowl to stop any further cooking.

When the squash has been in the oven for 45 minutes, cook the pasta in salted boiling water according to the packet instructions. Drain, reserving a little of the cooking water.

While the pasta is cooking, heat 2 tablespoons of oil in a frying pan. Add the onion and cook on a low heat for 10 minutes, until soft. If it looks like catching at any stage, add a splash of water. Add the garlic and chilli and fry for a further 2 minutes.

Add the pasta to the pan with a drizzle of extra virgin olive oil and a splash of the reserved pasta water and toss gently. Take the squash out of the oven. Holding it in a tea towel, use a fork to scrape across the flesh in noodle-like strands. Add these to the pasta with the lemon zest and half of the cheese and parsley. Season to taste and sprinkle with the remaining cheese and parsley before serving.

VARIATIONS
* For an earthy flavour, replace the parsley with finely chopped rosemary needles or sage, cooked with the onion.
* Toss the pasta and cooked squash with a little reduced double cream, and some crumbled blue cheese.

butternut, red onion and pumpkin seed salad

quick & easy

vegan

Pair the sweetness of butternut and roasted red onions for a fantastic winter side salad. To turn it into a full meal, add cooked Puy or dark green lentils, goat's cheese or feta and perhaps some strips of roasted red peppers.

SERVES 4 AS A SIDE

3 red onions, sliced into
  1cm-thick discs
6–7 tbsp olive oil
1 tbsp balsamic vinegar
1 medium butternut squash,
  peeled and cut into chunks
  (see page 200)
a few thyme sprigs (optional)
30g pumpkin seeds
pinch of hot smoked paprika
1 tbsp red or white wine
  vinegar (or use more
  balsamic)
1 tsp Dijon mustard,
  or to taste
¼ tsp crushed garlic,
  or to taste
1 bag of mixed salad leaves
  (100–150g)
salt and black pepper

Heat the oven to 190°C/Gas 5.

Keeping the onion discs whole, place them in a roasting tin and drizzle with a tablespoon or two of olive oil, the balsamic vinegar and a splash of water. Season with salt and pepper.

Cover the tin with foil and roast for 30–40 minutes on a low shelf in the oven, until the onions are soft and sweet.

Meanwhile, place the squash chunks in another roasting tin, toss with a further tablespoon or so of oil to coat and a good sprinkling of salt and roast for around 30 minutes, until tender and lightly caramelised, throwing in the sprigs of thyme halfway through the cooking time (if using).

While the vegetables are roasting, put the pumpkin seeds in a small pan with a teaspoon of olive oil, a pinch of salt and a pinch of paprika. Toast over a medium heat, stirring or tossing frequently, until lightly browned, then transfer to a plate to stop them toasting further.

Make a simple vinaigrette: whisk together the vinegar, around 3 tablespoons of olive oil, the mustard and garlic to taste. Season with salt and pepper.

Put the salad leaves in a large salad bowl, pour over the dressing and toss to combine. Scatter over the butternut, onions and seeds.

crown prince, goat's cheese and spinach pie

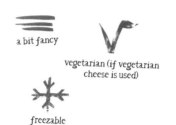

a bit fancy

vegetarian (if vegetarian
cheese is used)

freezable

SERVES 4

1 medium crown prince
    squash, peeled and cut into
    chunks (see page 200)
light olive oil, for roasting
    and frying
2 red onions, thinly sliced
2 garlic cloves, finely
    chopped
500g fresh spinach
150g hard goat's cheese
    or feta, crumbled
3–4 thyme sprigs, leaves
    stripped
scant grating of nutmeg
a few tbsp crème fraîche
    or mascarpone (optional)
600g puff or flaky pastry
    (2 x 300g packets)
knob of butter, for greasing
1 egg, beaten with a fork
salt and black pepper

Crown prince has a rich orange flesh that holds its shape beautifully when cooked, giving a good texture to the filling. This pie goes well with a simply dressed salad of bitter leaves and toasted hazelnuts or late-season cobnuts, or a pile of warm kale seasoned with fried garlic on a colder day.

Heat the oven to 200°C/Gas 6 then roast the squash with a good drizzle of oil and salt (see page 201).

Slowly fry the onions in a good glug of oil over a low–medium heat for 30 minutes, stirring occasionally, until very soft and sweet. Add the garlic for the last 5 minutes of cooking.

Bring a deep pan of salted water to a rolling boil. Put the spinach into the water and stir. Cook for 20–30 seconds then remove with a slotted spoon and plunge into very cold water. This stops the cooking process and helps retain the verdant colour. When cool, drain the spinach and squeeze dry thoroughly, then roughly chop.

In a large bowl, gently mix the squash, onions, spinach, cheese, thyme, a few twists of pepper and a scant grating of nutmeg. If the mix seems dry, moisten it with a few tablespoons of crème fraîche or mascarpone. Taste and season.

Reduce the oven temperature to 190°C/Gas 5.

Divide the pastry in half and roll out one half on a floured surface until 3mm thick. Butter the inside of the pie dish and line with the pastry, leaving a bit of overhang. Roll out the remainder of the pastry until 5mm thick and the right size for the lid. Return both to the fridge for 30 minutes to chill. If your pastry is pre-rolled you don't need to bother with this stage of chilling – just line the pie dish then fill it straightaway.

Fill the pie dish to the brim with the filling mix. Brush the overhanging pastry with a little water, place the lid on top and press down. Cut off the overhang and crimp the pastry edges together with your thumb and forefinger. Brush the lid with the beaten egg, lightly score it with a criss-cross pattern and a couple of vents in the top to let the steam escape. Bake for 20–25 minutes or until golden and crisp.

VARIATION

* Instead of spinach, use kale. Strip it from its stems and boil as described above but giving it a few minutes longer to ensure the leaves are totally tender.
* If for you a pie is not a pie without meat, add cubes of crisply fried bacon or a few slices of cooked sausage or chorizo. This will push up the saltiness, so either reduce the cheese by 50g or exercise caution in your seasoning.

TIP: FREEZING PIES

Most pies are best frozen before they are baked. They can then be baked straight from the freezer but will need an extra 30 minutes in the oven. A metal pie dish is best for freezing, since other materials risk shattering if exposed to such a dramatic temperature change.

squashy bottom soup bowls

easy

vegetarian (if vegetarian
cheeses are used)

This easy-to-make squash soup doesn't even require any bowls
– just eat it straight out of the shell, saving on the washing up
and adding to the entertainment. It's a great child-pleaser for
Hallowe'en and has endless variations with different garnishes –
some fried shiitake or chestnut mushrooms would up the
earthy autumnal feel.

SERVES 4

4 small squash (onion
    squash is ideal)
300g Ogleshield cheese
    (or a good melting cheese
    such as Gruyère or
    Cheddar), grated
100g Parmesan (or
    vegetarian equivalent),
    grated
about 40g butter
few gratings of nutmeg
4 small thyme sprigs
800ml double cream
salt and black pepper

Heat the oven to 190°C/Gas 5.

Slice the tops off the squash and scoop out the seeds and pulp,
then place the squash bowls, cut-side up on a baking tray
(reserve the lids).

Divide the cheeses and butter between the squash and add a
grating of nutmeg and a small sprig of thyme to each, then pour
in the cream to two thirds of the way up each squash bowl.

Season with generous amounts of black pepper and a cautious
amount of salt – bear in mind the saltiness of the cheeses. Put
the lids on, place on a baking tray and bake for 45 minutes to
1 hour, depending on the size of your squash, until tender.
Eat by scraping the soft flesh into the hot cream.

- -

VARIATION
Serve this in a large single squash, such as a crown prince. Treat
it like a large fondue pot, dipping in toast soldiers or leftover roast
potatoes. You will need to up the cooking time – this will take
at least 1 hour, and it's worth reducing the oven temperature
to 180°C/Gas 4 and/or wrapping the squash loosely with foil
so the outside doesn't brown too much before it cooks through.
The flesh should give to the tip of a knife.

- -

Thai squash curry

Making curry paste is quick and easy, and really gives your dish an extra edge, but if you prefer, buy a good-quality tub instead. Thai basil has a pronounced anise taste, but you can use sweet basil instead. Serve with steamed or boiled rice or noodles.

SERVES 4

1 large butternut squash, peeled and cut into 2.5cm chunks

2 tbsp sunflower or veg oil

300ml vegetable or chicken stock

1 x 400g can coconut milk

2–3 tbsp nam pla (Thai fish sauce), or to taste

juice of 1 lime

a small bunch of Thai basil, leaves only

a small bunch of coriander, roughly chopped (if not making the curry paste)

salt

For the curry paste

2 shallots, peeled and roughly chopped

3 garlic cloves, roughly chopped

5cm piece of fresh ginger, peeled and chopped

2 fresh Thai green chillies, stalks discarded, roughly chopped

2 lemongrass sticks, outer leaves discarded, thinly sliced

5 lime leaves

large bunch of coriander, roughly chopped

Heat the oven to 200°C/Gas 6.

Toss the squash with about a tablespoon of the oil and a pinch of salt, then roast in the oven until just tender (see page 201). Be careful not to overcook it – you want the chunks to retain their shape.

Make the curry paste using a blender or hand blender. Purée the shallot, garlic, ginger, chilli, lemongrass, lime leaves and most of the coriander. Whizz until really smooth, adding a little water if necessary, until you have a bright green paste.

In a wok or large pan, lightly fry the curry paste (if you're using shop-bought you'll need around 2 tablespoons, depending on the brand strength) in the remaining oil over a medium heat for 1–2 minutes to release its flavours. Add the stock and bring to a gentle boil.

Add the chunks of roasted squash then the coconut milk. Don't let it boil again as this will kill the flavour of the coconut – you're just aiming to heat the milk through. Remove from the heat and season, first with nam pla (which is very salty), then with salt if necessary, the lime juice, Thai basil and the remaining coriander. You are aiming for a fragrant combination of sweet, sour, salty and spicy. Serve piping hot.

VARIATIONS

* Add quick-cooking vegetables such as bean sprouts, mangetout and small florets of broccoli along with the squash to cook them for just a few minutes.
* Fry vegetables that need more cooking, such as thin slices of mushroom or pepper, in the oil a couple of minutes before adding the curry paste.
* For a quicker version, add raw chunks of squash to the stock, pour over the coconut milk and let everything simmer together for around 20 minutes, until the squash is tender.

squash and black bean chilli

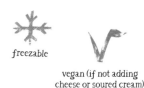

freezable

vegan (if not adding
cheese or soured cream)

SERVES 4

1 medium butternut, large
onion or smallish crown
prince squash
2 tbsp olive oil, plus extra
for roasting
1 large onion, chopped
4 celery sticks, finely chopped
1 red pepper, deseeded
and chopped
1 green pepper, deseeded
and chopped
3 large garlic cloves, crushed
1–2 tsp crushed chipotle
chillies (if you can't source
them, substitute another
fresh or dried red chilli)
1 tsp dried marjoram or
handful of fresh oregano
2 bay leaves
2 tsp ground cumin
1 x 400g can chopped
tomatoes
2 x 400g cans black beans,
rinsed and drained
juice of 1 lime (approx. 2 tbsp)
small bunch of coriander,
finely chopped
salt and black pepper
grated cheese and/or soured
cream, to serve (optional)

Either stuff a whole squash with the chilli, or dice and roast the squash and add it to the chilli. The latter opens up a whole variety of serving suggestions: eat it with rice or in a baked potato; top it with a dollop of soured cream, some spicy tomato salsa or some guacamole; stuff it in a taco with some grated cheese; or spread it over a tortilla. If you are stuffing the squash you will need to use one that is a suitable size and will hold its shape when cooked, such as onion squash (see page 198 for varieties).

Heat the oven to 180°C/Gas 4. If stuffing a whole squash, cut it in half and follow the instructions for baking whole (page 201); if roasting in chunks, follow the roasting instructions on page 201.

Heat the oil in a large heavy pan over a medium–high heat. Add the onion and celery. Reduce the heat to medium, and cook, stirring occasionally, for about 10 minutes until soft.

Add the peppers and continue cooking for a further 10 minutes or so, stirring frequently.

Stir in the garlic, and cook for another minute. Add the chilli, 1–2 teaspoons of salt, 1 teaspoon of black pepper, the herbs and cumin. Give everything a good mix then add the tomatoes. Simmer, uncovered, for about 30 minutes.

Stir in the beans and continue to simmer for a further 10 minutes. Remove the bay leaves, stir in the lime juice and coriander and adjust the seasoning to taste. If using roast squash, add it now, heat through, then serve. If stuffing a whole squash, fill each roasted squash half with the filling mixture. Top with grated cheese or soured cream (or both), if you like.

beef shin and pumpkin stew with gremolata

long, slow cook

freezable

SERVES 6-8

olive oil, for frying

1.5kg beef shin, cut
into large dice

3 large red onions, sliced

4 garlic cloves, finely
chopped

4 salted anchovy fillets,
finely chopped

½ bottle of white wine

1 tbsp tomato purée

2 bay leaves, fresh if possible

3 largish thyme sprigs,
leaves stripped

1 x 400g can of chopped
tomatoes

1 litre good chicken or
beef stock

1 dried chilli, or a good pinch
of cayenne pepper

1 small pumpkin, peeled and
cut into 2.5cm chunks, raw
or roasted (see page 201)

salt and black pepper

For the gremolata

pared zest of 1 unwaxed
lemon (with as little white
pith as you can)

2 garlic cloves

leaves and stems from a small
bunch of flat-leaf parsley

A rich, flavoursome stew that is easy to make and can be made ahead of time. Once you've browned the shin meat and made the onion base, you simply leave this slow-cooking cut on a low simmer to work its magic. This is a wonderful dinner on a cold day, paired with warm butter beans. Or eat it in the warmer months with boiled new potatoes. We've served this at our annual pumpkin days for the last two years and it's one of the first things to sell out (after the toffee apples!). Like all meaty stews it is even better the next day and you can easily halve or double the quantities to have leftovers – use them as a rich sauce for pasta. It also freezes well.

Heat a little oil in a frying pan until nearly smoking. Season your beef well with salt and pepper then fry, stirring frequently, in small batches until well browned on all sides. Set the meat aside on a plate and keep all the browning juices in the pan.

Place the red onions in a large, deep casserole or ovenproof pan with a good glug of oil and cook gently over a low–medium heat, stirring occasionally for 10 minutes, until soft. Add the chopped garlic and anchovy and cook for a further 5 minutes.

Reheat the meat frying pan, add the wine and let it bubble up. Scrape the pan with a spatula to mix the meaty residue into the wine. Pour this into the onions and add the tomato purée, bay and thyme leaves. Turn up the heat and allow the mix to bubble and reduce down by half to take away the raw taste from the wine.

Add the tomatoes and the browned beef and top up with the stock so that the meat is covered by at least a centimetre of liquid. Add the dried chilli or cayenne then leave on a low heat, half covered with a lid, to cook at a bare simmer for 3–4 hours, or until the beef is tender and flakes into shreds when pressed with a wooden spoon.

While the beef is cooking, make the gremolata: chop the lemon zest, garlic and parsley very finely together.

Add the pumpkin to the stew for the final 30–40 minutes (or, if you are adding roasted chunks, add them at the very end, giving them just long enough to warm them through). If it looks as though the stew is drying out, add water to top up the liquid. The sauce should be rich and thick, with a nice gloss from the beef's melted connective tissue. Taste and season as needed, then serve the stew scattered with the gremolata and accompanied by seasonal veg.

purple
sprouting
january to may
broccoli

Purple sprouting broccoli's wild florets are the despair of quality control supervisors across the country. 'PSB' is a delicacy that's equal, if not superior, to asparagus; and it has the great advantage of coming into season from January to May, when other home-grown greens are in short supply. At the height of the season, in March and April, we make no apologies for including it in virtually every veg box and every meal in the Field Kitchen.

For most people, broccoli has come to mean Calabrese: the chunkier, more uniform variety from Calabria in southern Italy. Purple sprouting broccoli is less highly bred, more winter hardy and has much more flavour. There are now varieties which will crop through the summer and autumn but at the time of writing we are sticking to the traditional late winter and spring varieties. The varieties we grow come mostly from Tozer, one of the last independent English seed producers. We start the season with Rudolf, then move on to Redhead and Red spear. There is always a glut in late March and April, as the highest-yielding Claret comes into season. To my great delight, such is the popularity of purple sprouting broccoli with our customers that over the last few years we've been trying to breed our own variety to allow us to continue picking a little later into the spring 'hungry gap'.

Guy

purple sprouting broccoli

storage

Purple sprouting broccoli keeps for 4–6 days in a plastic bag in the fridge, but like most greens it's best eaten as fresh as possible. It gets stressed at higher temperatures, so don't let it linger too long in a warm room.

prep

The slightly wild aspect of PSB is all part of its charm and it doesn't need much trimming: the florets, leaves and stem are all edible and delicious. Just pick off any discoloured leaves and, towards the end of the season, trim the bottoms of the stalks if they seem at all woody. If any of your spears are particularly large (possibly because we have got a bit behind with the picking), split them down the middle with a sharp knife so that they cook at the same speed as the more delicate florets – evenly-sized pieces are best for even cooking.

cooking

PSB is like asparagus – the less you do to it the better. Boil, steam or stir-fry for a quick, fresh finish, or roast or griddle to intensify its taste. Many of the methods that work with PSB will also be good with the less strong-tasting Calabrese (aka broccoli).

boil/steam

At its freshest, PSB should take no more than 5 minutes to boil in an unlidded pan. To keep them as green as possible, make sure your pan is large enough to hold the spears without crowding, so they don't halt the boiling action when added. Lift them out with tongs or a slotted spoon to protect the delicate florets.

Steaming will hold in more nutrients but takes a fraction longer than boiling (up to 5 or 6 minutes. Cook the spears in a single layer or in batches so they cook through evenly.

When steamed or boiled, serve PSB straight away or, if you're serving it cold or later on, plunge into cold water to stop the cooking process and help preserve its colour.

IDEAS FOR STEAMED OR BOILED PSB
There are few things more delectable than a pile of quick-cooked PSB with a knob of butter and a sprinkle of sea salt and pepper. Once you get tired of that (if ever):

* Flavour the butter: lightly cook a finely chopped garlic clove or a finely chopped chilli in it, or melt a couple of anchovy fillets, or all three, together. A squeeze of lemon is also a good addition.

* For a lovely toasted flavour, heat the butter until it goes nutty brown then drizzle it over the broccoli.

* Eat your broccoli cold, substituting the butter with salad dressing – almost any will work (see page 296 for tips on vinaigrettes).

* Heat some double cream in a small saucepan, letting it bubble gently for a few minutes, then crumble in some blue cheese, such as Stilton, Gorgonzola or Roquefort. Let it melt, then pour the sauce over the broccoli.

* Toss chopped broccoli with pasta, crumbled blue cheese, toasted walnuts and a dash of olive oil.

roast

A lovely way of intensifying PSB's distinctive flavour, roasting also allows you to add aromatics. It is best done with smaller spears so they cook right through without the outside burning. Heat the oven to 200°C/ Gas 6 and toss the spears in a roasting tin with a little olive oil. Season well with salt and pepper and roast for 8–10 minutes. Watch the PSB carefully: the stalks should be just tender and very slightly coloured. See Roasted Purple Sprouting Broccoli with Chilli, Lemon and Garlic, page 222.

purple sprouting broccoli

fry

Fry young, tender spears of purple sprouting broccoli for 4–5 minutes on a medium heat in oil or butter. Or cut the spears into small pieces and add to a stir-fry: get your wok really hot, add oil with a high smoking point (e.g. sunflower or groundnut), immediately add some finely chopped garlic, ginger and sliced chilli, then, seconds later, some finely sliced veg, including the broccoli. Toss frequently until the vegetables are as tender as you like, usually just a few minutes. Finish with seasonings such as soy sauce, hoisin, oyster sauce and sesame oil and serve immediately with rice or noodles. See Purple Sprouting Broccoli and Shiitake Stir-fry on page 227.

griddle

Griddling PSB adds a smoky flavour and a nice bit of extra colour and texture. Steam or boil it first for 2–3 minutes (see above), then finish on a hot griddle brushed with oil, cooking for less than a minute on each side.

eating PSB raw

Broccoli is rich in iron and vitamins A, B and C and eating it raw preserves these nutrients well. Choose the smallest, most tender shoots and dress with salt and pepper, olive oil, and lemon juice or balsamic vinegar a few minutes before serving.

works well with...

* chillies and black pepper
* citrus – lemon and orange
* dairy – butter, cheese (blue, sheep's, goat's and Parmesan)
* eggs – hollandaise sauce and poached eggs (including duck eggs)
* ginger
* mustard
* nuts – almonds, hazelnuts, peanuts and walnuts
* pork – bacon, pancetta and salami
* salty flavours – anchovies, capers, oyster sauce and soy sauce
* sesame   seeds, oil and tahini

roasted purple sprouting broccoli with lemon, chilli and garlic

quick & easy

vegan

Simple, zesty and bright, this speedy side pairs well with fried tofu but would go equally with chicken or white fish.

SERVES 4 AS A SIDE

200g purple sprouting
   broccoli, trimmed if
   necessary and cut into
   equal-sized stems
3–4 tbsp olive oil
1 thumb-sized red chilli,
   deseeded and finely
   chopped, or a couple
   of pinches of dried
   chilli flakes
3 garlic cloves, finely
   chopped
finely grated zest and
   juice of 1 lemon
salt

Heat the oven to 200°C/Gas 6.

Put the broccoli into a roasting tin, season lightly with salt and mix with a good slosh of olive oil until well coated. Roast for 4 minutes then add the chilli, garlic and lemon zest and mix well. Return to the oven for a further 3–4 minutes, or until the broccoli is tender to the point of a knife. Mix again and check the seasoning. Finish with a pinch more salt if needed and a splash of lemon juice to taste.

VARIATION

For an Asian-style twist, replace the lemon with a lime, add a small amount of finely grated ginger and top with toasted sesame seeds.

purple sprouting broccoli, bacon and poached egg on toast

quick & easy

An excellent start to the day. Since any dish that involves bringing together poached eggs and hot toast is an exercise in precision, the instructions are carefully ordered to help you achieve perfect timing. If you're wary of poaching, fry your eggs instead.

SERVES 2

1 tbsp white wine vinegar
6 rashers of streaky bacon (smoked or unsmoked as you prefer)
25g butter
100g purple sprouting broccoli, trimmed if necessary and cut into small florets
2 thick slices of sourdough bread
2 eggs (the fresher the better for poaching)
salt and black pepper

Bring a pan of water to the boil, adding a tiny splash of vinegar to help set the egg white.

Fry the bacon in a frying pan over a medium heat until crispy then set aside.

Heat the butter in the bacon frying pan, add the purple sprouting broccoli and fry until just tender, 4–5 minutes. Toast the bread.

While the broccoli's cooking, turn the heat under the egg pan down so that the water is barely simmering, then gently crack in the eggs. After 3–4 minutes, carefully remove them with a slotted spoon – the white should be cooked and the yolk runny.

Push the broccoli to one side of the pan and soak up the buttery bacony juices by pressing the toast into them. Place a piece of toast on each serving plate. Stack the purple sprouting broccoli and bacon on top then add the poached eggs, a pinch of salt and a twist of pepper.

VARIATIONS
* Use black pudding in place of bacon.
* Replace the toast with potato latkes (see pages 190).
* If you're after something more elaborate and indulgent, spoon over home-made hollandaise sauce (see page 231) to make this a twist on eggs Benedict.
* Duck eggs will give you a higher yolk-to-white ratio.

purple sprouting broccoli with roasted garlic, capers, shallots and anchovies

quick & easy

A loud, punchy dressing for those who love strong, piquant flavours. For a vegetarian version replace the anchovies with a teaspoon or two of smooth Dijon mustard.

SERVES 2

1 scant tbsp of capers
(small if possible, if not,
chop them roughly)
1 bulb of roasted garlic
(see page 284)
2 tbsp olive oil
2 tsp cider vinegar
150g purple sprouting
broccoli, trimmed if
necessary and divided
into similar-sized pieces
2 small shallots, very
finely sliced or diced
3 or 4 anchovy fillets,
finely chopped
salt and black pepper

If your capers are brined, soak them in cold water for 20 minutes or so to remove the excess salt (skip this step if they come in oil).

Squeeze the roasted garlic flesh out of its skin and mash to a purée using the back of a fork. Add the olive oil and cider vinegar and mix into a paste.

Steam or boil the broccoli for 3–4 minutes, until just cooked (see page 218).

Gently toss the warm broccoli with the garlic paste, shallots, anchovies and capers and add salt and pepper to taste.

pasta with purple sprouting broccoli, chilli and poor man's Parmesan

quick & easy

In Italy, *pangrattata*, or poor man's Parmesan - breadcrumbs with garlic and chilli - is traditionally sprinkled over pasta to give flavour and texture. You could also use it on salad, fish or chicken.

SERVES 2

200g pasta (linguine, spaghetti or fusilli would all be good)

4 tbsp olive oil, plus extra for drizzling

2–4 anchovy fillets (depending on how much you like them)

1 large or 2 small garlic cloves, finely chopped

4 tbsp coarse dried breadcrumbs

finely grated zest of ½ lemon

½–1 red chilli (depending on the size and heat and your preference for it), deseeded and finely chopped

200g purple sprouting broccoli, trimmed if necessary and cut into even-sized pieces

small handful of parsley leaves, chopped

salt and black pepper

Cook the pasta in a large pan of salted boiling water, according to the packet instructions, until al dente.

Meanwhile, heat the oil in a frying pan on a medium–low heat. Add the anchovies and mash them with a wooden spoon so they dissolve into the oil. Add the garlic and breadcrumbs and fry, stirring, until crispy, then add in the lemon zest and chilli and fry for a minute more.

Steam or boil the broccoli for 3–4 minutes, until just tender (see page 218).

Once the pasta is drained, stir in a good drizzle of olive oil and the parsley. Toss with the broccoli and fried breadcrumbs and season with salt and pepper before serving.

purple sprouting broccoli and shiitake stir-fry

quick & easy

vegan

Tamarind has a sweet-sour, slightly plum-like flavour, often used in Eastern and African cooking. If you can't find it, this will work without but you may need to add a little extra lime juice. You can request shiitake mushrooms as part of your Riverford order, but you can also replace them with a punnet of closed-cup or Portobello mushrooms.

SERVES 4

200g noodles (use buckwheat
  for gluten-free)
2 tsp sesame oil, plus
  extra to finish
3 tbsp sunflower or
  groundnut oil
400g purple sprouting
  broccoli, trimmed if
  necessary and cut into
  similar-sized small pieces
150g shiitake mushrooms,
  roughly chopped
5cm fresh ginger, peeled and
  sliced into fine matchsticks
1–2 red chillies (depending
  on your heat preference),
  deseeded and finely sliced
2 garlic cloves, finely sliced
  or chopped
2 tsp tamarind paste mixed
  with 2 tbsp hot water
2 tbsp soy sauce, or to taste
250g marinated tofu,
  cut into cubes
juice of 2 limes
handful of coriander leaves
handful of toasted cashew
  nuts or peanuts (see page
  136 for how to toast them),
  roughly chopped

Cook the noodles according to the packet instructions. Drain and toss in just enough sesame oil to coat. Leave to one side.

Heat the sunflower or groundnut oil in a wok or large frying pan. Add the purple sprouting broccoli and stir-fry on a high heat for 2 minutes. Add the mushrooms, ginger, chilli and garlic and fry for a minute more.

Stir in the tamarind and soy sauce and a couple of tablespoons of water and cook, stirring, for a further minute. Add the tofu, lime juice, coriander and cooked noodles and toss everything together. Taste and add more soy sauce or sesame oil if desired, then sprinkle over the toasted nuts.

TIP: BEST MUSHROOM PRACTICE
To clean your mushrooms, wipe them with a damp piece of kitchen paper or a clean cloth – washing can make them a bit slimy.

wheatberries and purple sprouting broccoli with crispy garlic and chilli

quick & easy

vegan

A hearty and healthy lunch combining toothsome wheatberries, clean greens and crispy fried onions (page 160). Wheatberries are the entire wheat kernel except for the hull. They take a while to cook but have a good nutty texture, lending real substance to a dish.

SERVES 2

100g purple sprouting
  broccoli, trimmed
  if necessary
100g wheatberries (or one
  of the alternatives below)
4 tbsp sunflower or vegetable
  oil (or use the oil you
  used to fry the onions)
1 fresh red chilli,
  very finely sliced
2 garlic cloves, very
  finely sliced
handful of Crispy
  Fried Onions (see
  page 160; optional)
salt and black pepper

Boil the purple sprouting broccoli for 3–4 minutes, until just tender (see page 218). Remove with a slotted spoon and plunge into very cold water before draining.

Add the wheatberries to the same water and cook for 25 minutes, or until cooked but still chewy. Drain in a colander. Wipe out the pan and heat the oil in a frying pan on a medium heat. Add the chilli and garlic and fry, stirring, until the garlic has turned golden.

Add the broccoli and fry for a couple more minutes, then add the drained wheatberries and a handful of crispy fried onions, if using. Mix everything together, check the seasoning and add a dash more onion oil if it seems dry. Serve warm.

VARIATION
Pearled spelt or barley work as substitutions for the wheatberries, or, to save time, choose couscous or bulghur.

Purple sprouting broccoli with maltaise sauce

a bit fancy

vegetarian

The French have many variations on their classic hollandaise; in a *sauce maltaise* it is flavoured with blood orange. It's distinctively tangy and sweet. A regular orange gives different but also delicious results. Once made, the sauce will only hold for about 5 minutes before it is liable to split, so make sure your broccoli is prepped and ready to be cooked and served immediately.

*SERVES 4 AS A
LUNCH OR STARTER*

finely grated zest of
  1 blood orange
125ml blood orange juice
  (about 2 oranges)
2 large egg yolks
200g butter, melted (but
  no longer piping hot)
lemon juice, to taste
350–400g purple sprouting
  broccoli, trimmed if
  necessary and cut into
  equal-sized stems
salt

To make the maltaise sauce, put the orange zest and juice in a small saucepan and bring to the boil, then bubble to reduce the liquid to 2–3 tablespoons. Strain through a piece of muslin or a small sieve and discard the zest.

Put the egg yolks and 2 tablespoons of cold water into a heatproof bowl that sits snugly over a pan of barely simmering water. Whisk until doubled in volume and the mixture has thickened. Remove from the heat and whisk for a further 20–30 seconds.

Return the bowl and pan to the heat and very gradually whisk in the melted butter until the sauce has the consistency of thick double cream. If your sauce starts to feel too sticky, add a splash of the orange juice.

Whisk in the reduced orange juice and season with salt to taste. Add a squeeze of lemon juice if you want to sharpen the flavour. The sauce will hold for 5 minutes or so in the bowl over the pan of water, but off the heat. Don't leave it much longer, as it is prone to splitting.

Steam or boil the broccoli for 3–4 minutes, until just tender. Serve immediately with the maltaise sauce drizzled over the top.

VARIATION: HOLLANDAISE SAUCE

Instead of the blood orange juice and zest use the juice of a lemon. Start by whisking the egg yolks with a scant 2 tablespoons of the lemon juice (instead of water), as described above. When the hollandaise is made, taste and add more lemon juice if needed. With the salt added at the end you can also include a pinch or two of cayenne pepper.

TIPS FOR MAKING HOLLANDAISE/MALTAISE

* Don't have the water in the pan too hot; a bare simmer is all you need. Your whisking bowl should fit snugly over the pan but not touch the water.
* If your sauce starts to thicken too much and looks as if it might curdle, take it off the heat for a minute and keep whisking in the melted butter to let it cool slightly.
* If the sauce splits, you can try to rescue it by taking it off the heat, adding a drop of water and whisking briskly. If that fails, put another egg yolk in a clean bowl and set it over the water, then gradually whisk in the split mixture.

Purple sprouting broccoli with chorizo and potatoes

quick & easy

Simple and full-flavoured, this relies on the paprika flavour of good cooking chorizo for its success. Smaller, more waxy potatoes are best as they'll hold their shape. Serve this dish on its own or with roasted chicken, fish or a fried egg.

SERVES 2

300g potatoes, scrubbed but
  left whole and unpeeled
200g purple sprouting
  broccoli, trimmed
  if necessary
1 tbsp light olive or
  sunflower oil
1 cooking chorizo
  (about 100g), skinned
  and crumbled
juice of ½ lemon
handful of parsley leaves,
  chopped
salt and black pepper

Bring the potatoes to the boil in a pan of cold, salted water. When simmering, cook for 15–20 minutes, depending on size, until tender. Drain and leave to dry.

Boil or steam the purple sprouting broccoli for 3–4 minutes, until just tender (see page 218). Drain and refresh in very cold or iced water to stop the cooking process and preserve the colour, then drain again.

Cut the cooked potatoes into wedges. Heat the oil in a frying pan. Add the chorizo and potato and fry on a medium heat for a few minutes to cook the chorizo through and crisp the potato. Add the broccoli and fry for a minute or two more to warm it through. Season with salt and pepper. Serve with a squeeze of lemon juice and a sprinkling of chopped parsley.

radicchio
(and other
bitter leaves)
october to december

I am a huge fan of radicchio and the entire family of bitter leaves. This passion was confirmed when I met Geetie Singh, a fellow bitter-leaves fan, in a radicchio field; two years later our wedding cake was decorated with their leaves. In recent years I have been on a bit of a mission to convert more of our customers, extending the range we send out with boxes, to include small doses of dandelion leaves, pain de sucre and others. It is the red radicchio you will see most – and we always make sure that some boxes each week are free of them so you can avoid them if you are not a convert .

Dandelion greens, radicchio, escarole, curly endive, Belgian endive, and pain de sucre all share the characteristic bitterness derived from their wild dandelion-like ancestors and, to varying extents, have retained a hardiness that allows most to thrive even in a dismal Devon winter. Radicchio can be in season from July to December and, in the mild south west, sometimes through to March. They are at their best and most useful in the boxes from October to December and definitely decline in bitterness as the winter progresses. In Italy you find many types of radicchio and many more regional recipes for using them, but we do best with the solid, round Chioggia or lighter, more erect and less dense Treviso types. Both are good cooked and raw and we would say they're interchangeable, though Italians might be appalled to hear us say so!

Raw in salads, griddled, roasted or cooked into risottos and pastas, they have the potential to revive a stew-jaded pallet through the winter months as well as acting as a diuretic, digestive stimulant and cleanser of the liver and intestines. As well as loving them, instinctively I just know they are good for me.

Guy

storage

Like other bitter leaves, radicchio should keep well in the fridge as a whole head for at least a week and possibly two. If you're using them in several sittings, peel off the outer leaves first, rather than cutting them in half.

prep

Wash the leaves well before use: tip them into a big bowl of cold water, swill around a couple of times then leave to sit a moment while any dirt sinks to the bottom of the bowl. Lift the leaves out with your hands and dry them in a salad spinner, or gather them in a clean tea towel and shake this around to drive off the excess water. Washed and dried leaves will store in the fridge for a day or two: ideally layer them with kitchen paper and seal in a plastic box.

eating radicchio raw

Raw radicchio goes beautifully with sweet, salty and creamy flavours. Cut the heads into quarters lengthways, cut out the core, then slice into ribbons. The cut edges will go brown fairly quickly, so make the salad just before you serve. Dress it first, in a sweet–sour vinaigrette made with sherry or balsamic vinegar (see page 296). Then add in sweet seasonal fruits such as ripe pears or persimmons and a salty cheese such as Roquefort or Stilton (see page 242 for our recipe). Toasted nuts also work well.

OTHER BITTER LEAVES

Sharp, bitter winter leaves are a lovely way to pep up cold-weather cooking. Whether you eat them cooked or raw, all these leaves share the characteristic bitterness of radicchio (derived from their wild dandelion-like ancestors), and can often be used interchangeably with it in recipes:

BELGIAN ENDIVE (sometimes called chicory or just endive) are pale green, tightly wrapped buds or 'chicons' that are commonly grown in northern Europe. They are traditionally served wrapped in ham and smothered in béchamel sauce, or eaten in a mixed salad with boiled egg. Green chicory is first grown in the field to produce roots; these are then harvested in the autumn and transferred to forcing sheds for the winter. They are kept in the dark and 'forced' to produce their shoots without light, just as rhubarb is forced in the Yorkshire triangle. The heads go green and become more bitter if you store them in the light.

CURLY ENDIVE (sometimes called frisée) has frilly, deeply indented green leaves with a pale heart. Huge amounts of this are eaten in France, where they enhance the natural tendency towards a pale centre by putting caps on the plants for a few days before harvest. It's less bitter than radicchio and is good raw in salads.

PAIN DE SUCRE is a solid chicory with tightly wrapped leaves. This is the hardiest of the family and can stand in the field through to February. The pale hearts have a mild flavour and crunchy texture similar to Belgian endive, graduating to greener, more bitter outer leaves which are better suited to cooking.

cooking

Cooking radicchio softens its bitterness considerably, and is often a good place to start if you aren't used to eating it.

fry/wilt

Slice the radicchio into thin ribbons and let them wilt in a hot pan with some melted butter and finely chopped garlic. Stir frequently; it should only take a few minutes. Use in omelettes or pasta and bean dishes with cream and cheese.

Sliced raw radicchio can also be added directly to hot dishes as they cook; it will wilt in a few minutes. For a simple, elegant risotto, cook the rice with red wine rather than white, and be generous with it. Fold in sliced raw radicchio for the last 10 minutes of cooking and finish with lots of Parmesan.

radicchio

roast/griddle

Cut the heads into quarters or sixths lengthways, depending on their size, leaving the core intact so the leaves hold together. Gently rub with olive oil and salt.

To roast, heat the oven to 200°C/Gas 6 and place the oiled wedges on a lined tray. Roast for about 15 minutes, until starting to wilt and colour, turning them over halfway through cooking.

To griddle, heat a cast-iron griddle pan until very hot, then lay the wedges inside in batches. Turn them once or twice with tongs, until just wilted and colouring in places. Gently transfer to a shallow bowl or platter containing a sweet–sour vinaigrette (see page 296) and let them soak it up. Serve warm or at room temperature.

(see page 296)

IDEAS FOR ROASTED/ GRIDDLED RADICCHIO

* Griddled (or fried) radicchio is smoky and tender and can either be eaten as a side or in a salad. It goes well topped with a few curls of pecorino and eaten with a grilled steak, chicken, or Italian-style sausages.

* Dress in vinaigrette made with sweet vinegars such as balsamic and sherry vinegar, adding crushed garlic and/ or a little smashed anchovy. (See page 296 for vinaigrette recipes.)

* Turn into a light meal in its own right by adding fresh buffalo mozzarella and ham.

(See page 296 for vinaigrette recipes.)

works well with…

* anchovies
* cheese – blue cheese, Parmesan and sharp goat's cheese
* cream and crème fraîche
* eggs
* lemon
* mustard
* nuts – hazelnuts and walnuts
* pork – bacon and ham
* sweet fruits – apples, figs, pears, persimmons and poached quinces
* vinegar – especially sweet ones such as balsamic and sherry

bitter leaf salad with lemon, anchovy and mustard dressing

quick & easy

A vibrant salad with a sharp, salty dressing to wake up your tastebuds and counterbalance the usual comforting winter fare.

SERVES 4 AS A SIDE

6 salted anchovy fillets, rinsed well in cold water
½ garlic clove, roughly chopped
1 tbsp lemon juice
1 tsp Dijon mustard
4–5 tbsp olive oil
200g mixed winter leaves, such as radicchio, land cress, mustard leaf, chicory
salt

Grind the anchovies and garlic in a pestle and mortar, or chop both very finely.

Stir in the lemon juice and mustard until well combined. Slowly whisk in the olive oil, a little at a time, until you have a rich emulsified dressing. Taste and add some salt if needed.

Put the mixed leaves into a salad bowl, pour over the dressing and toss to combine just before serving.

VARIATIONS

* Add some sliced ripe pear and toasted walnuts to make this a complete meal.
* Turn the dressing into a green sauce by adding a few handfuls of chopped capers and lots of finely chopped green herbs such as parsley, tarragon, basil and chervil. This is very good with lamb or fish.
* Try the dressing over warm roast or griddled radicchio (see opposite) or chicory leaves.
* For a vegetarian option, replace the anchovies with capers: they'll have the same salty, savoury effect.

bacon and radicchio omelette

quick & easy

A perfect speedy lunch. You can make one large omelette and split it or two smaller ones to serve.

SERVES 2

2 tbsp light olive or other
    mild oil
6 rashers of smoked streaky
    bacon, diced
4 large eggs
1 small tightly packed head
    of radicchio, or half
    a large head, roughly
    chopped
a generous knob of butter
    (about 30g)
1 garlic clove, finely chopped
squeeze of lemon juice
a few snipped chives
salt and black pepper
hot buttered toast, to serve
    (optional)

Heat a tablespoon of the oil in a frying pan on a medium heat. Add the bacon and fry until it starts to brown. Meanwhile, beat the eggs together using a fork along with a small dash of water and a pinch of salt.

When the bacon has started to brown, turn up the heat and add the radicchio. Keep it moving as it starts to wilt. Add half the butter and the garlic and cook for a further 2–3 minutes, making sure the garlic doesn't burn. Season with salt, pepper and a squeeze of lemon juice. Set aside and keep warm.

Wipe the pan clean and heat the remaining tablespoon of oil and the other half of the butter over a medium heat until hot and foaming. Add the beaten egg, swirl quickly with a fork and let it settle into the pan. Cook your omelette to your liking; the egg continues to cook with residual heat so slightly underdone is good.

Spread the radicchio and bacon mix across the omelette, scatter over some chives and fold the omelette in half. Eat with hot buttered toast, if you like.

VARIATIONS
* Add a dollop of soured cream or crème fraîche or a crumble of blue cheese along with the chives.
* Serve the radicchio and bacon mix as a side dish to accompany a game bird, roast chicken or veal.

radicchio and persimmon salad

quick & easy

**SERVES 4 AS A SIDE
OR STARTER**

1 small shallot, peeled
    and finely diced
2 tsp red wine vinegar
2 tsp sherry vinegar (or
    use all red wine vinegar)
1 head of radicchio
4 ripe fuyu persimmons
    (or ripe pears)
4 tbsp olive oil
a pinch of sugar
50g (a couple of good
    handfuls) watercress, baby
    spinach, rocket or other
    dark green leaves
a good handful of walnut
    halves or hazelnuts,
    toasted (see page 136)
    and roughly chopped
120g blue cheese, such
    as Stilton or Roquefort,
    crumbled
salt and black pepper

Resembling squat, orange tomatoes, and with an exotic fruity flavour, persimmons are available at the same time as radicchio, usually around November. An alternative is to use ripe pears or poached and sweetened quinces. This recipe comes from Riverford Cook Anna who discovered sweet fuyu persimmons while working in restaurants in California. She recommends serving the salad on its own as a starter or with bread and cold meats, especially pâté.

Put the diced shallot into a small bowl or jug and pour over the vinegars. Set aside.

Cut the radicchio into quarters lengthways, remove each core and slice the leaves into ribbons on the diagonal. Remove any tough stems from the leaves.

Try eating a small wedge of persimmon. If the skin feels tough, peel the fruit. If not, don't bother. Cut the persimmons into wedges.

Make vinaigrette by whisking the oil, sugar and salt and pepper into the shallots and vinegar. Taste and adjust the seasoning as necessary.

Put the salad leaves and persimmon wedges into a large bowl, pour over the dressing and toss to combine. Scatter the nuts and cheese over the top.

sautéed radicchio and borlotti beans

quick & easy (if using tinned beans)

vegan

This dish is a good accompaniment to scallops, pork or steak. You could also just serve it on toast, perhaps with some goat's cheese crumbled on top. It is especially nice if you cook your own borlotti beans (see box below), but if you are short on time use good canned ones.

SERVES 4 AS A SIDE OR
2 AS A MAIN WITH TOAST

1–2 tbsp olive oil

2 garlic cloves, finely chopped

leaves from a good sprig of rosemary, very finely chopped

1 head of radicchio, cut into quarters, core removed, then finely shredded

2 tbsp balsamic vinegar, or more to taste

1 x 400g can borlotti beans or 130g shelled fresh beans, cooked as below

salt and black pepper

Heat a tablespoon of the oil in a heavy-bottomed pan on a medium heat, then add the garlic and rosemary and fry for 2–3 minutes, until the garlic is just starting to colour.

Add the radicchio, stir well and sweat down for about 5 minutes, until wilted. Season with salt and pepper and add the balsamic vinegar and the beans. Cook for a few more minutes until the excess water has evaporated and the flavours mellow.

Check the seasoning and add more balsamic vinegar to taste – the sweetness of the balsamic should counterbalance the bitterness of the radicchio. Serve drizzled with the remaining olive oil.

HOW TO COOK BORLOTTI BEANS
Place beans in a pot and cover with cold water by 2.5cm. Add the aromatics you have to hand (peeled onion, a few peeled garlic cloves, a good glug of olive oil, a dried chilli and parsley stalks, bay leaves or thyme sprigs) and a generous pinch of salt. Bring to a boil then reduce the heat and simmer, partially covered, until the beans are tender. Add more water as needed to keep the beans covered, but try not to stir as they may break up. They will take around 30–40 minutes to cook. Test several beans to be sure. Fish out the aromatics and check the seasoning.

chargrilled radicchio with squash and goat's cheese

vegetarian

A beautiful balance of bittersweet griddled radicchio, sweet roasted squash and salty cheese.

SERVES 4

2 heads of radicchio
2 tbsp balsamic vinegar,
    plus extra to serve
about 5 tbsp olive oil
1 large butternut or crown
    prince squash, peeled and
    cut into wedges no more
    than 2cm wide
leaves from a small bunch of
    flat-leaf parsley, chopped
100g hazelnuts, toasted and
    roughly chopped
150g hard goat's cheese
salt and black pepper

Heat a cast-iron griddle pan until really hot. Heat the oven to 190°C/Gas 5.

Cut each radicchio head into eight wedges, keeping the root end intact. Put into a shallow bowl and season all over with a few pinches of salt, the balsamic vinegar and a drizzle of olive oil. Gently rub the radicchio wedges so that all sides are lightly oiled.

In batches, lay the squash on the hot griddle and cook for a minute or two on each side until lines appear (you are not trying to cook the squash through, just mark it).

Transfer the squash to a roasting tin and gently toss with salt, pepper and just enough oil to lightly coat. Roast for 20 minutes, or until cooked through.

Meanwhile, griddle the radicchio in batches – again just a minute or two on each side to give the wedges colour. As each piece is done, lay it in the oil and vinegar in the bowl so it can soak up more of the dressing.

Add the griddled radicchio to the roasting pan along with the squash for the final 10 minutes of cooking.

Put even amounts of squash and radicchio on to individual plates, sprinkle over the chopped parsley and hazelnuts, then use a vegetable peeler to shave strips of goats' cheese over the top. Put extra balsamic vinegar on the table for those who'd like more.

VARIATION:
Add a generous handful of winter leaves to turn it into a salad, or some robust cooked grains (pearl barley or spelt) for something a bit more substantial.

radicchio and bacon pasta

quick & easy

SERVES 4-5

1 large onion, finely diced

1–2 tbsp olive oil

400 long pasta (linguine,
   spaghetti, fettuccine and
   pappardelle work well)

25g butter

250g smoked streaky bacon
   or pancetta, rind removed
   and cut into thin strips

1 head of radicchio
   (about 150g), shredded

50–100ml cream

juice of 1 lemon

80–100g Parmesan,
   finely grated

salt and black pepper

flat-leaf parsley, finely
   chopped, to serve
   (optional)

Sweet onions, salty Parmesan, crisp, smoky bacon and a little cream temper radicchio's pleasant bitterness. If you are particularly fond of its sharpness, use two heads rather than one. To save time, you could also omit the onion, adding a little garlic with the bacon instead.

In a heavy-bottomed pan over a medium heat, fry the onion in a tablespoon of the oil and the butter for 10 minutes, or until translucent.

Add the bacon to the onion and continue to fry gently until the fat runs and it begins to colour. Add the radicchio, stir and cook for a minute or so, until collapsed, adding a little more oil if necessary.

Meanwhile, cook the pasta according to the packet instructions.

Just before the cooking time of the pasta is up, stir the cream into the radicchio, then add the lemon juice, a little at a time, tasting as you go. Add the Parmesan, season to taste, then toss the sauce with the drained pasta. Scatter over the parsley, if using.

VARIATIONS

* Add torn sage leaves to the bacon and cook for 2 minutes before adding the radicchio.
* Add blue cheese or fried mushrooms with the cream.

salsify

october to january

Salsify is a beautiful name for a vegetable that most resembles a small gnarled walking stick. It was a Victorian favourite but they often gave it the same unappetising treatment as scalloped oysters and served it in thin slices, drowned in white sauce, which is perhaps why it fell out of fashion.

We started to cultivate it after asking our customers for suggestions from their own allotments - a large number of you grow your own veg - and I'm glad we did. Its delicate creamy flesh has been compared to everything from oysters to parsnips, but I think it's most like another vegetable that is close to my heart - globe artichokes; subtle and delicate and not too sweet. They are both part of the *Asteraceae* or sunflower family, which includes a number of unusual and delicious edible species, ranging from thistles to chicory and water lotus.

Salsify is a doddle to grow but its peak season is quite short, so grab it while you can. We sow it between April and May, and carefully pull up the long thin roots between October and January. It is closely related to scorzonera, also known as black salsify, which has darker skin and crisper flesh, and can be used interchangeably with it in recipes.

Guy

storage

Salsify should be firm and smooth and it often comes with the green tops still on. Keep it in a sealed container or plastic bag in the fridge and use within a week.

prep

Salsify can be peeled before or after cooking. If you peel it before, put it straight into cold water acidulated with a good squeeze of lemon juice or a dash of vinegar added so that its creamy flesh doesn't discolour. Dice or slice it, as the recipe requires, returning the pieces to the acidulated water until you are ready to use them.

cooking

Although salsify can be grated or sliced very thinly and eaten raw, it tends to discolour and its flavour is best brought out by cooking.

boil

Depending on the thickness of your salsify, it will take between 20 and 45 minutes to cook, put into salted boiling water. You want it just tender so keep testing by inserting the tip of a sharp knife: it should meet no resistance. Salsify has a waxy bite and it's better well cooked than al dente. Add a dash of lemon juice and olive oil to the water to help keep its creamy colour.

To boil in its skin, soak the salsify for a few minutes in cold water then scrub it clean and top and tail it. Cut into even lengths and place it directly into a saucepan of cold salted water. Bring slowly to the boil and simmer until tender to the point of a knife. Drain and cool in a bowl of cold water before peeling. This is a good technique for recipes that then call for frying or roasting.

fry

Grated raw salsify can be fried with no need to boil it first (see Salsify Fritters, page 254). For crunchy chips to dip in a lemony mayonnaise, boil batons of salsify until tender, drain and leave in the colander to steam-dry, then coat with a light batter (45g plain flour, 1 teaspoon cornflour, 80ml cold water, salt and ½ teaspoon bicarbonate of soda) and deep-fry at 180°C (see page 88 for notes on deep-frying.) Alternatively, coat the boiled and drained salsify in flour, then beaten egg, then breadcrumbs, and deep-fry in the same way.

roast

Heat the oven to 200°C/Gas 6. Peel and cut the salsify into lengths. Place in a roasting dish along with a few gently bashed garlic cloves and a bay leaf and toss with a drizzle of olive or rapeseed oil and salt and pepper. Roast for about 20 minutes, until tender. It's good sprinkled with zingy gremolata (see page 214).

braise

An alternative to boiling or roasting is to slow-cook salsify in the oven for a couple of hours with a little added moisture (see our recipe overleaf). It can also be added to a stew or braise: let it simmer away with all the other ingredients for the last 30–45 minutes, until tender.

IDEAS FOR BOILED SALSIFY

* Toss with melted butter and eat straight away, or sauté in butter for a couple of minutes.

* Make salad: dress while still warm (not hot), with a sharp vinaigrette (see page 296) or a creamier, mayonnaise-based dressing. Lots of chopped parsley makes a good addition.

* Turn it into soup (see page 292 for our guidelines). A dash of cream and cheesy croutons make it even better.

braised salsify

long, slow cook

vegan

freezable

SERVES 6 AS A SIDE

1kg salsify
4 tbsp olive oil
juice of 1 large lemon
    (about 4 tbsp)
1 tsp sugar
salt

Cubes of silky-tender salsify make a good winter side dish for slow-roast lamb or pork shoulder, which can go in the low oven at the same time. This is Riverford Cook Anna's favourite way to cook salsify.

Heat the oven to 170°C/Gas 3. Scrub and peel the salsify then cut into chunky pieces. If you have an extra moment, roll-cut for attractive pointy shapes that are best at caramelising (see page 69). Keep them in a bowl of water acidulated with some lemon juice if not cooking immediately.

Put the salsify in a roasting tin with the oil and lemon juice and season with salt and sugar. Toss everything together then cover the pan tightly with foil. Bake in the oven for 2–3 hours, until the salsify is tender, sweet and translucent. It's best when it starts to caramelise in places. Check on it every half an hour or so: toss around in the pan then replace the foil and continue baking. Taste, season if necessary, and serve hot or at room temperature.

sautéed salsify, mushrooms, garlic and parsley on toast

quick & easy

vegan (depending on bread used)

This recipe makes for a luxurious Sunday breakfast, though it would work just as well for a light lunch or dinner. Hearty, thick-sliced sourdough toast is a very good vehicle for salsify due to its slight tang and robust texture, but don't be put off if you don't have it – more or less anything goes.

SERVES 2

250g salsify
juice of 1 lemon
2 tbsp olive oil, plus extra
for drizzling
250g mushrooms, sliced
2 garlic cloves, crushed
handful of parsley leaves,
chopped
slices of sourdough bread
salt and black pepper

Peel the salsify, chop into chunks and boil with a pinch of salt and half the lemon juice for 5 minutes, then drain.

Heat half the oil in a frying pan over a medium heat, add the salsify and season well with salt and pepper. Fry until the salsify is tender and golden, turning the pieces regularly. Add the mushrooms and fry for a further 10 minutes, or until all the liquid has evaporated and they are beginning to crisp and turn golden.

Add the garlic and fry for a further minute, then take off the heat and add the parsley and more lemon juice, salt and pepper to taste.

Toast the bread and drizzle with a little more olive oil. Pile the salsify and mushrooms on top then serve piping hot.

salsify fritters

quick & easy

vegetarian

These addictive little fritters are a lovely alternative to bubble and squeak or hash browns for a proper brunch. They go well with all the usual brunch pillars - crisp bacon, a fried or poached egg, black pudding or sausages. Alternatively, eat them as a light lunch dish with a salad or greens.

SERVES 4

400g salsify
1 garlic clove, finely chopped
leaves from a small bunch
   of thyme, finely chopped
2 tbsp plain flour
2 large eggs, lightly beaten
generous knob of butter
salt and black pepper

Peel and coarsely grate the salsify (a food processor saves effort). In a large bowl, mix the salsify with the garlic, thyme and some salt and pepper. Add the flour and mix well, then pour in the beaten eggs and mix again.

Warm a generous knob of butter in a large frying pan over a medium heat. Form the mixture into fritters about the size of the palm of your hand and no more than 0.5cm thick so they cook right through. Put the fritters into the frying pan and turn the heat down low. Flip a couple of times during cooking and, as they absorb the butter, add a little more. Cook slowly for 10–15 minutes, until deep golden brown on both sides. Serve hot.

november to april

spinach
and
chard

june to september

I'm a fan of spinach year round, but perhaps most of all when the tenderest of the spring and summer leaves give way to something a bit more robust and earthy. It presents endless eating possibilities, and the only thing to bear in mind is that what might look like a wheelbarrow full of uncooked leaves will always wilt down to quite a modest portion. You can never start with enough spinach. In your boxes, outside the UK season, you may see spinach in whole heads, rather than as individual leaves. These are grown for us by Pepe Aguilera in Spain and have revolutionised the greens contents of boxes in the winter months; I am very proud of their flavour.

Chard can be treated pretty much like spinach and substituted for it in many recipes. I regard chard as a pretty good second to spinach, especially the white ribbed Swiss variety.

Spinach and chard are very easy to grow; we plant them directly into the ground and normally take a single harvest, which gives the best quality and fastest picking. If you choose the right varieties for your garden, especially if sown from July onwards when they'd have less tendency to bolt, they'd can be picked all year. They are both members of the amaranth family, which also includes beetroot, quinoa and common edible garden weeds such as fat hen (*Chenopodium album*) and Good King Henry (*Blitum bonus-henricus*), both of which can be foraged and used as a substitute for spinach or chard in most recipes. All the greens in this group are a treasure trove of nutritional wonders, including vitamin K, vitamin A, vitamin C, minerals and lots of fibre.

Guy

identifying

We grow two types of spinach, true and perpetual. True spinach is dark green and highly succulent with smaller spear- or spade-shaped leaves and thin, tender leaf stalks. Perpetual has larger, paler leaves; it is also more robust in texture and taste than true spinach, but still well worth it and a lot easier to grow.

Chard is hardier again than perpetual spinach. It has large, succulent, dark green leaves with thick fleshy stems, which can be white (Swiss chard), reddish (ruby chard), yellow or a mixture of all three (rainbow chard). Swiss chard has the best flavour, though we occasionally grow the others for colour and variety.

storage

True spinach has a short shelf life. Keep it in a plastic bag in the fridge and eat it as soon as possible, and certainly within a couple of days. Perpetual spinach and chard keep better and will last 4–5 days in a plastic bag in the fridge. A bit of wilting won't damage the flavour, so unless it's accompanied by discolouration, it'll still be good to eat.

prep

Greens need a good wash to get rid of dust and grit: put them in a big bowl of cold water and swish around a few times. Leave to sit for a couple of minutes to allow the dirt to sink to the bottom of the bowl, and then lift the leaves out with your hands and drain in a colander.

You can eat true spinach stalks and all, unless the stalks are very big, in which case give them a trim. Perpetual spinach is tougher. The ribs are best snipped or torn out and discarded (unlike chard, they are not particularly good to eat).

Your chard may arrive as a whole head or as loose leaves. Either way, you'll usually have to separate out the stalks and leaves as the former take far longer to cook. Strip the leaves away from the stalks by pinching at the base and pulling the stalk through your fingers. Slice or dice the stalks as required and leave in some water lightly acidulated with lemon juice or vinegar to prevent them turning brown.

eating spinach and chard raw

When spinach or chard leaves are small (often described as 'baby spinach' etc.) they are delicious raw tossed into a mixed green leaf salad.

cooking

Chard and spinach are both quick and easy to cook. It's pleasant (though not essential!) to maintain their glorious bright green colour, so we've shared a few tips on that here too.

blanch and squeeze

Spinach and very tender young chard don't need blanching, but it's a good technique to use for most chard. Blanch the stems in boiling water for 6–10 minutes, until tender, adding the leaves for the last 2–3 minutes or blanching them separately. Lift out the chard with a spider strainer or slotted spoon and plunge it into very cold water to cool, then drain. This stops it cooking further and fixes the colour. Give the leaves a squeeze to remove excess water then try using it in one of the following ways:

* Re-heat in a pan with oil or butter and flavourings such as garlic, chilli and spices.

* Muddle through warm chickpeas or white beans.

* Make a simple gratin: mix with cream and top with grated cheese and breadcrumbs then bake at 150°C/Gas 2 for 20 minutes.

* Pile on toast rubbed with garlic and drizzle with extra virgin olive oil.

* Whizz chard stems into a hummus along with tahini, garlic, lemon juice and olive oil.

HANDY HINT
If a recipe calls for chard leaves but not their stems, go ahead and blanch the stems too, then refrigerate or freeze them for making a cheesy gratin another day. Add a pinch of bicarbonate of soda to the water to stop white stems turning grey and help rainbow chard stems keep their vibrant hues.

slow braise

Slow-cooked chard loses its bright green colour but is full of flavour. Slice the stems finely and the leaves into wide ribbons by making a pile of leaves, rolling them up into a fat cigar and slicing them crossways. Heat a little oil or butter in a pan and fry a few aromatics – onion, garlic, chilli and spices – then mix in the chard and fry for a few minutes more. Add enough water or stock to about 1cm depth and simmer over a low-medium heat, covered, for 10–20 minutes, until the chard stems are tender. Remove the lid towards the end of cooking to boil off excess water. Finish with some lemon juice or vinegar to brighten the flavour. For a heartier dish, include a tin of chickpeas or beans.

work well with...

* Asian flavourings – chilli, ginger, sesame and soy sauce
* cheese – especially ricotta and feta, also hard cheeses
* dairy – butter, cream and crème fraîche
* dried fruit – raisins and currants
* garlic
* lemon
* mustard
* olives and olive oil
* pork – bacon, chorizo and ham
* spices – cayenne, chilli, mace, nutmeg and paprika

fast cook

Tear or slice spinach or chard leaves into ribbons, or leave them whole if small. Cook quickly in a hot pan with a little heated oil or butter and a dash of water. Keep them moving in the pan; they should wilt within moments. Season to taste with salt and pepper. You could add finely chopped garlic, chilli or anchovies to the hot fat and fry for a couple of minutes before adding the greens. A dash of lemon juice at the very end is good to brighten the flavour.

Add finely sliced raw chard stems to a stir-fry along with other quick-cooking vegetables. Or blanch the stems as described on the previous page then slice or dice them finely and add them to your fast-cooked chard leaves to heat through.

korean-style spinach

quick & easy

vegan

freezable

This side dish is called *sigeumchi namul* and is usually eaten with other vegetable dishes and rice. You can use either sort of spinach for this, though we'd recommend true if you have it. It is best dressed just before serving.

SERVES 2 AS A SID

200–250g spinach
2 small garlic cloves,
    finely chopped
1 spring onion, finely sliced
2 tbsp soy sauce
1 tbsp sesame oil, or to taste
1 tsp toasted sesame seeds
salt

Trim the spinach stems if they're large, and wash thoroughly. Blanch and squeeze the spinach (see page 259) then roughly chop.

Put the garlic, spring onion, soy sauce and sesame oil in a large bowl and mix well. Add the spinach and mix again, using your hands to make sure each leaf is coated. Taste and adjust the salt. Serve at room temperature topped with the sesame seeds.

flageolet bean stew with chard

long slow cook   vegan

freezable

A simple bean stew from Riverford Cook Anna that can be endlessly adapted by adding other veg or meat. It's good with sausages or leftover roast meat or on its own with crusty bread and a drizzle of olive oil. Using tinned beans (three 400g tins) instead of dried will speed up the cooking, but the flavour of dried beans is generally better.

SERVES 6 (OR MORE IF SERVED AS A SIDE)

500g dried flageolet beans
2 onions, peeled and halved
2 carrots, peeled and halved
2 celery sticks, halved
4 garlic cloves, peeled
bouquet garni (2 bay leaves
    and a few sprigs of fresh
    parsley and thyme tied
    together with string)
4–6 tbsp light olive oil
2 heads of Swiss chard,
    or 1 if huge
1 tbsp paprika (optional)
1 tbsp tomato purée
    (optional)
salt and black pepper

Soak the dried beans in three times their volume of cold water for 8 hours or overnight.

Drain and rinse the soaked beans then put in a large pan and cover with cold water by about 2cm. Add one onion, carrot and celery stick, each cut in half, half the garlic, the bouquet garni and 2–3 tablespoons of olive oil. Bring to the boil then reduce to a simmer and cook slowly until tender, adding more water if needed so the beans are always covered. The cooking time will depend on the freshness of your beans and can be anything from 45 minutes to 1½ hours. When the beans are nearly soft, season well with salt, and then continue cooking until all the beans have creamy insides, but are still holding their shape.

While the beans are cooking, separate the chard leaves from their stems and set the leaves aside. Cut the stems and the remaining onion, carrot and celery into fine dice and cook in a large pan over a medium heat in 2–3 tablespoons of olive oil and a pinch of salt. Finely chop the remaining garlic and add it after 6–8 minutes, when the vegetables are half cooked.

Continue cooking for a further 6–8 minutes, until everything is soft, sweet and golden, but not browned. If using, add the paprika and tomato purée now and cook for a few more minutes.

Drain the beans, reserving their cooking liquid. Pick out the veg and herbs used as flavourings and discard. Stir the beans through the onion base. Add some of the bean cooking liquid and around 2 tablespoons of olive oil to loosen. Shred the chard leaves and stir them through. Bring everything to a simmer and cook for 3–4 minutes, until the leaves are tender. Check the seasoning. Drizzle with a little olive oil for extra shine and flavour.

Jansson's temptation with chard

a bit fancy

SERVES 4 AS A SIDE

500ml double cream
1 tsp rosemary leaves,
    finely chopped
3 garlic cloves, thinly sliced
250g bunch of chard
2 tbsp olive oil
6–8 anchovy fillets (rinsed
    very well if the salted kind)
500g large potatoes (a waxy
    or all-rounder which will
    hold its shape), very
    finely sliced
salt and black pepper

This lovely gratin is a variation on the traditional Swedish potato and onion dish called Jansson's temptation. It replaces the onion with a layer of chard whose strong earthy flavours partner beautifully with the anchovies. Good served with roast lamb.

Heat the oven to 180°C/Gas 4.

Pour the cream into a large saucepan and add the rosemary and garlic. Bring the cream to the boil then turn the heat down and simmer very gently for about 20 minutes.

Meanwhile, blanch and squeeze the chard stems and leaves (see page 259) then roughly chop.

Heat the olive oil in a frying pan, add the anchovies and stir over a low heat until they break up. Add the chard stalks and leaves. Season with salt and pepper and stir well to coat in the anchovy butter. Taste for seasoning.

Arrange half the potato slices on the bottom of a gratin dish, cover with the chard mixture and then top with the remaining potato. Press the layers down firmly with a spatula. Taste the infused cream mixture, season well, then pour over the potatoes.

Cover the gratin with foil and bake in the oven for 1–1½ hours, until the potatoes are tender (a blunt knife should easily sink through to the bottom). Remove the foil for the last 10 minutes of the cooking time to colour the top lightly. Serve hot.

Spanish-style Swiss chard with chickpeas

quick & easy

vegan

freezable

Swiss chard is a favourite in Spanish kitchens and in this recipe Riverford Cook Anna pairs it with classic Hispanic ingredients – smoked paprika, chickpeas and garlic. It's lovely warm out of the pan, but even better if left to infuse for an hour and eaten at room temperature.

SERVES 4-6 AS A MEZZE
OR LIGHT LUNCH

2 large heads or bunches of
   Swiss chard (500g 600g)
2–3 tbsp olive oil, plus a little
   extra for garnishing
1 onion, thinly sliced
3 garlic cloves, thinly sliced
1 x 400g can chickpeas,
   drained
1½ tsp smoked paprika
¼ tsp cayenne pepper
2 tsp sherry vinegar,
   or to taste
salt and black pepper

Detach the chard leaves from the stems. Cut the stems into 2cm lengths and the leaves into 5cm-wide ribbons. Blanch and squeeze the chard stems and leaves (see page 259).

Heat the olive oil in a wide frying pan and cook the onion with a pinch of salt on a medium heat for about 10 minutes, until soft. Add the garlic and cook a further 2 minutes. Add the chickpeas, chard stems, paprika and cayenne and cook for 3–4 minutes, stirring often. Finally, stir in the chard leaves and cook for a further 3–4 minutes.

To finish, season with salt and pepper, a drizzle of olive oil and a couple of splashes of sherry vinegar to brighten the flavour.

VARIATION
Make a more substantial meal by adding thickly sliced Spanish cooking chorizo near the beginning, along with the onions, or tinned sardines near the end, along with the chard leaves.

spinach and feta filo pie

a bit fancy

vegetarian (if a
vegetarian cheese is used)

Riverford Cook Anna found many versions of this pie during
her culinary travels across Greece and Turkey. Her recipe here
is for a nice and simple form, easily assembled with shop-bought
filo pastry. The filling is generous in quantity and moist in
consistency – you want it to be bursting with succulent greens.

SERVES 6-8

400g spinach, well washed,
    dried and finely chopped
200g feta cheese, crumbled
1 small bunch spring onions,
    white and pale green parts
    only, finely sliced
2 eggs
225ml thick plain yoghurt,
    plus optional extra to serve
2 tsp sumac or lemon juice,
    to taste
½ tsp chilli flakes, to taste
125g butter
1 x 250g pack ready-made
    filo pastry
1 egg yolk
salt and black pepper

Heat the oven to 180°C/Gas 4 with a rack in the lower third.

Mix the spinach, feta, onions, whole eggs and yoghurt together in
a bowl, then add sumac or lemon juice, chilli and salt and pepper
to taste. You want a fairly acidic mix with a hint of piquancy.

Melt the butter in a small saucepan and brush the base and sides
of a round, square or rectangular metal baking tin (about 25cm
across and 2.5cm deep) with a little melted butter.

Line the tin with a sheet of filo, gently easing it into the corners.
Let its edges hang over the side – you'll deal with those later. Brush
the sheet with butter, and repeat the filo layers and buttering until
you've used half of your sheets. Keep the waiting sheets under
a damp tea towel at all times so they don't dry out. If your tin is
round, lay each sheet at a different angle to the last one, so that
their corners hang over evenly all round the tin.

Spoon the filling mixture into the tin and even out the surface.
Cover with the remaining layers of filo and butter, forming a lid,
until all the pastry is used up. Trim off the edges by running a sharp
knife around the outside edge, holding it vertically against the tin.
Mix the egg yolk with a few drops of water and then brush over
the top of the pie.

Carefully cut the top of the pie into squares or diamonds using
a sharp knife. It works well if these are around 5cm wide. Only
go as deep as the filling, not right through the base layer.

Bake in the lower half of the oven for around 1 hour, until the pie
has puffed right up and turned a rich golden brown all over. You
may need to rotate the pie occasionally to ensure it browns evenly.

If your oven doesn't have a heat source at the bottom, the base of the pie may not be browned (and therefore a bit soggy). Crisp it up by placing the tin directly on the stove over a medium-low heat for a few minutes, moving it around so that it cooks evenly all over. Let the pie cool in its tin on a wire rack. It's much easier to cut out the sections and serve once it's cool. Serve at room temperature on its own or with more yoghurt.

VARIATIONS

* Finely chop the tender stems and leaves from a bunch of dill and a bunch of parsley and add these to the filling mix.
* Substitute edible wild greens such as nettles for the spinach. Nettles will need to be well washed (wear rubber gloves!), boiled, drained and chopped.

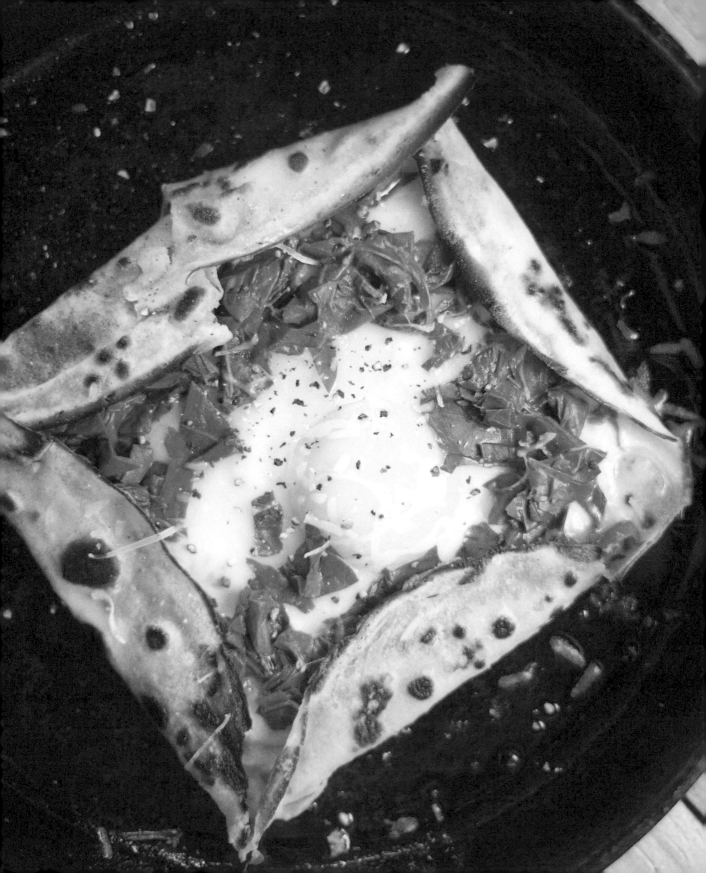

galettes with chard and Gruyère

a bit fancy

vegetarian (if a
vegetarian cheese is used)

Melted cheese, an egg and fresh greens housed in a nutty-flavoured gluten-free buckwheat pancake. These look impressive, but they're simple to cook. This is also good with spinach, Comté, ham, or sweet pancake fillings. The pancakes can be made in advance and frozen between sheets of greaseproof paper.

SERVES 4

For the galettes
100g buckwheat flour
good pinch of salt
1 egg
300ml milk
50g butter, melted
sunflower oil, for oiling
   the pan

For the filling
400g chard, leaves stripped
   from their stalks
4 eggs
125g Gruyère or Cheddar,
   grated
salt and black pepper

To make the galette batter, sift the flour and salt into a mixing bowl. Make a well in the centre and add the egg, then whisk, adding the milk a little at a time, until you have a smooth batter. Leave to rest for at least 1 hour.

Meanwhile, blanch and squeeze the chard leaves (see page 259) then roughly chop.

Stir the melted butter into the batter. Heat a lightly oiled non-stick frying pan over a medium-high heat. Put a quarter of the batter into the pan, rolling it around to cover the surface of the pan. Cook for about a minute until golden on the underside, then carefully flip the galette over.

Crack an egg into the centre. Scatter a quarter of the chopped chard and grated cheese over the whole galette and season with salt and pepper. When the underside is cooked to golden brown, use a spatula then your fingertips to lift then fold the edges of the galette into the centre to form a square. Serve immediately, repeating with the remainder of the batter and filling.

lemony chicken and spinach curry

quick & easy

freezable

This is a healthy curry with no creamy sauce which freezes really well. A pile of basmati rice and a good dollop of yoghurt will make it into a meal.

SERVES 4

1 tsp cumin seeds
1 tsp coriander seeds
1 tbsp sunflower, light olive
    or coconut oil, plus
    a little extra if necessary
600g diced chicken
    (leg, thigh or breast)
1 large or 2 small onions,
    finely sliced
3 garlic cloves, finely
    chopped, crushed
    or grated
5cm piece of fresh ginger,
    peeled and finely chopped
    or grated
1–2 fresh chillies, finely
    chopped (add the seeds
    too if you like it hot)
1 tsp turmeric
10 cardamom pods
juice of 2–3 lemons,
    depending on size
400ml vegetable or
    chicken stock
300g spinach, tough stalks
    removed and leaves
    roughly chopped if large
large handful of coriander,
    roughly chopped
salt and black pepper

Lightly toast the cumin and coriander seeds in a dry frying pan until you just start to smell their aroma, then grind them with a pestle and mortar.

Heat the oil in a large, heavy-based pan. Add the chicken pieces and fry over a high heat, turning once, until golden brown. (Don't overcrowd the pan – cook in batches if you need to.) Transfer the chicken to a plate.

Add the onion to the pan with a splash more oil if needed. Fry gently for 10 minutes, stirring now and then, until soft. Add the garlic, ginger, chillies and all the ground spices and fry, stirring, for another 2 minutes.

Return the chicken to the pan with the lemon juice and stock. Bring to the boil, reduce the heat and simmer for 15 minutes or so, until the chicken is cooked through. Stir in the spinach and let it wilt for just a minute or two before seasoning and stirring in the chopped coriander.

swede

october to march

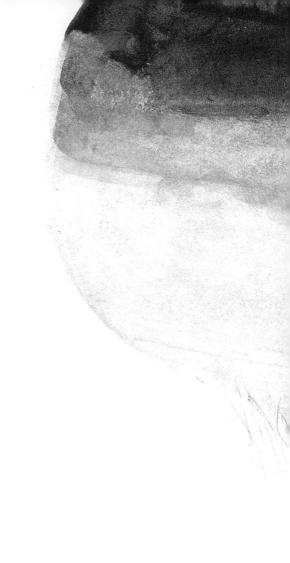

Much as I love my vegetables I am not going to write an ode to the swede. For me its virtues are humble, lying largely in its dependable storability, its cheapness, its winter season and its glorious combination with butter and pepper. I do also love haggis, but only once a year: a pasty would not be the same without them and nothing goes quite as well with roast beef as mashed swede and horseradish.

There is a surprising amount of variation in flavour between varieties, and I would be tempted to wax more lyrical if we could still buy our local variety Devon Champion but this is no longer available, the market having been taken over by quicker-growing, more uniform varieties – a travesty indeed. We really should have saved some of our own seed.

We sow our swedes around Midsummer's Day on our more exposed fields that rise towards Dartmoor, giving slower growth and more flavour. Our hardy teams walk the crop three or four times from October to early March, taking the swedes as they reach the desired 1kg. By April they start to go woody and are more fit for the cows than the kitchen.

Guy

swede

storage

A freshly harvested swede without any damage to the skin should be good for between two and four weeks stored in the bottom of the fridge.

prep

Peel your swede with a robust peeler or a sharp knife. If the latter, create a flat surface by cutting off the bottom before you start so that it sits firmly on the chopping board, then follow the natural curve of the swede with your knife, working from top to bottom, turning as you go. Cut the peeled swede into cubes, chunks or slices as required, ensuring an even size so they cook at the same rate. Swede is very dense and can take longer to cook than you expect, so don't make your pieces too chunky.

eating swede raw

Crisp, juicy and piquant, a bit like a carrot without the sweetness, swede can be eaten raw. It's good in slaws, combined with other winter veg (see page 54); or grated finely and added to salad.

cooking

It might seem natural to roast swede, as it's a technique that works so well with other root veg. However, its high water content prevents it from caramelising as satisfactorily and it's generally better to slow-cook it. Swede has a tendency to disintegrate if cooked for too long, which is fine for mash, but if you want it to hold its shape, watch it carefully when boiling or slow-cooking so that you can remove it from the heat when just tender.

slow-cook

Swede responds well to a long, gentle simmer – 45 minutes or even more. The larger the pieces and the slower the simmer, the better it will hold its shape. It's good in winter stews, and its peppery flavour pairs especially well with beef. For a Turkish-style vegetarian option, gently simmer cubes of swede with plenty of olive oil and lemon juice (see page 278). Or add tiny cubes to pearled spelt or barley and cook like a risotto, but for a bit longer (see page 295).

boil and mash

Buttery mashed neeps is a Burns' Night classic for the Scots, an essential

accompaniment to haggis (along with whisky). It's a wonderfully comforting side on other winter evenings as well, and is especially good with sausages and greens.

Boiling takes anywhere between 15 and 30 minutes, depending on the size you've chopped your veg. Drain once tender, return to the pan, mash and cook for a few minutes on a low heat to drive off excess water (it risks being watery if you skip this step). Afterwards, mash again, adding plenty of butter, pepper, salt and nutmeg.

bake

Swede works well baked in gratins and pies, but beware its tendency to give off water. If you are substituting it for another root vegetable, reduce the amount of liquid in the recipe as well.

works well with...

* bacon
* carrots
* delicate herbs – dill and parsley
* dairy – butter, cream, crème fraîche
* meats that go well with pepper and mustard – beef, pork, rabbit
* robust herbs – rosemary, sage, thyme
* sweet spices – anise, nutmeg
* white and black pepper

root veg and blue cheese pasties

a bit fancy

vegetarian (if a vegetarian cheese is used)

freezable

MAKES 8 PASTIES

For the pastry
500g plain flour
250g cold unsalted butter,
    cut into small dice
1 tsp fine salt
2 large egg yolks

For the filling
500g swede and other root
    veg (about 250g swede,
    and the remainder a
    mix, e.g. parsnip, celeriac
    and/or carrot), peeled
    and cut into 1cm dice
100g onion, cut into
    small dice
150g Stilton or other
    blue cheese, crumbled
1 large egg, beaten
salt and black pepper

To glaze
1 egg, beaten with
    a pinch of salt

At our farm in Devon we make pasties with the crimping on top, but feel free to make a Cornish version with the crimping on the side. These can be made up to the point of baking, frozen, and cooked straight from the freezer, adding 30 minutes to the cooking time. To save time, use shop-bought shortcrust pastry.

To make the pastry, put the flour, butter and salt in a food processor and pulse until the mixture looks like fine breadcrumbs. Add the egg and pulse briefly to combine, but don't overmix. Gradually add 6–8 tablespoons of cold water, stopping the pulsing the moment the mixture starts to come together. Transfer the pastry dough to your work surface or a bowl and form into a ball with your hands (press it together rather than kneading it). Wrap in cling film and chill in the fridge for a minimum of 30 minutes, an hour if you have time.

Heat the oven to 170°C/Gas 3.

Mix the filling ingredients together in a large bowl. Season well, particularly with pepper.

Divide the pastry into 8 similar-sized pieces. On a lightly floured work surface, roll out each piece into a circle approximately 18cm in diameter. Use a plate as a template if you need to.

Divide the filling between the pastry circles, leaving about 2cm clear around the edges. Fold up the edges of each pastry circle and use your fingers to press and crimp them together. If the pastry splits slightly, press it back together or patch it with a small offcut.

Place the pasties on a baking sheet lined with parchment, brush with the beaten egg and bake for 45–50 minutes, until golden.

- -
GOOD PASTRY PRACTICE
Many recipes tell you to chill your pastry for 30 minutes, but we recommend you give it at least 1 hour if you have time. Brushing the pastry with the beaten egg before it goes in the oven gives it a beautiful golden crust; the pinch of salt helps enrich the colour.
- -

baked swede with slow-cooked onions

quick & easy

vegetarian

freezable

SERVES 6 AS A SIDE

6 onions, sliced

170g butter

2 swede, peeled, cut in half
   and then into 3mm slices

salt and black pepper

Both the swede and onions are sweet enough to counter a
fatty meat dish without the pudding sweetness of parsnips
so we often serve it in place of potatoes with beef, lamb or
duck. Any leftovers can be cooled, pressed and fried in slices
the next day (see 'variation' below).

Heat the oven to 190°C/Gas 5.

In a frying pan set over a low–medium heat, slowly fry the
onions in the butter, stirring occasionally, until very soft and
tender, about 15 minutes.

Mix the swede with the onions in a big bowl and season well
with salt and black pepper.

Pack into a roasting tin or gratin dish as layered and flat as you can.
Cover the tin with baking parchment and then tightly with foil and
bake in the oven for about 30 minutes, or until the vegetables yield
easily to the point of a knife. Remove the foil and parchment and
cook for a further 15–20 minutes, until the top is golden brown.

VARIATION

Once baked, the whole thing can be pressed and cooled. Put a
flat baking sheet or roasting tin on top, weigh it down with a few
tins and cool overnight in the fridge. Turn it out on to a chopping
board and cut it into generous slices or wedges, then either dust
lightly with flour and fry in a pan until browned on both sides or
put the slices into a medium oven for 10 minutes to warm through.
Serve as a side dish or treat it like a rösti and top with a poached
egg and bacon for a stonking breakfast.

swede, celeriac and carrots braised in olive oil

long, slow cook

vegan

SERVES 4-6 AS A SIDE

½ large swede (about 500g)

½ large celeriac (about 500g)

2 large carrots (about 250g)

juice of 2 lemons, or to taste

125ml good olive oil

2 tsp sugar, or to taste

1½ tsp salt, or to taste

1 fresh bay leaf

4 peppercorns

leaves and tender stems
    from a bunch of parsley
    (about 30g), chopped

leaves and tender stems
    from a bunch of dill
    (about 30g), chopped

This is a Turkish method, common along the Aegean coast, that's used for cooking lots of different vegetables. The idea is to braise them slowly with lemon juice, olive oil, salt and a little sugar to concentrate and accentuate their natural flavours. It is definitely best served at room temperature, and preferably the next day. This recipe comes from Riverford Cook Anna, who likes it served as part of a mezze spread.

Scrub and peel the vegetables. Cut the carrots into thickish slices on a sharp angle. Cut the swede and celeriac into 1cm slices, and then into 1cm batons. Cut these into cubes or diamonds.

Put the veg into a large, wide pan and add the lemon juice, olive oil, sugar, salt, bay leaf and peppercorns. Add cold water until they are almost but not quite submerged. Cover with baking paper pressed to the surface and a lid and set over a medium heat. When it comes to a simmer, turn the heat down and cook slowly for about 1 hour, until the vegetables are completely tender. Try to avoid stirring too much so that the vegetables hold their shape. Halfway through the cooking time, taste the braising liquid and decide if it needs more lemon, oil or seasonings.

When the vegetables are done, lift them out with a slotted spoon into your serving dish and discard the bay leaf and peppercorns. With the pan uncovered, boil the braising liquid until reduced and syrupy. Taste it occasionally and stop it from boiling if it's becoming too salty.

Add the herbs to the liquid, then pour it over the vegetables and let cool. Serve at room temperature.

warming beef stew with swede

freezable

long, slow cook

SERVES 4

sunflower oil, for frying

4 thick pieces of beef
    braising steak or beef
    shin (700–800g)

1 onion, sliced

2 garlic cloves, finely
    chopped or crushed

50g piece of fresh ginger,
    peeled and finely grated

2 tsp paprika

3 large carrots, peeled and
    chopped into large bite-
    sized pieces

1 medium swede, peeled
    and chopped into large
    bite-sized pieces

500ml bottle of ale

1 x 400g can chopped
    tomatoes

salt and black pepper

This is Riverford Cook Kirsty's alternative to a Sunday roast, which she serves with lots of greens and mash on the side. If you don't have a casserole that will go on the hob, prepare it in a saucepan and then bake it in an ovenproof dish covered with foil. You can also cook it very gently on the hob from start to finish, keeping a fairly close eye on it and topping up with some water if it starts to dry out. Once ready, the stew can be left in the oven at a low temperature (100–110°C/Gas ¼). It reheats and freezes very well.

Heat the oven to 150°C/Gas 2. Heat 2 tablespoons of oil in a heavy-based flame- and ovenproof casserole. Fry the beef on both sides over a high heat to brown it. Transfer to a plate.

Turn the heat down. Fry the onion in the same pan for 10 minutes, until soft, adding a splash more oil and/or water if needed to stop it catching and burning.

Stir in the garlic, ginger, paprika, carrot and swede, then add the ale and chopped tomatoes and return the beef to the pan. Season with salt and pepper.

Heat until bubbling, then cover and transfer to the oven. Cook for 2–3 hours, until the beef is very tender (stewing beef can vary in the time it takes to soften, depending on the cut and age of the animal). Check the seasoning before serving.

swede, leek and bacon gratin

freezable

long slow cook

The leeks in this gratin could easily be replaced with boiled greens such as cabbage or kale. Leave out the bacon and it makes a flavoursome vegetarian main course.

SERVES 6-8

100ml milk
500ml double cream
2 garlic cloves
1 large rosemary or
    thyme sprig
150g smoked streaky
    bacon, cut into lardons
1–2 tbsp olive oil
3 leeks, white and pale
    green parts cut in rings
knob of butter (about 30g),
    plus extra to grease the
    gratin dish
1 swede, peeled and sliced
    paper thin (use a mandolin
    if you have one)
salt and black pepper

Heat the oven to 170°C/Gas 3.

Put the milk, cream, garlic and rosemary or thyme in a pan over a low–medium heat. Slowly bring to a boil and then gently simmer for 5 minutes, being careful not to let it boil over. Season with salt and pepper and remove from the heat.

Fry the bacon in the oil in a frying pan over a medium heat until really crispy. Add the leeks and a knob of butter and cook on a low heat for 20–30 minutes, until the leeks are soft and just beginning to caramelise. Season well with salt and pepper.

Arrange half the sliced swede on the bottom of a greased gratin or shallow ovenproof dish and season. Add the sautéed leeks and then top with the remaining swede and season again. Press the layers down with the back of a spoon. Using a sieve, strain over the infused milk and cream mixture and cover the dish with foil.

Bake in the oven for about 1 hour, until a blunt knife can be easily inserted through to the bottom. Uncover and bake for 15 minutes until the gratin is golden around the edges. Leave to stand for 10 minutes before serving.

VARIATION
Top the gratin with a hard grating cheese such as Parmesan, Cheddar, pecorino or Gruyère and return to the oven for the last 10 minutes.

garlic october to january

We don't generally include garlic in the veg boxes, though we occasionally add a bulb as a free item, and you will also occasionally see immature 'wet' garlic, as well as a free hit of wild garlic, in spring boxes.

After years of struggling to grow garlic in our damp Devon climate we have given up; half our crop is grown on our farm near Peterborough and the rest on our farm in the French Vendée. Cloves are planted in November and the harvest starts in April with fresh or 'wet' garlic; the first bulbs are fully dry in August.

Garlic goes with everything, intensifying the flavour of savoury dishes in a way nothing else seems capable of. But garlic needn't only play a supporting role. Slow-cooked into sweet submission it can take the lead, particularly when paired with mild canvasses such as bread, rice, potatoes and pasta. We haven't given it a full chapter but have included a few ideas here.

Along with onions, leeks and chives, garlic belongs to the genus *Allium* and is the most pungent of the lot. The strong flavour is caused by a chemical reaction when the garlic cells are broken so garlic is at its most intense after it has been chopped or crushed. But the pungency of garlic varies - keep tasting as you go when adding to dips etc.

storage

Keep garlic somewhere dry and airy and, if well dried, it'll last for several months, though it may show tendency to sprout as spring approaches. Leftover crushed or chopped garlic can be stored covered with oil in the fridge for up to a week and is good in salad dressing or stirred through wilted greens.

prep

There are lots of gadgets out there to help you prepare garlic but you only need a sharp knife. Cut the base off the clove, press it lightly with the flat of your knife and the skin should come off easily. Either chop finely or, to crush without the bother of a garlic crusher, sprinkle a peeled clove with coarse salt (which acts as an abrasive) and use the flat of your knife to press it down hard on a chopping board a few times, until puréed.

cooking

Gently fried garlic and onion form the base for thousands of recipes, from soups and stews to pasta sauce, but you can also roast or poach your garlic, making it more the star of the show.

Mellow and caramel, roasted garlic is so versatile that it's a good idea to make quite a bit at once: take several heads of garlic and cut off the top centimetre, exposing the flesh. Nestle them upright in an ovenproof dish, drizzling with olive oil, salt and a dash of water. Cover tightly with foil and roast at 170°C/Gas 3 for 1 hour. Once cool, squeeze out the sweet, sticky pulp. Spread straight on toast for a snack or canapé. This is also excellent stirred into dressing or mayonnaise, soups or stews, folded into mash, or stirred into a hot tray of roast potatoes (see page 184 for tips on roasting). Store leftover roasted garlic in a jar of olive oil in the fridge.

To soften garlic's texture and flavour, poach it in milk. Put a handful of cloves (peeled or unpeeled) into a small saucepan, cover with milk and simmer very gently for 20–30 minutes, until completely soft. You can use both the cloves and the garlic-flavoured milk – they're particularly good in mash.

garlic butter

quick & easy

vegetarian

freezable

This will keep in the fridge for a week or in the freezer for months, to be sliced off as needed. Smear on good crusty bread and bake in the oven; add to a tray of veg for the last few minutes of roasting; pop into a pot of wine-steamed mussels; or add to the sizzling juices of a fried steak, fillet of fish or pan of mushrooms for an easy sauce. Play with the contents of your butter: a pinch of chilli or cayenne pepper will pep things up and the parsley can be exchanged for most other fresh herbs.

SERVES 3–4

3–4 garlic cloves
pinch of salt
200g butter, at room temperature
small handful of parsley, finely chopped
dash of pastis (aniseed-flavoured aperitif),
   or a small squeeze of lemon juice

Peel and crush the garlic into a fine paste with a pinch of salt (see page 282). Add to the butter with the parsley and the pastis or lemon juice. Beat everything together, place on a sheet of baking parchment or cling film and roll into a sausage shape, twisting both ends like a Christmas cracker.

Castilian garlic soup

quick & easy   freezable

This satisfying, really simple garlic soup – *sopa de ajo castellana* in its native Spanish – is often served with a poached egg in it.

SERVES 4

½ loaf of good-quality white bread such
    as sourdough, cut into 1cm-thick slices
2 garlic bulbs, peeled and cut in half crossways
120ml extra virgin olive oil
1 litre chicken stock
salt and black pepper
poached eggs, to serve (optional)

Heat the oven to 170°C/Gas 3.

In a roasting tray, lay out the slices of bread and the halved garlic bulbs and douse in olive oil. Roast for about 45 minutes, until the bread is toasted golden brown and the garlic is completely soft. Check frequently, as the bread may need to come out earlier than the garlic.

When the garlic bulbs are cool enough to handle, squeeze the flesh into a blender. Add the toasted bread, any olive oil left in the roasting tray and the stock. Season with salt and plenty of pepper and blend until smooth and creamy. Pour into a saucepan and simmer for a few minutes, until heated through. Check the seasoning and add a poached egg to each bowl if you like.

aillade

quick & easy   Vegan

The combination of garlic and parsley has a unique ability to lift a dish, transforming it into a show-stopper. It's particularly good for cutting through oily or fatty meat and fish.

This works as a sort of winter pesto. It goes well with lamb, or transform it into a pasta sauce or a mezze dip (see variations).

SERVES 3-4

4 garlic cloves, roughly chopped
100g toasted walnuts
100ml olive oil
handful of parsley
30ml walnut oil
salt

Bash the garlic into a paste in a pestle and mortar (you can also use a food processor or work on a chopping board). Add two thirds of the walnuts, grinding them into a rough paste and adding a dash of olive oil to loosen.

Finely chop the parsley and roughly chop the rest of the walnuts. Put all the ingredients into a bowl, mix and season well with salt.

VARIATIONS
* For an easy pasta sauce: very gently heat the aillade in a pan to take the raw edge off the garlic, stir in a spoonful of crème fraîche and some grated sheep's cheese or Parmesan.
* Stir in a dollop of yoghurt, a squeeze of lemon and a pinch of cumin to make a dip.

fresh herbs

Fresh herbs can transform a dish by adding depth or brightness to the flavour, as well as adding interest to the overall look.

basil
Basil is a delicate herb that bruises easily so treat it with care. Spicy and fresh in equal measure, basil pairs beautifully with tomatoes – raw, roasted or cooked into a sauce. To avoid it going black, store it somewhere cool rather than cold and slice the leaves with a very sharp knife, or tear them with your hands. Once you've picked off the leaves, keep the stalks and throw them into a bubbling tomato sauce to infuse, then fish them out before serving.

chervil
The flavour of chervil is somewhere between mild parsley and tarragon, with a note of aniseed. It pairs well with delicate flavours such as poultry, fish, eggs and summer vegetables. Use chervil as a garnish, or blitz with tarragon, chives, parsley, oil and capers to make a vibrant green sauce that is fantastic on salmon.

chives
Chives have a mild oniony flavour that makes them very useful in the kitchen. Pair them with eggs, potatoes, cheese, fish or anything else that usually benefits from a dose of onion or garlic. Chop them finely to release their flavour and add them at the end of cooking, or use them in salads or as a garnish. Mixed into sour cream, chives make a lively dip for potato wedges. The purple flowers are edible, too: break them up and sprinkle them over a potato salad.

coriander
Grassy, cooling and citrussy, coriander leaf is a match for hot and spicy food – Indian, Thai, Vietnamese and Mexican. Try it, too, on tomato salads, in guacamole or with fatty meats such as lamb and pork. Coriander's flavour dies when cooked, so use it raw as a garnish or add it to a dish right at the end of cooking. Coriander stalks can be whizzed, along with garlic, ginger or galangal, green chilli and shallots, into a vibrant green Thai curry paste (see page 210).

dill
Feathery dill's mild aniseed flavour is underrated in the UK. Try it in salads such as tomato, cucumber and radish, or with beetroot and feta. Dill also pairs brilliantly with sour dairy produce – soured cream, yoghurt and cream cheese – and enhances simply cooked salmon, chicken, new potatoes and eggs.

mint
Mint has a fresh, sweet flavour and cooling aftertaste. It works well with fatty foods such as lamb or spicy Middle Eastern dishes. It is particularly good with feta, yoghurt, cucumber, melon, peas, oranges and aubergine. Mint is also great in drinks, from a soothing mint tea to a refreshing mojito. Mint leaves bruise easily: a good way to cut them, which avoids this, is to stack a few in a neat pile, roll up tightly like a cigar and then slice crossways into thin ribbons.

oregano and marjoram
These herbs are closely related and can be used interchangeably. Quite strongly flavoured, especially when dried, oregano and marjoram can stand up to spicy flavours, for example in a Mexican-style beef or bean chilli. They work well with meat, fish and vegetables to be grilled or roasted, along with some garlic and olive oil. They also enhance tomato sauces for pasta and pizza, especially with a little red chilli in the mix.

As strong herbs, they are generally not used as a garnish and are better off added early, to give them time to cook and infuse.

parsley (flat-leaf or curly)

Fresh, cool and green, parsley's powerful flavour is versatile, be it in flat-leaf or curly form. Stronger flavoured flat-leaf is perhaps more favoured, but unless you particularly want the flat leaves for decoration, they're pretty interchangeable in recipes. Just use a little more curly for the same flavour.

sorrel

Common sorrel has arrow-shaped leaves, which look a little like miniature dock leaves. Its flavour is strongly acidic and sour. Combine young sorrel with other leaves for a zingy green salad, but go easy on the vinegar in the dressing. Use it to brighten up buttery mashed potatoes, meat or cheese pies, or rich, spicy stews, as is done in parts of West Africa.

tarragon

A little tarragon goes a long way so use its distinctive anise flavour with care. It goes well with fish, chicken and egg dishes. It suits certain vegetables too, especially asparagus, and carrots. Try it in a simple omelette or an asparagus quiche. Tarragon excels in creamy sauces for chicken and rabbit, and in Béarnaise sauce for steak. Cut tarragon will quickly blacken, so chop it at the last minute. Tarragon vinegar is delicious in chicken salads: infuse a few sprigs in a bottle of white wine vinegar or cider vinegar for a week or so.

STORING HERBS

To lengthen the life of fresh herbs, remove any rubber bands or ties and swish the herbs around in a big bowl of cold water. Let them sit for a few minutes while any dirt sinks to the bottom. Lift out then spin dry in a salad-spinner or by shaking in a clean tea towel. Layer the herbs in a plastic box with sheets of kitchen paper to absorb the remaining water. Finish with a final sheet of paper, then seal and store in the fridge. Many herbs will keep like this for a week or even two.

basil

coriander

dill

bay

chives

chervil

mint

sage

thyme

rosemary

parsley (flat-leaf)

parsley (curly)

oregano
(marjoram looks very similar)

tarragon

useful basics,
including stocks, soups, risottos and dressings

stocks

Homemade stock is really worth having and can, at its most basic, be constructed in half an hour from the humblest ingredients. It freezes well and if space is at a premium, you can boil it once strained until it's reduced right down to a strong-tasting liquor, then pour into an ice cube tray. When you come to use, add quite a bit of water. And if you're also short on ice cube trays, transfer the frozen cubes to a plastic bag.

vegetable stock

Use what you have. It could be the guts of a butternut squash with a couple of onion ends to make a quick squash stock for a squash risotto, or it could be a medley of odds and ends collected over the week and kept in a plastic container or bag in the bottom of the fridge. There are, however, a few basic rules:

* Leave out potatoes and brassicas (e.g. cabbage, Brussels sprouts and broccoli).

* Try to include an extra carrot, onion, leek and celery stick, peeled as needed and roughly chopped. Together these provide a particularly good base of flavour.

* Certain herbs are good too, especially parsley, thyme and bay, but avoid the stronger ones such as rosemary and sage as they'll overpower the delicate flavour of a veg stock. This is a good use of herb stalks, so next time a recipe calls for parsley leaves, keep the stalks in a bag in the fridge: they will last easily for a week or two.

* A few peppercorns will add a subtle peppery note, but hold off on the salt as you can add it later when using your stock. Reducing your stock at the end concentrates its flavour and you may find it too salty.

* A squirt of tomato purée (or a fresh tomato), chopped mushroom stalks and Parmesan rind all add an extra umami dimension. Parmesan rinds wrapped in cling film will keep in the fridge for weeks, or they can be stored in the freezer for months.

* Coarsely chop any veg that's still whole and place everything in a large saucepan covered with cold water. Bring to a boil then reduce the heat and simmer for as long as you have – anything from 30 minutes to a couple of hours. Strain through a sieve and you're done. Let the stock cool before storing in the fridge (for up to 5 days) or the freezer (for several months) in a plastic container or as ice cubes (see above).

chicken stock

You can either use a raw chicken carcass or the remains of a roast chicken. In either case, break it up a bit before putting it in the pot. If you don't have time to make stock immediately, freeze your carcass and wait until you have two or three stored up to make a big batch. Chicken wings are a fantastic addition for flavour, and are cheap. As with veg stock, use a selection of vegetables and herbs – carrots, onion and celery plus parsley, bay and thyme are the classic combination.

Put the chicken into a large pot and cover with cold water. Slowly bring to a boil and skim off the scum that rises.

Now add the vegetables and herbs, reduce the heat and simmer very gently for at least 1 hour and preferably 3. In professional kitchens stock is never covered, since this can cause it to go cloudy, but it won't harm the flavour if you do.

Lift out the bigger bits of carcass with a slotted spoon or tongs then strain the stock through a sieve.

You might not want to bother to remove the fat: it tastes great and is full of nutrients. But if you'd like to, let it rise to the surface and then skim it off with a spoon. A good chef's tip is to swirl the bottom of a ladle over the surface of the stock in ever-increasing circles to push the fat to the edges, then quickly use the ladle to scoop it up. Or chill the stock overnight and lift the solidified fat off the top. This can be saved for frying potatoes. Reduce the stock and store as described above.

soups

For seasoned veg box users, soup-making is often a weekly routine - typically a scramble to use up the last leek before the next veg box arrives. Most vegetables can be turned into good soup: choose your main veg, follow the steps below, and, once you have mastered the basics, experiment with all manner of flourishes and variations.

1. Create your base flavour

Take all or some of: 1 onion or leek, 1 celery stick, 1 carrot per 300-400g of main veg. Avoid or go easy on carrots if you want a light coloured soup. Chop finely and sweat over a medium heat in butter or oil for at least 10 minutes, until soft and sweet, but not coloured.

2. Add hardy herbs, aromatics and seasoning (fresh, soft herbs are better added at the end)

Add your chosen herbs and spices. A bay leaf and a clove or two of chopped garlic rarely go amiss – cook for a couple of minutes to allow them to release their flavour, without colouring.

3. Introduce the main character

Add the main vegetable – around 300g – peeled and chopped. Stir to coat it in the fat and start its cooking. Leafy veg, such as spinach, kale and cabbage, are best added toward the end of cooking to retain the colour and avoid overcooking.

4. Add liquid

Choose your liquid – water, veg stock or chicken stock are the most versatile – and pour in enough to cover the veg. Simmer until the veg is good and tender (usually 30–45 minutes).

Sieve or blitz or not, or half and half, depending on the consistency you want A chunky pottage is often apt for cabbage and kales in particular. Roots most readily lend themselves to a smooth purée, but be cautious not to over-blend potatoes – they can go a little gluey as they release their starch.

5. Bulk it out (optional)

Towards the end of cooking you can add leafy veg, cooked peas or beans, drained tinned pulses, cooked grains or torn up bread to thicken the soup and add different textures. Cook a few minutes or enough to heat through.

6. Finishing touches

Swirl or sprinkle any finishing touches into the serving bowls – yoghurt, crème fraîche, seeds, nuts, fresh herbs, garnishes etc. (see some suggestions opposite) to improve flavour or appearance.

Companions and complements

Some pairings work particularly well in soups, each ingredient enhancing or lifting the other's flavour. In general, combinations that you have seen matched in other dishes will work well in a soup. Here are some of the best:

* **beetroot:** sharp and acidic flavours, such as orange zest/juice or balsamic vinegar. Or warm spicing from cumin, star anise or caraway. Or a little ginger or horseradish. A swirl of dairy at the end.

* **cabbage, greens and kale:** spice up with bacon, chorizo, caraway, chilli or curry spices. Use a sturdy root, pulse or grain as the main body of the soup (potato, celeriac, cannellini), adding cabbage or kale towards the end. Cabbage and kale soups are best left chunky rather than blended. Lemon is a good finishing touch.

* **carrot:** happy with spices such as paprika, cumin, coriander, chilli and cardamom; sweetness in the form of honey; or sharpness, such as citrus; top with toasted nuts or seeds or crumbled black pudding.

* **cauliflower and romanesco:** pair well with Asian flavourings: try simmering in coconut milk and adding cumin, turmeric or caraway. Crispy bacon or a blob of coarse mustard make apt additions; or mascarpone, crème fraîche or crumbled blue cheese for a comforting creamy finish.

* **celeriac:** good with other earthy flavours, such as chestnuts, mushrooms and hardy herbs like thyme and rosemary; finish with toasted hazelnuts or walnuts or crisp bacon.

* **Jerusalem artichokes:** horseradish will give it some kick; also pairs well with earthy flavours such as mushrooms and chestnuts. Season with woody herbs (rosemary, thyme and bay). Will cope well with almost any form of dairy.

* **parsnip:** warming spices (ginger, turmeric, curry powder, cumin) are perfect partners; as are mutually sweet flavours, like apple, almonds and maple syrup.

* **potatoes:** beyond the classic leek, potatoes pair well with mushrooms, kale and watercress. Bacon, or any type of cured pork product gets a tick, as do most cheeses, herbs and leafy greens.

* **pumpkin and squash:** Asian flavours, such as chilli, lime, coconut and lemongrass all work well; as do warming aromatic spices, (cumin, coriander and garam masala). Dried fruit such as raisins and dates complement their natural sweetness; while a tangy feta or goat's cheese contrasts well.

* **spinach and chard:** aside from classic nutmeg, season these with chilli, Parmesan and lemon; other dairy, such as yoghurt and cream; add leaves at the last minute so as not to overcook them.

risottos

Risottos count among the most comforting of foods. They offer infinite possibilities for variation, using up leftovers, and debate about method and desirable texture. Below is our suggested basic approach.

basic risotto recipe

FOR 2, BUT CAN BE SCALED UP AS NECESSARY

up to 1 litre vegetable, chicken or fish stock
   (you may not need it all)
knob of butter and/or slug of olive oil
1 onion, finely diced (or use 2 shallot or 1 leek)
1 celery stick, finely diced (optional)
1 large garlic clove, finely minced (optional)
160–200g risotto rice (e.g. Arborio, carnaroli
   or vialone nano), depending on appetite
140ml white wine or white vermouth (optional)
20–30g cold butter, cut into small cubes
large handful of Parmesan (about 50g), grated
salt and black pepper

Heat the stock in a saucepan. Heat the butter and/or oil in a heavy-based wide pan then add the onion and celery and fry on a low–medium heat for at least 10 minutes, until soft, stirring frequently. Add the garlic and fry for a further couple of minutes.

Add the rice and continue cooking and stirring for a couple of minutes to toast it. Stir in the wine and let the rice absorb it all, then start adding the hot stock, a ladle at a time, stirring constantly and adding the next ladleful only when the previous one has almost all been absorbed. Keep the risotto at a constant bubble. After about 20 minutes the rice should be nearly cooked through – tender with a little bite; taste it to check. If you run out of stock before the rice is cooked, add boiling water from the kettle.

Remove the pan from the heat and rapidly stir in several cubes of the butter and the Parmesan. Cover and leave the risotto to sit for just a couple of minutes (any longer and it will become stodgy). If it's too thick for your liking, stir in a little more stock. Check the seasoning and serve.

flavour it

The default way to add your veg is to cook them separately and then stir them into the rice shortly before the risotto is ready. So, for example, you could fry a mixture of sliced mushrooms, roasted chunks of squash (see page 201) or shredded and blanched kale (see page 128).

* For quick-cooking vegetables, such as finely grated beetroot and shredded tender greens, you can get away with throwing them straight in with the rice. Add frozen peas in for the last few minutes.

* Chopped herbs are good additions, too. Add strong ones at the start with the onion: sage works a treat with squash, and thyme is good with mushrooms. Save delicate herbs, such as parsley, for stirring in or sprinkling on top as a garnish.

* Spices are unusual in risottos, but a touch of chilli or saffron in with the onions can be delicious.

bored of rice?

With a nutty flavour and more robust texture, pearled or wholegrain spelt and barley grains are excellent alternatives to risotto rice, though they take a bit longer to cook.

Follow the method opposite, toasting the grains in the hot fat once you've fried the onions and celery. They'll go a shade darker and gain extra nutty flavour. These grains generally need less liquid and more time than rice, and you don't need to add stock gradually: start with about half and top up with more towards the end if necessary. Allow around 25 minutes for pearled grains and up to 45 minutes for wholegrain spelt or barley (follow the packet instructions and just keep tasting and checking).

You can finish with a little cream if you like; letting it bubble up and thicken slightly, then stir in the Parmesan (omit the butter if you use cream) and check the seasoning.

Or for a lighter alternative, try quinoa, using 75–100g per person. Rinse in a sieve under cold water, then simmer in stock or water until just cooked – around 13–15 minutes. Add the quinoa to the fried onions along with whatever cooked veg and herbs you are using.

salad dressings

There are two main things to bear in mind when making dressings: firstly, everyone has their favourite, so adjust quantities in a recipe to find your perfect mix; secondly, the flavour is diluted when tossed with your leaves, so when tasted neat, it should be punchy.

basic vinaigrette

Vinaigrette keeps in the fridge for a week or so. Taste it again before using as it will likely have lost some of its zing and may need a little more vinegar. This quantity of vinaigrette will do two or three salads.

2 tbsp red wine vinegar
2 tsp Dijon mustard
½ garlic clove, crushed (optional)
pinch of sugar
pinch of salt
a few grindings of black pepper
6 tbsp extra virgin olive oil

Whisk everything except the oil together until well combined.

Pour in the oil while continuing to whisk; it should emulsify into a thick, creamy consistency. Alternatively, vigorously shake everything together in a jam jar.

Taste and add more sugar, salt, pepper or mustard according to your taste.

VARIATIONS

* For a **lemon vinaigrette**, replace the vinegar with lemon juice, or a mixture of lemon and orange juice.

* For a **nut or seed vinaigrette**, substitute some of the olive oil with walnut or toasted sesame oil. A good rapeseed oil also provides a nice nutty flavour.

* For a **herb vinaigrette**, whizz the vinaigrette in a blender or food processor to incorporate soft herbs such as basil, tarragon, chives or chervil: it will go bright green and taste amazing.

* Make **creamy vinaigrette** by substituting buttermilk, yoghurt, crème fraîche, soured cream or a mix of these for the oil. You may want to reduce the vinegar slightly.

* Make **brown-butter vinaigrette**, which is good on green leaves and on cooked veg such as broccoli: melt around 50g butter in a frying pan and continue cooking until the milk solids turn nut brown. Whisk together with the vinegar and seasonings and use immediately, before the butter solidifies.

* Or simply play around with the types of ingredient: try different vinegars – cider, balsamic, sherry and walnut are good ; vary the mustard, replace it with a teaspoon of horseradish, or leave it out altogether. Try honey or maple syrup instead of sugar.

dried beans

Tinned beans and chickpeas are a marvellous labour-saving invention and we use them all the time. However, the texture and flavour of dried beans tends to be a little superior, and occasionally it's definitely worth cooking them from scratch. They'll last in the fridge for 5 days, so cook more than you need then use them as the base for a few quick meals.

dried beans (haricot, flageolet, cannellini, butter, or black eyed beans; about 75g per person)
1 carrot
1 onion, peeled and halved
1 celery stick,
a few garlic cloves, peeled
1 dried or fresh chilli (optional)
parsley stalks, bay leaves, sprigs of thyme (optional)
olive oil
salt

Place the beans in a big plastic container or stainless steel pot, cover with three times their volume of cold water and soak for 8 hours or overnight.

Drain and rinse the beans, place in a big pot and cover with fresh cold water by 2–3cm. Add the aromatics (see suggestions above) and a good slug of olive oil. Do not add salt now as this may make the beans tough.

Bring to a boil then reduce the heat and simmer gently, partially covered, until the beans are nearly tender, adding more water as needed to keep the beans covered. This will take anything from 45 minutes to 1½ hours, depending on the age of your beans. If they need more than 2 hours they are probably ancient and may not have the best flavour – dried beans should be used within a year or two of being harvested.

When tender, add a generous quantity of salt and continue simmering for a few minutes until the beans have no hint of chalkiness. Test several to be sure. Don't stir much or they will break up.

Fish out the vegetables and herbs and check the seasoning. Use straight away or store in the fridge with enough of the cooking liquor to just cover the beans.

USES FOR COOKED BEANS

* Hearty stew: add vegetables and/or meat. Chorizo and other pork products work especially well. Wilt spinach straight into the stew just before serving.

* Cold bean salad: add finely diced red onion, parsley and vinaigrette.

* A side dish for a big roast or braise – they are particularly good with lamb and pork – perhaps with extra fried onions and garlic muddled through, and plenty of fresh herbs.

* Purée and spread on toast with a good drizzle of olive oil. Fried sage leaves are great on top of this.

* Purée with extra garlic, tahini, chilli and lemon juice for an alternative to hummus.

* Mix into pasta and serve hot with grated Parmesan and plenty of black pepper.

Index

a

aillade 285
aloo gobi 96–7
anchovy 214–15, 226, 263
    lemon, anchovy and mustard
        dressing 239
    pasta with kale, anchovies and
        chilli 137
    purple sprouting broccoli, with
        roasted garlic, capers, shallots
        and anchovies 224–5
apple 63, 110
    celeriac, apple, parsley and
        walnuts 111
    parsnip, apple and ginger soup 177

b

bacon 93, 191, 194
    bacon and radicchio omelette 240–1
    Jerusalem artichoke and bacon
        gratin 116
    parsnip, Brussels sprout and bacon
        potato cakes 174–5
    purple sprouting broccoli, bacon
        and poached egg on toast 223
    radicchio and bacon pasta 246–7
    roasted celeriac with mustard and
        bacon 109
    swede, leek and bacon gratin 281
basil 286, 288
bean(s)
    dried 297
    see also specific beans
béchamel sauce 139
beef
    beef cottage pie 194
    beef shin and pumpkin stew
        with gremolata 214–15
    beef stew with swede 280
    North African spiced beef and
        root vegetable stew 172–3
beetroot 16–31
    beetroot, potato and horseradish
        röstis 26–7
    beetroot dip 21
    beetroot and pink peppercorn
        gratin 30–1

beetroot salad with cottage cheese
    and horseradish 24
beetroot soup 293
borscht-style stew with soured
    cream 23
cooking beetroot 19–21
preparation 18
raw beetroot 19
roast beetroot and potatoes with
    red onions, balsamic vinegar
    and rosemary 29
roasted beetroot, carrot, lentil and
    cumin seed salad 22–3
spiced pickled beetroot 28
storage 18
Belgian endive 237
black bean and squash chilli 212–13
borlotti bean and radicchio,
    sautéed 243
borscht-style stew with soured
    cream 23
broccoli see purple sprouting broccoli
bruschetta, slow-cooked cavolo
    nero 130
Brussels sprouts 32–45
    Brussels sprout salad with balsamic
        and Parmesan 40
    Brussels sprouts with cream,
        lemon and parsley 37
    Brussels sprouts and pancetta
        pasta with sage and roast garlic
        cream 42–3
    cooking 34–6
    Indian spiced pan-fried Brussels
        sprouts 44–5
    parsnip, Brussels sprout and bacon
        potato cakes 174–5
    preparation 34
    raw Brussels 34–5
    roasted Brussels, sage and chestnut
        butter 38–9
    sausage, sprout and potato hash
        with poached eggs 41
    storage 34
bubble and squeak 187
bulghur wheat salad with carrot, date
    and pomegranate 75
butter 90–1

brown-butter vinaigrette 296
chestnut butter 38–9
garlic butter 284
Savoy, brown butter and red
    onions 55
butter bean, cauliflower and kale 94–5

c

cabbage 46–63, 293
    braised red cabbage 62–3
    Celtic/green 48–9
    cooking 51
    Hispi 48, 50, 51, 56
    identification 48–9
    January King 48–9, 51, 59, 60, 123
    Keralan cabbage thoran 56–7
    preparation 50
    raw cabbage 50–1
    red cabbage 48, 50–1, 54, 63
    sausage and Jerusalem artichoke
        bake with cabbage 122–3
    Savoy 47–9, 51, 53, 55, 59–60, 123
    Savoy, brown butter and red
        onions 55
    smashed potatoes, cabbage crème
        fraîche and chives 59
    spicy greens with mung beans 58
    storage 50
    toasted seed and tahini slaw 52–3
    Tundra 48–9
    turkey meatball broth with greens
        60–1
    Vietnamese-style carrot and
        cabbage slaw 80–1
    white cabbage 48–9, 50, 54
    winter rainbow coleslaw 54
    see also spring greens
carrot 52–3, 64–81, 67, 280, 293
    bulghur wheat salad with carrot,
        date and pomegranate 75
    carrot braised with cider and
        thyme 71
    carrot and coriander soup 72–3
    carrots in a bag 78–9
    cooking 67–70
    Keralan cabbage thoran 56–7
    leftover carrots 70

Moroccan carrot salad with
cumin and orange 74
preparation 66
raw 66
roast carrots with honey and
fennel 76–7
roasted beetroot, carrot, lentil
and cumin seed salad 22–3
roll-cut carrot 69
storage 66
swede, celeriac and carrots braised
in olive oil 278–9
Vietnamese-style carrot and
cabbage slaw 80–1
cauliflower 82–99, 293
aloo gobi 96–7
cauliflower butter beans and
kale 94–5
cauliflower couscous 84, 86
cauliflower 'Polonaise' 92
cooking 86–8
deep-fried Szechuan cauliflower 89
parsnip, cauliflower and chickpea
korma 178–9
preparation 84
puréed cauliflower 86–8
raw 84–6
roast cauli, butter, lemon and
cumin 90–1
Sicilian romanesco 98–9
storage 84
taffy cauliflower cheese 93
cavolo nero (black kale) 106–7, 126–7,
132, 138, 139–41
slow-cooked cavolo nero
bruschetta 130
celeriac 100–11, 194
celeriac, apple, parsley and
walnuts 111
celeriac, kale and mushroom pie
106–7
celeriac mash 104
celeriac rémoulade 103
celeriac soup 104, 293
cooking 103–5
potato and celeriac gratin 108
preparation 102
raw 102
roasted celeriac with mustard and
bacon 109
'smashed' celeriac 104–5

smoked mackerel, celeriac and
watercress salad 110
storage 102
swede, celeriac and carrots braised
in olive oil 278–9
chard 256–72, 293
cooking 259–60
flageolet bean stew with chard 262
galettes with chard and Gruyère
268–9
identification 258
Jansson's temptation with chard 263
preparation 258–9
raw 259
Spanish-style Swiss chard with
chickpeas 264–5
storage 258
cheese 138, 162–3, 176, 191,
208–9, 242
baked potatoes with cheesy kale
filling 192–3
cheese sauce 93
galettes with chard and Gruyère
268–9
leek and smoked cheese macaroni
154–5
root veg and blue cheese
pasties 276
see also specific cheeses
chervil 147, 286, 288
chestnut butter 38–9
chicken
chicken, artichoke and leek filo
pie 118–20
chicken, leek and tarragon
pasta 152
chicken stock 291
lemony chicken and spinach
curry 270–1
chickpea 172–3
parsnip, cauliflower and chickpea
korma 178–9
Spanish-style Swiss chard with
chickpeas 264–5
chilli 137, 203, 222, 226
chives 59, 286, 288
chorizo 132–3
kale, spelt and chorizo big
soup 140–1
purple sprouting, chorizo and
potatoes 232–3

coleslaw
winter rainbow 54
see also slaw
coriander 72–3, 286, 288
cottage cheese, horseradish
and beetroot salad 24
cottage pie, venison/beef 194
couscous, Sicilian romanesco 98–9
cumin 74, 90–1
cumin seed 22–3
curly endive 237
curry 178–9, 210–11, 270–1

d
date, pomegranate and carrot with
bulghur wheat salad 75
dill 286, 288
dressings 54, 80, 147, 296
lemon, anchovy and mustard 239

e
egg 92, 148–9, 240–1, 268–9
baked eggs with kale and cream
138
purple sprouting, bacon and
poached egg on toast 223
sprout and potato hash with
poached eggs 41

f
fennel, honey and roast carrots 76–7
feta
leek and feta fritters 148–9
spinach and feta filo pie 266–7
fish (smoked), sour cream and potato
latkes 190
flageolet bean stew with chard 262
French onion soup 162–3
fritters 148–9, 254–5

g
galettes with chard and Gruyère
268–9
garlic 159, 188–9, 222, 224–5,
253, **282–5**
aillade 285

Castilian garlic soup 285
cooking 284
garlic butter 284
garlic cream 42–3
preparation 282
storage 282
goat's cheese
chargrilled radicchio, squash
and goat's cheese 244–5
crown prince, goat's cheese and
spinach pie 206–7
grains 14, 295
gratins 30–1, 108, 116, 146, 186–7,
195, 281
gremolata 214–15

h

hashes 41, 132–3
herbs 286–9, 292–3
herb vinaigrette 296
hollandaise sauce 230–1
horseradish 24, 26–7

j

Jansson's temptation with chard 263
Jerusalem artichoke 112–23, 293
artichoke and leek soup 117
chicken, Jerusalem artichoke and
leek filo pie 118–20
cooking 114–15
Jerusalem artichoke and bacon
gratin 116
mashed artichoke 115
preparation 114
raw 115
sausage and artichoke bake with
cabbage 122–3
sautéed Jerusalem artichokes 121
storage 114

k

kale 47, **124–41**, 293
baked eggs with kale and cream 138
baked potatoes with cheesy kale
filling 192–3
cauliflower butter beans and
kale 94–5

celeriac, kale and mushroom
pie 106–7
cooking 128–9
curly kale 126–7, 131–2, 135,
138–40
fruit and nut pilaf 134–6
Guy's kale hash 132–3
identification 126
kale crisps 129
kale and mushroom lasagne 139
kale with raisins and sherry
vinegar 131
pasta with kale, anchovies and
chilli 137
preparation 127
raw 126–7
red Russian kale 126, 129, 131, 135
spelt and chorizo big soup 140–1
slow-cooked cavolo nero
bruschetta 130
storage 126
kitchen kit 15
korma, parsnip, cauliflower and
chickpea 178–9

l

lasagne, kale and mushroom 139
latkes (potato), smoked fish and sour
cream 190
leek 59, 93, **142–55**, 177
artichoke and leek soup 117
chicken, Jerusalem artichoke and
leek filo pie 118–20
chicken, leek and tarragon pasta 152
cooking 145–6
griddled leeks, wild rice and
quinoa with chervil 147
leek and feta fritters 148–9
leek gratin 146
leek and Parmesan tart 150–1
leek pasta 146
leek and potato soup 145
leek and smoked cheese
macaroni 154–5
leek vinaigrette 146
mussels with leeks 153
preparation 144
raw 142
storage 144
swede, leek and bacon gratin 281

lemon 37, 90–1, 188–9, 203, 222,
278–9
lemon, anchovy and mustard
dressing 239
lemon vinaigrette 296
lemony chicken and spinach
curry 270–1
lentil 122–3
roasted beetroot, carrot, lentil and
cumin seed salad 22–3

m

macaroni, leek and smoked
cheese 154–5
mackerel (smoked), celeriac and
watercress salad 110
maltaise sauce 230–1
marjoram 286–7
meatball broth and greens 60–1
mint 286, 288
mung bean and spicy greens 58
mushroom
celeriac, kale and mushroom
pie 106–7
cleaning 227
kale and mushroom lasagne 139
purple sprouting broccoli and
shiitake stir-fry 227
sautéed salsify, mushrooms,
garlic and parsley on
toast 253
mussel with leeks 153
mustard 109, 239

n

noodles, purple sprouting broccoli
and shiitake stir-fry 227
nuts 227, 242, 244–5, 285
kale, fruit and nut pilaf 134–6
nut vinaigrette 296
toasted nuts 136
see also specific nuts

o

omelette, bacon and radicchio 240–1
onion 67, **156–67**, 177, 191, 206–7,
214–15

baked swede with slow-cooked
     onions 277
butternut, red onion and pumpkin
     seed salad 204–5
cooking 159–60
crispy fried onions 160
French onion soup 162–3
identification 158
onion gravy 161
onion sauce 161
preparation 158–9
raw 159
red onion 29, 55, 158, 165, 204–5
roast beetroot and potatoes with
     red onions, balsamic vinegar
     and rosemary 29
roast onions and thyme 164–5
Savoy, brown butter and red
     onions 55
slow-fried onions with rosemary
     and cream 161
and stock 159
storage 158
yellow onion 158, 161–2, 165
orange 74, 230–1
oregano 286 7, 289

p
pain de sucre 237
pancetta and Brussels sprout pasta
     with sage and roast garlic
     cream 42–3
pangrattata (poor man's Parmesan),
     purple sprouting and chilli with
     pasta 226
Parmesan 108, 137, 139, 208–9, 246–7
     Brussels sprout salad with balsamic
     and Parmesan 40
     leek and Parmesan tart 150–1
parsley 37, 111, 203, 253, 287, 289
parsnip 168–81, 293
     cooking 171
     leftover parsnips 171
     North African spiced beef and
          root vegetable stew 172–3
     parsnip, apple and ginger soup 177
     parsnip, Brussels sprout and bacon
          potato cakes 174–5
     parsnip, cauliflower and chickpea
          korma 178–9

parsnip chips 171
parsnip mash 171
parsnip skordalia 180–1
parsnips Molly Parkin 176
preparation 170
raw 170
storage 170
pasta 42–3, 137, 139, 146, 152,
     154–5, 226, 246–7
pasties, root veg and blue
     cheese 276
pearl barley risotto 295
persimmon and radicchio salad 242
pies 106–7, 118–20, 194, 206–7, 266–7
pilaf, kale, fruit and nut 134–6
pomegranate, date and carrot with
     bulghur wheat salad 75
potato 23, 72–3, 96–7, 132–3,
     182–95, 187, 263, 293
     baked potatoes with cheesy kale
          filling 192–3
     beetroot, potato and horseradish
          röstis 26–7
     cooking 184–7
     Cosmos 184
     creamy tartiflette 191
     Desiree 184
     gratin dauphinois 195
     identification 184
     King Edward 184
     leek and potato soup 145
     leftover potato 187
     Marfona 184
     mashed potato 186
     Orla 184
     parsnip, Brussels sprout and
          bacon potato cakes 174–5
     Pink Fir Apple 184
     potato and celeriac gratin 108
     potato latkes with smoked fish
          and sour cream 190
     potato salad 187
     preparation 184
     purple sprouting, chorizo and
          potatoes 232–3
     roast beetroot and potatoes with
          red onions, balsamic vinegar
          and rosemary 29
     roast potatoes 184–5, 188–9
     smashed potatoes, cabbage,
          crème fraîche and chives 59

sprout and potato hash
     with poached eggs 41
storage 184
Triplo 184
venison/beef cottage pie 194
pulses 14
pumpkin 196–215, 293
     beef shin and pumpkin stew
          with gremolata 214–15
     cooking 201–2
     preparation 200
     storage 199
     sugar pumpkin 198
pumpkin seed 199, 204–5
purple sprouting broccoli
     216–33
     cooking 218–20
     pasta with purple sprouting
          broccoli, chilli and poor man's
          Parmesan 226
     preparation 218
     purple sprouting, chorizo and
          potatoes 232–3
     purple sprouting, bacon and
          poached egg on toast 223
     purple sprouting broccoli with
          maltaise sauce 230–1
     purple sprouting broccoli and
          shiitake stir-fry 227
     purple sprouting, roast garlic,
          capers, shallots and
          anchovies 224–5
     raw 220
     roasted purple sprouting,
          lemon, chilli and garlic 222
     storage 218
     wheatberries, purple sprouting,
          crispy garlic and chilli 228–9

q
quinoa, griddled leeks and wild rice
     with chervil 147

r
radicchio 234–47
     bacon and radicchio omelette 240–1
     bitter leaf salad with lemon,
          anchovy and mustard
          dressing 239

chargrilled radicchio, squash
and goat's cheese 244–5
cooking 237–8
preparation 236
radicchio and bacon pasta 246–7
radicchio and persimmon
salad 242
raw 236
sautéed radicchio and borlotti
beans 243
storage 236
rémoulade, celeriac 103
rice
griddled leeks, wild rice and
quinoa with chervil 147
kale, fruit and nut pilaf 134–6
risotto 201, 202, 294–5
risotto 294–5
squash risotto 201, 202
romanesco 82–99, 293
cauliflower 'Polonaise' 92
cooking 86–8
preparation 84
puréed romanesco 86–8
raw 84
Sicilian romanesco 98–9
storage 84
rosemary 29, 161, 188–9
röstis, beetroot, potato and
horseradish 26–7

S

sage 38–9, 42–3
salads
beetroot salad with cottage cheese
and horseradish 24
bitter leaf salad with lemon,
anchovy and mustard
dressing 239
bulghur wheat salad with carrot,
date and pomegranate 75
butternut, red onion and pumpkin
seed salad 204–5
Jerusalem artichoke salad 114
potato salad 187
radicchio and persimmon
salad 242
roasted beetroot, carrot, lentil and
cumin seed salad 22–3

roasted beetroot salads 20
salsify salad 251
smoked mackerel, celeriac
and watercress salad 110
salsify 248–55
cooking 250–1
preparation 250
salsify fritters 254–5
salsify salad 251
salsify soup 251
sautéed salsify, mushrooms,
garlic and parsley on
toast 253
storage 250
sausage
sausage, sprout and potato
hash with poached eggs 41
sausage and artichoke bake
with cabbage 122–3
seeds 14
seed vinaigrette 296
toasted seed and tahini slaw 52–3
see also pumpkin seed
shallot 156–67
identification 158
preparation 158–9
purple sprouting, roasted garlic,
capers, shallots and anchovies
224–5
shallot tarte tatin 166–7
storage 158
skordalia, parsnip 180–1
slaw
toasted seed and tahini 52–3
Vietnamese-style carrot
and cabbage 80–1
see also coleslaw
soffrito 67
sorrel 287
soup 292–3
artichoke and leek 117
carrot and coriander 72–3
Castilian garlic 285
celeriac 104
French onion 162–3
kale, spelt and chorizo 140–1
leek and potato 145
parsnip, apple and ginger 177
salsify 251
squashy bottom soup
bowls 208–9

spaghetti
spaghetti squash spaghetti, chilli,
parsley and lemon 203
squash spaghetti 198, 203
spelt
kale, spelt and chorizo big
soup 140–1
spelt risotto 295
spices 14, 159, 293
spinach 256–72, 293
cooking 259–60
crown prince, goat's cheese
and spinach pie 206–7
identification 258
Korean-style spinach 261
lemony chicken and spinach
curry 270–1
preparation 258–9
raw 259
spinach and feta filo pie 266–7
storage 258
spring greens 48–9, 50
squash 196–215, 293
acorn 198
butternut 198, 200, 204–5, 210–13,
244–5
butternut, red onion and pumpkin
seed salad 204–5
chargrilled radicchio, squash and
goat's cheese 244–5
cooking 201–2
crown prince 198–9, 206–7, 212,
244–5
identification 198
kabocha 198, 199, 201–2
mashed squash 202
onion squash 198–9, 208, 212
preparation 200
spaghetti squash 198, 199
spaghetti squash spaghetti with
chilli, parsley and lemon 203
squash and black bean chilli
212–13
squash risotto 201, 202
squash spaghetti 198, 203
squash stock 201
squashy bottom soup bowls 208–9
storage 199
stuffed squash 201
Thai squash curry 210–11
stew 23, 172–3, 214–15, 262, 280

stir-fry, purple sprouting broccoli
and shiitake 227
stock 159, 201, 290–1
store cupboard essentials 14–15
swede 271–82, 293
baked swede with slow-cooked
onions 277
beef stew and swede 280
cooking 274–5
mashed swede 274–5
preparation 274
raw 275
root veg and blue cheese
pasties 276
storage 274
swede, celeriac and carrots
braised in olive oil 278–9
swede, leek and bacon gratin 281

t

tahini and toasted seed slaw 52–3
tarragon 152, 287, 289
tart, leek and Parmesan 150–1
tarte Tatin, shallot 166–7
tartiflette, creamy 191
thyme 71, 164–5, 188–9
toast
purple sprouting, bacon and
poached egg on 223
sautéed salsify, mushrooms, garlic
and parsley on 253
tofu, purple sprouting broccoli and
shiitake stir-fry 227
tomato 23, 140–1, 176, 212–15, 280
peeling 140–1
turkey meatball broth with
greens 60–1

v

venison cottage pie 194
vinaigrettes 296

w

walnut, celeriac, apple and parsley 111
watercress, smoked mackerel and
celeriac salad 110
wheatberry, purple sprouting, crispy
garlic and chilli 228–9

Acknowledgements

The Riverford community is extensive. Over the years, the good will and generosity of countless customers, staff and friends have helped us evolve a cooking style and a bank of recipes to maintain our enthusiasm for season after season of beans and broccoli, courgettes and cardoons.

Special thanks for bringing this book to fruition to Kirsty Hale, the backbone of our recipe team for many years and tireless inventor of better ways with veg; to Anna Colquhoun, a founder Riverford Cook who gives generously of her time and shares her enthusiasm for the anthropology as well as the practicalities of food; and to Rob Andrew, longstanding Riverford chef with an inventive knowledge of veg built up in his years at Riverford (Field Kitchen, Travelling Field Kitchen, staff canteen) and before.

Imogen Fortes has been a firm, supportively critical and knowledgeable editor. Ariel Cortese, of Big Fish, has contributed the beautiful art work, and Alex and Emma Smith, of Smith & Gilmour, the design, cover and art direction.

Thank you to Martin Ellis for the rich bank of images he has built up to reflect life at Riverford through the seasons; to Jason Ingram and Ali Allen for wonderful food photography; to our trusty team of staff recipe testers, and Ed Watts for his help in the kitchen; and to Katie Sanderson and Anna Neima, reliable sources of support, criticism, writing and editorial assistance.

Cataloguing in Publication Data is available from the British Library

ISBN: 978-0-9932155-0-6

Design: Smith & Gilmour
Project editor: Imogen Fortes
Recipe photography: Ali Allen and Jason Ingram
Landscape and farm photography: Martin Ellis
Food styling: Linda Tubby and Kirsty Hale
Font design and illustration: Ariel Cortese at Big Fish
Linen: The Linen Works
Potter: Ali Herbert

Printed and bound in Italy by L.E.G.O.

www.riverford.co.uk

the veg new year

late May to early July

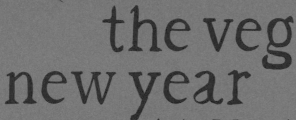

asparagus
broad beans
bunched carrots
bunched onions
bunched radishes
chard
globe artichokes
  and cardoons
kohlrabi
lettuce (Batavia;
  cos; Little Gem)
new potatoes
  (Lady Christl)

pak choi
salad leaves
salad potatoes
  (Alexia; Charlotte)
spring onions
spring and summer
  greens
summer turnips
watercress
wet garlic